THE SKETCHES
OF
LOUISA MAY ALCOTT

THE SKETCHES

OF

LOUISA MAY ALCOTT

With an Introduction by Gregory Eiselein

IRONWEED AMERICAN CLASSICS
IRONWEED PRESS · NEW YORK

Ironweed Press, Inc.
P. O. Box 754208
Parkside Station
Forest Hills, NY 11375

Manufactured in the United States of America.
Ironweed American Classics books are printed on acid-free paper.

Cover painting: Winslow Homer, "The Bridle Path,
White Mountains," 1868, oil on canvas.
Sterling and Francine Clark Art Institute,
Williamstown, Massachusetts.

Library of Congress Cataloging-in-Publication Data

Alcott, Louisa May, 1832–1888.
    The sketches of Louisa May Alcott / with an introduction by
Gregory Eiselein.
       p.   cm. — (Ironweed American classics)
    Includes bibliographical references.
    ISBN 0-9655309-8-1 (pbk. : alk. paper)
       I. Title.   II. Series.
PS1016   2001
818'.403—dc21

00-057259

CONTENTS

CONCORD, MASSACHUSETTS

FROM *THE YOUTH'S COMPANION* AND *MERRY'S MUSEUM*

ACKNOWLEDGMENTS

Special gratitude is owed to the following individuals and institutions for the courtesies extended: Philip Lampi, Dennis Laurie, and Russell Martin, Newspapers and Periodicals Department, American Antiquarian Society; Kathryn L. Schnaible; Microtext Department, Boston Public Library; and Library of Congress.

INTRODUCTION

Throughout her career Louisa May Alcott (1832–1888) used her own experiences as a source for plots, characters, and themes. The distinction between the autobiographical and the fictional is therefore often blurred in her writings. In the novels *Little Women* (1868–69) and *Work* (1873), she broadly translated aspects of her life into imaginative narratives and, in "Transcendental Wild Oats" (1873) and "How I Went Out to Service" (1874), fictionalized specific events from her early years. Such texts are sometimes the best or the only source of information about particular periods in Alcott's life, but she crafted them to be read as fiction rather than as firsthand accounts of actual events.

Her nonfiction sketches aim for a more direct and immediate presentation of her observations and experiences. This is not to say that these sketches are simply factual or objective. Their underlying purposes are often political or edificatory. Moreover, her settings at times resemble those of fiction: "Life in a Pension" (1867) and "A Visit to the Tombs" (1876), for example, both recall Gothic scenes. Similarly, her characters tend to be types rather than multidimensional individuals or impartially described real people. But these sketches are distinctive in that they provide in a spontaneous, seemingly artless manner Alcott's own perspective on the events around her. She writes in the 1869 Preface to *Hospital Sketches,* "These sketches, taken from letters hastily written in the few leisure moments of a very busy life, make no pretension to literary merit, but are simply a brief record of one person's hospital experience." Like an artist making pencil sketches, Alcott composed these pieces rapidly in an attempt to capture the immediacy of the events and did not strive for a polished style or a complex narrative structure, precisely because such deliberate artistry might have detracted from their unpremeditated quality—the sense of an eyewitness jotting down observations as the events unfold.

Alcott's sketches have important antecedents in Anglo-American literary tradition, notably Washington Irving's *Sketch Book of Geoffrey Crayon* (1819–20); Charles Dickens's *Sketches by Boz* (1836); and William Makepeace Thackeray's *Paris Sketch Book* (1840) and *Irish Sketch Book* (1843). Like Dickens and Thackeray, Alcott was part of the nineteenth-century movement toward realism in literature; like her predecessors, she saw herself not simply as an observer but also as a critic. But Alcott's sketches are not nearly as well-known as those of her male counterparts, even though she produced a considerable body of work in the genre. *Hospital Sketches* (1863), her best-known nonfiction work, is usually read as a Civil War piece rather than as a contribution to the literary form. Her achievements in the genre have not been fully appreciated, largely because most of the texts have never been collected and made readily available. But as evidenced in this volume, Alcott's lively style and democratic lack of pretension are well suited to the genre, and her ironic self-awareness highlights the important role of the observer in the literary sketch.

Most of the sketches were written during the middle of Alcott's life, when she was at the height of her literary productivity. All but two of the pieces deal with events that occurred between the summer of 1861, when she took a month-long vacation in the White Mountains of New Hampshire, and December 1875, when she visited a newsboys' home, an orphanage, and a prison in New York. During that period, roughly coinciding with the Civil War and Reconstruction, a great deal changed in Alcott's world.

At the beginning of this period Alcott was "writing and grubbing as usual," as she put it. Living in comfortable poverty with her family in Concord, Massachusetts, she sewed, taught kindergarten, and wrote. Although the distinguished publisher and editor James T. Fields advised her to give up writing and to teach instead, she eventually found writing to be far more lucrative, and by the end of this period had attained both fame and wealth as a writer. Her most important children's novels—*Little Women, An Old-Fashioned Girl* (1870), *Little Men* (1871), and *Eight Cousins* (1875)—and her adult novels *Moods* (1865) and *Work* were written during this time, as were most of her thrillers. In this fifteen-year span Alcott witnessed the abolition of slavery, the first impeachment of a U.S. President, and the completion of the trans-Atlantic cable and transcontinental railroad; she also made two year-long trips to Europe, one from 1865 to 1866, the other from 1870 to 1871.

Although the sketches are among the most straightforwardly autobiographical of Alcott's works, few center on her life, identity, or home; instead, their view is usually directed outward. Though published after "Hospital Sketches" (1863), "Letters from the Mountains" (1863) chronicles a trip Alcott made to New Hampshire in 1861, where she vacationed with her cousins Louisa and Hamilton Willis (who become Laura and Will in the text). These sketches do include details of her itinerary—her train ride from Boston to New Hampshire, her mountain walks, her difficulties with horseback riding—but the focus is on her many encounters with tourists and locals. She sardonically describes a young married couple as "a pair of dolls eloped from a baby house" and recounts with near-envious identification the antics of eight boisterous male college students, expressing the hope that she might be reincarnated as a "freshman" in a future life. In these portrayals Alcott often relies on stereotypes—for example, spinsters, dandies, and even national and ethnic stereotypes. But her assumptions and initial impressions are also questioned and often proved erroneous. She derides a young vendor selling drinks and snacks on the train, describing him as a "shrill boy" and imagining him to be "the ghost of some lad killed on the road, who haunts the cars and so avenges himself on the corporation for having made a corpse of him." Farther down the tracks, however, Alcott finds herself desperately wishing for his return: "The longing for him seems to lay him like a spell, for he appears no more; and I gasp for water and the noisy ghost in vain." As in many of her first-person narratives, Alcott turns the satire initially directed at others toward herself.

Her descriptions of landscapes follow a similar pattern of reversal. Preferring to explore on her own, Alcott bristles at the thought of following established or guided routes and complains about "being trotted from place to place and ordered to go into ecstasies because everyone else does." Yet as she reaches the summit of Mount Washington, her skepticism gives way to awe and exaltation: "Neither eye, brain, mind, nor body is half large or strong enough to take in the magnitude and significance of all about you." The reader has barely been swept up into the Romantic sublime when Alcott changes direction once again, offering bits of tourist conversation— "You dreadful boy! You've sat on the sandwiches and got the mustard all over you!" Such details abruptly dispel the rapturous mood and bring the scene back to the mundane; in the process, the sketch pokes fun not only at the tourists but also at the narrator. Flouting the conventions of travel writing, Alcott rarely dwells on scenery and in one instance excuses her reticence on the subject by saying simply, "I hope no one expects a description of the indescribable." At times she becomes willfully uninformative and laconic: "Pass a great river, ought to know its name, but don't."

Her mountain letters were originally composed for the amusement of friends and family back in Concord. But when "Hospital Sketches" appeared in the antislavery weekly *Commonwealth,* it proved to be such a hit that "people bought the papers faster than they could be supplied," and its editor Franklin B. Sanborn immediately asked Alcott for additional contributions. She reworked these two-year-old mountain letters into sketches and submitted them to Sanborn, although she later regretted her decision and terminated the series after just four installments. Although the letters were well received, the perpetually self-critical Alcott feared "they were not good" and resolved "never again to try to be funny lest I should be rowdy and nothing more." Her own censure of them notwithstanding, the pleasure of these sketches lies precisely in their rowdiness and their subversion of the conventions of the form.

Necessarily more somber is *Hospital Sketches,* a chronicle of Alcott's experiences as an army nurse, which appeared serially in May and June of 1863 before being published as a book in August. In December 1862, Alcott traveled to Washington, D.C., to assume her post at Georgetown's Union Hotel Hospital, renamed Hurly-burly House in the sketches. Spurred by a patriotic and humanitarian desire to serve, "Nurse Tribulation Periwinkle," as Alcott calls herself, performs her duties with zeal. But her initial enthusiasm soon gives way to horror when the wounded from Fredericksburg are brought in and she sees "several stretchers, each with its legless, armless, or desperately wounded occupant." Like many of her other sketches, these are marked by dramatic shifts in tone—from cheerful enthusiasm to horror, from comedy to tragedy. In *Hospital Sketches* and the lesser-known "Hospital Lamp" (1864), a poignant character sketch, Alcott depicts the tenderness and affection that ordinary soldiers feel for one another. Ned's farewell to John in *Hospital Sketches* and Hunt's description of his friend Tom in "Hospital Lamp" are among the most moving scenes in all of Alcott's sketches.

Alcott had not worked long at the hospital when she contracted a debilitating case of typhoid. The doctors' treatment seemed to exacerbate her condition, and eventually the staff sent for her father to escort her back to Massachusetts. A few months after her return, Sanborn approached her and suggested that her hospital letters to her family be recast as a series of sketches for his newspaper. Lured by the prospect of earning money, and perhaps flattered at being treated like a professional writer, Alcott revised the letters for publication. They were immediately popular with the readers of the *Commonwealth,* who were eager for details about the war and appreciated Alcott's uncompromising abolitionism. After three installments she was pressed for a fourth, and was subsequently persuaded to expand them into a book. *Hospital Sketches* sold well and brought her a measure of critical acclaim; even Fields expressed admiration for the sketches. Perhaps more important, the success of *Hospital Sketches* encouraged Alcott to develop her own style—one that was marked by energy and spontaneity, drew heavily on her own experiences, and mixed politics with pathos, didacticism with irreverence, the serious with the comic.

After the war Alcott was presented with an opportunity to tour Europe, although the arrangement was not ideal, as it required her to serve as a nurse for a difficult patient, Anna Weld. Alcott, Weld, and Weld's brother, George, arrived in Liverpool on July 29, 1865, and Alcott spent the next year in Europe, visiting England, Germany, France, and Switzerland, before returning to the United States in July 1866. The trip became an important source for a number of her later writings. Her accounts of nurse-patient relations in *Work,* for instance, were based on her experiences with Anna Weld. On the trip Alcott also met Ladislas Wisniewski, a young man who had recently fought in the January Insurrection, an unsuccessful Polish rebellion against Russian domination; he would later serve as the model for Alcott's most famous male character, Laurie in *Little Women.* It is in her sketches, however, that these two first appear: Weld as the "Mademoiselle" in "Up the Rhine" (1867) and Wisniewski as the "captivating and romantic" young pianist in "Life in a Pension."

Seven of the sketches in this volume detail incidents from Alcott's trips through Europe. The first, "Up the Rhine," recounts a brief river voyage she took in August 1865. It begins predictably enough, with comments on the picturesque German landscape and the national characteristics of the various tourists, but the sketch takes a comic turn when "poor little Mademoiselle" insists on going ashore to rest. Left behind in a quaint German village ill equipped for tourists, Alcott struggles with her inability to speak German, the townspeople's inability to understand English, and Mademoiselle's willful invalidism. In "Life in a Pension," Alcott describes her experiences with another "motley collection" of tourists—this time at a Swiss hotel on the northeastern shore of Lake Geneva during the fall of 1865. Although the setting is European, almost Gothic, and the characters multinational, the focus of the sketch is on a simmering feud between two Americans: Alcott, "an observing spinster" with "the blood of a born abolitionist," and Colonel Polk, a former slave owner from South Carolina, who maligns Northerners and tells racist tales about his erstwhile slaves. And later in Nice, Alcott encounters the colorful Madame Rolande, the subject of "A Royal Governess" (1868), from whom the Weld party rents several rooms. At first the prying, overbearing Rolande, a former governess for Queen Victoria's children, seems ridiculous, her life apparently devoted to paying homage to the Queen's family and reliving memories of her association with the royals. But at the end of the sketch Alcott subverts the satire and transforms Rolande from an object of ridicule into a rather sympathetic figure.

Intended for a relatively well-educated adult audience, these three travel sketches appeared in the pages of the New York weekly *Independent* in 1867 and 1868. After the stunning success of *Little Women,* Alcott continued to draw on the events of this trip for her nonfiction, but with a younger audience in mind. With meandering narratives that resemble open-ended adventures, three sketches recounting her unconventional explorations of greater London later appeared in the children's magazine *Youth's Companion.*

After leaving Rolande and Weld in Nice, Alcott arrived in London on May 17, 1866, and stayed in Wimbledon visiting with Ellen and Moncure Daniel Conway, an American couple she knew from Concord. "The Maypole Inn: A Place of Holiday Stories" (1882) chronicles a countryside expedition undertaken by Alcott and a certain "C——" soon after her arrival. "C——," like "Mr. C." in *Shawl-Straps* (1872) and "C." in "London Bridges" (1874), is most likely Moncure Conway, Alcott's chief guide to London. In the sketch the pair head to Chingford, just northeast of London, to visit an ancient Norman church and the Maypole Inn, a site made famous by Dickens's *Barnaby Rudge* (1841). The sketch is replete with Dickensian references, from the anti-Catholic Gordon Riots of 1780, so vividly depicted in *Barnaby Rudge,* to the raven, Barnaby's companion. Although she thoroughly enjoyed this day trip, Alcott waited sixteen years to publish her account of it.

Other sketches about Alcott's 1866 excursions in London had appeared earlier. "How We Saw the Shah" (1873) is an amusing report of a desultory June outing. The title is somewhat misleading: Although the narrator and her party do catch a glimpse of the Shah and his entourage, the event is of only secondary importance in the sketch. Indeed, Alcott expresses, though somewhat disingenuously, her disdain for the Persian king. "London Bridges," an account of a moonlight trip to the Thames and its bridges, offers yet another glimpse of the city. Although the setting is well suited for a romantic or tragic tale, Alcott keeps the tone light and ends the sketch on a comic note.

Much of Alcott's second trip to Europe is treated in *Shawl-Straps,* in which she invents fictional personas for her traveling companions and herself and weaves into the plot events from the first European trip (the Dickens pilgrimage with the Professor, for example, is based on Alcott's sightseeing excursions with Moses Coit Tyler in 1866). Perhaps in part to dispel rumors circulating in Boston that she had grown seriously ill or had died, during the second tour Alcott published in the *Boston Daily Evening Transcript* "Recent Exciting Scenes in Rome" (1871), a journalistic sketch about a flood in Rome and a visit by King Victor Emmanuel. She later revised this sketch, dressing up the prose and changing the characters' names, and incorporated it into the *Shawl-Straps* narrative.

Although that trip would be her last one to Europe, Alcott remained an active traveler, at least in the Northeast. In late 1875, she was living in New York, mingling with the city's literati and exploring various philanthropic projects. Sometime after Thanksgiving she visited the Newsboys' Lodging House and wrote a spirited report, "An Evening Call" (1876), about the home and the 180 children who lived there. Like Horatio Alger's novel *Ragged Dick* (1868), this sketch draws attention to a grave social problem of the late-nineteenth-century United States—the thousands of homeless children who roamed the nation's urban alleyways and avenues. Although the subject is a dark one, the tone of this sketch is cheerful and optimistic, perhaps because she so liked the boys she met.

Subsequent philanthropic visits were not quite so sunny. On Christmas Day in 1875, Alcott and the social reformer Abby Hopper Gibbons visited a large orphanage on Randall's Island, in the East River. In "A New Way to Spend Christmas" (1876), Alcott seems at a loss while visiting the children, many of whom were ill or physically or mentally disabled. Faced with the suffering at the Union Hotel Hospital, "Tribulation Periwinkle" energetically threw herself into her work, tending to the wounded and the dying, but in the orphanage Alcott seems less sure of herself, finding little to do beyond passing out gifts. At one point she remarks, "Alas, how sad it was to see such suffering laid on such innocent victims and to feel how little one could do to lessen it!" Instead of reflecting on the limits of benevolence, as she does in *Hospital Sketches,* Alcott falls back on the conventional language of pity and piety, lamenting the "innocent victims" and praising Gibbons's "heaven-born charity." On the following Wednesday, December 29, 1875, she accompanied Gibbons on a tour of "the Tombs," the infamous prison on Manhattan's Lower East Side, her impressions of which are recorded in "A Visit to the Tombs." The tone of "A Visit to the Tombs" is rather grave and mysterious. Although the sketch was intended for a younger audience, the dramatic events, the hints of violence, and the narrator's voyeuristic "desire to see what lay behind" the prison walls recall the mood of Alcott's thrillers.

Alcott was often an outspoken advocate for the disenfranchised and the destitute. Her upbringing in an abolitionist family, her father's philosophical idealism, her mother's lifelong commitment to charitable pursuits, and her childhood in Concord all shaped her social and political consciousness. Alcott's reformist proclivities are evident not only in her adult pieces but in her children's pieces as well. Published in *Merry's Museum,* her first children's sketch, "A Visit to the School Ship" (1869), chronicles a visit to a progressive reformatory for juvenile criminals. In "Little Boston" (1873), Alcott introduces the subject of women's suffrage to the readers of the *Youth's Companion*. In the sketch she watches from her window a group of children playing and notices that they imitate adult social behavior. While playing "election," however, the children—in contrast to their grown-up counterparts—decide that "the ladies" should also participate. The humor of this sketch arises from the mimicry of the children, but the satire is directed at adults.

In the spring of 1875, Alcott published in the *Woman's Journal* another comic feminist piece, "Woman's Part in the Concord Celebration," an account of the town's Centennial celebration. The organizers, through incompetence and deliberate design, all but exclude the women from the day's events, although the group includes "the great-granddaughters of Prescott, William Emerson, John Hancock, and Dr. Ripley." Instructed to wait for their escorts to lead them to the celebration, the women patiently stand in the cold until they finally realize that they have been forgotten. In keeping with the spirit of the day, the "free and independent citizenesses" of Concord decide to take matters in their own hands and walk unescorted to the festivities.

In this piece, as in many of the other sketches pertaining to events from the middle of her life, Alcott is an observer rather than the primary focus. Many of the pieces have a

distinctly journalistic quality, as though they were spontaneous dispatches. In later years Alcott's sketches would become more personal and reflective. In "Reminiscences of Ralph
Waldo Emerson" (1882), written on the day of his funeral,
and "Recollections of My Childhood" (1888), a posthumously
published memoir, Alcott turns her attention to the past, particularly her childhood in Concord. She recalls how important
Emerson's essays were to her and how generous he was in
sharing books from his library when "the book mania" seized
her as an adolescent. She also recounts her experiences with
the abolitionist movement and Emerson's commitment to
women's rights, which he steadfastly maintained despite the
unpopularity of the position. These two intimate, almost wistful pieces were among the last sketches to be written. Perhaps
Alcott, whose final years were marred by poor health, sought
to preserve a picture of herself and her beloved Concord by
which she wanted both to be remembered.

Gregory Eiselein
Kansas State University

HOSPITAL SKETCHES

CHAPTER I

OBTAINING SUPPLIES

"I want something to do."

This remark being addressed to the world in general, no one in particular felt it their duty to reply. So I repeated it to the smaller world about me, received the following suggestions, and settled the matter by answering my own inquiry, as people are apt to do when very much in earnest.

"Write a book," quoth the author of my being.

"Don't know enough, sir. First live, then write."

"Try teaching again," suggested my mother.

"No, thank you, ma'am. Ten years of that is enough."

"Take a husband like my Darby, and fulfill your mission," said sister Joan, home on a visit.

"Can't afford expensive luxuries, Mrs. Coobiddy."

"Turn actress, and immortalize your name," said sister Vashti, striking an attitude.

"I won't."

"Go nurse the soldiers," said my young brother, Tom, panting for "the tented field."

"I will!"

So far, very good. Here was the will—now for the way. At first sight not a foot of it appeared, but that didn't matter, for the Periwinkles are a hopeful race. Their crest is an anchor with three cock-a-doodles crowing atop. They all wear rose-colored spectacles and are lineal descendants of the inventor of aerial architecture. An hour's conversation on the subject set the whole family in a blaze of enthusiasm. A model hospital was erected, and each member had accepted an honorable post therein. The paternal P. was chaplain, the maternal P. was matron, and all the youthful P.'s filled the pod of futurity with achievements whose brilliancy eclipsed the glories of the present and the past. Arriving at this satisfactory conclusion, the meeting adjourned, and the fact that Miss Tribulation was available as army nurse went abroad on the wings of the wind.

In a few days a townswoman heard of my desire, approved of it, and brought about an interview with one of the sisterhood which I wished to join, who was at home on a furlough and able and willing to satisfy all inquiries. A morning chat with Miss General S.—we hear no end of Mrs. Generals, why not a Miss?—produced three results: I felt that I could do the work, was offered a place, and accepted it, promising not to desert but to stand ready to march on Washington at an hour's notice.

A few days were necessary for the letter containing my request and recommendation to reach headquarters and another containing my commission to return; therefore, no time was to be lost. And heartily thanking my pair of friends, I tore home through the December slush, as if the rebels were after me, and like many another recruit, burst in upon my family with the announcement:

"I've enlisted!"

An impressive silence followed. Tom, the irrepressible, broke it with a slap on the shoulder and the graceful compliment:

"Old Trib, you're a trump!"

"Thank you, then I'll *take* something." Which I did, in the shape of dinner, reeling off my news at the rate of three dozen words to a mouthful, and as everyone else talked equally fast and all together, the scene was most inspiring.

As boys going to sea immediately become nautical in speech, walk as if they already had their "sea legs" on, and shiver their timbers on all possible occasions, so I turned military at once, called my dinner my rations, saluted all new-comers, and ordered a dress parade that very afternoon. Having reviewed every rag I possessed, I detailed some for picket duty while airing over the fence; some to the sanitary influences of the washtub; others to mount guard in the trunk; while the weak and wounded went to the Workbasket Hospital to be made ready for active service again. To this squad I devoted myself for a week; but all was done, and I had time to get powerfully impatient before the letter came. It did arrive, however, and brought a disappointment along with its good-will and friendliness, for it told me that the place in the Armory Hospital that I supposed I was to take was already filled and a much less desirable one at Hurly-burly House was offered instead.

"That's just your luck, Trib. I'll tote your trunk up garret for you again; for of course you won't go," Tom remarked with the disdainful pity which small boys affect when they get into their teens. I was wavering in my secret soul, but that settled the matter, and I crushed him on the spot with martial brevity:

"It is now one. I shall march at six."

I have a confused recollection of spending the afternoon in pervading the house like an executive whirlwind, with my family swarming after me, all working, talking, prophesying, and lamenting, while I packed my "go-abroady" possessions, tumbled the rest into two big boxes, danced on the lids till they shut, and gave them in charge, with the direction:

"If I never come back, make a bonfire of them."

Then I choked down a cup of tea, generously salted instead of sugared by some agitated relative, shouldered my knap-sack—it was only a traveling bag, but do let me preserve the unities—hugged my family three times all around without a vestige of unmanly emotion till a certain dear old lady broke down upon my neck, with a despairing sort of wail:

"Oh, my dear, my dear, how can I let you go?"

"I'll stay if you say so, Mother."

"But I don't. Go, and the Lord will take care of you."

Much of the Roman matron's courage had gone into the Yankee matron's composition, and in spite of her tears, she would have sent ten sons to the war, had she possessed them, as freely as she sent one daughter, smiling and flapping on the doorstep till I vanished, though the eyes that followed me were very dim and the handkerchief she waved was very wet.

My transit from the Gables to the village depot was a funny mixture of good wishes and good-byes, mud puddles and shopping. A December twilight is not the most cheering time to enter upon a somewhat perilous enterprise, and but for the presence of Vashti and neighbor Thorn, I fear that I might have added a drop of the briny to the native moisture of—

"The town I left behind me,"

though I'd no thought of giving out—oh, bless you, no! When the engine screeched "Here we are," I clutched my escort in a fervent embrace and skipped into the car with as blithe a farewell as if going on a bridal tour—though I believe brides don't usually wear cavernous black bonnets and fuzzy brown coats, with a hairbrush, a pair of rubbers, two books, and a bag of gingerbread distorting the pockets of the same. If I thought that anyone would believe it, I'd boldly state that I slept from C. to B., which would simplify matters immensely. But as I know they wouldn't, I'll confess that the head under the funereal coal hod fermented with all manner of high thoughts and heroic purposes "to do or die"—perhaps both— and the heart under the fuzzy brown coat felt very tender with the memory of the dear old lady, probably sobbing over her army socks and the loss of her topsy-turvy Trib. At this juncture I took the veil, and what I did behind it is nobody's business. But I maintain that the soldier who cries when his mother says "good-bye" is the boy to fight best and die bravest when the time comes, or go back to her better than he went.

Till nine o'clock I trotted about the city streets, doing those last errands which no woman would even go to heaven without attempting, if she could. Then I went to my usual refuge and, fully intending to keep awake, as a sort of vigil appropriate to the occasion, fell fast asleep and dreamed propitious dreams till my rosy-faced cousin waked me with a kiss.

A bright day smiled upon my enterprise, and at ten I reported myself to my General, received last instructions and no end of the sympathetic encouragement which women give, in look, touch, and tone more effectually than in words. The next step was to get a free pass to Washington, for I'd no desire to waste my substance on railroad companies when "the boys" needed even a spinster's mite. A friend of mine had procured such a pass, and I was bent on doing likewise, though I had to face the president of the railroad to accomplish it. I'm a bashful individual, though I can't get anyone to believe it; so it cost me a great effort to poke about the Worcester depot till the right door appeared, then walk into a room containing several gentlemen, and blunder out my request in a high state of stammer and blush. Nothing could have been more courteous than this dreaded president, but it was evident that I had made as absurd a demand as if I had asked for the nose off his respectable face. He referred me to the Governor at the State House, and I backed out, leaving him, no doubt, to regret that such mild maniacs were left at large. Here was a Scylla-and-Charybdis business—as if a president wasn't trying enough, without the Governor of Massachusetts and the hub of the hub piled on top of that. "I never can do it," thought I. "Tom will hoot at you if you don't," whispered the inconvenient little voice that is always goading people to the performance of disagreeable duties and always appeals to the most effective agent to produce the proper result. The idea of allowing any boy that ever wore a felt basin and a shoddy jacket with a microscopic tail to crow over me was preposterous. So, giving myself a mental slap for such faintheartedness, I streamed away across the Common, wondering if I ought to say "Your Honor" or simply "sir," and decided upon the latter, fortifying myself with recollections of an evening in a charming green library, where I beheld the Governor placidly consuming oysters, and laughing as if Massachusetts was a myth and he had no heavier burden on his shoulders than his host's handsome hands.

Like an energetic fly in a very large cobweb, I struggled through the State House, getting into all the wrong rooms and none of the right, till I turned desperate and went into one, resolving not to come out till I'd made somebody hear and answer me. I suspect that of all the wrong places I had blundered into, this was the most so. But I didn't care, and though the apartment was full of soldiers, surgeons, starers, and spittoons, I cornered a perfectly incapable person and proceeded to pump for information with the following result:

"Was the Governor anywhere about?"

No, he wasn't.

"Could he tell me where to look?"

No, he couldn't.

"Did he know anything about free passes?"

No, he didn't.

"Was there anyone there of whom I could inquire?"

Not a person.

"Did he know of any place where information could be obtained?"

Not a place.

"Could he throw the smallest gleam of light upon the matter in any way?"

Not a ray.

I am naturally irascible, and if I could have shaken this negative gentleman vigorously, the relief would have been immense. The prejudices of society forbidding this mode of redress, I merely glowered at him; and before my wrath found vent in words, my General appeared, having seen me from an opposite window and come to know what I was about. At her command the languid gentleman woke up and troubled himself to remember that Major or Sergeant or something McK. knew all about the tickets and his office was in Milk Street. I perked up instanter, and then, as if the exertion was too much for him, what did this animated wet blanket do but add:

"I think McK. may have left Milk Street now, and I don't know where he has gone."

"Never mind. The newcomers will know where he has moved to, my dear, so don't be discouraged. And if you don't succeed, come to me, and we will see what to do next," said my General.

I blessed her in a fervent manner and a cool hall, fluttered around the corner, and bore down upon Milk Street, bent on discovering McK., if such a being was to be found. He wasn't, and the ignorance of the neighborhood was really pitiable. Nobody knew anything, and after tumbling over bundles of leather, bumping against big boxes, being nearly annihilated by descending bales and sworn at by aggravated truckmen, I finally elicited the advice to look for McK. in Haymarket Square. Who my informant was I've really forgotten; for, having hailed several busy gentlemen, some one of them fabricated this delusive quietus for the perturbed spirit, who instantly departed to the sequestered locality he named. If I had been in search of the Koh-i-noor diamond, I should have been as likely to find it there as any vestige of McK. I stared at signs, inquired in shops, invaded an eating house, visited the recruiting tent in the middle of the Square, made myself a nuisance generally, and accumulated mud enough to retard another Nile. All in vain, and I mournfully turned my face toward the General's, feeling that I should be forced to enrich the railroad company after all, when suddenly I beheld that admirable young man, brother-in-law Darby Coobiddy, Esq. I arrested him with a burst of news, and wants, and woes, which caused his manly countenance to lose its usual repose.

"Oh, my dear boy, I'm going to Washington at five, and I can't find the free ticket man, and there won't be time to see Joan, and I'm so tired and cross I don't know what to do—and will you help me, like a cherub as you are?"

"Oh, yes, of course. I know a fellow who will set us right," responded Darby, mildly excited, and, darting into some kind of an office, held counsel with an invisible angel, who sent him out radiant. "All serene. I've got him. I'll see you through the business and then get Joan from the Dove Cote in time to see you off."

I'm a woman's rights woman, and if any man had offered help in the morning, I should have condescendingly refused it, sure that I could do everything as well, if not better, myself. My strong-mindedness had rather abated since then, and I was now quite ready to be a "timid trembler," if necessary. Dear me, how easily Darby did it all. He just asked one question, received an answer, tucked me under his arm, and in ten minutes I stood in the presence of McK., the Desired.

"Now my troubles are over," thought I, and as usual was direfully mistaken.

"You will have to get a pass from Dr. H. in Temple Place before I can give you a pass, madam," answered McK., as blandly as if he wasn't carrying desolation to my soul. Oh, indeed! Why didn't he send me to Dorchester Heights, India Wharf, or Bunker Hill Monument, and done with it? Here I was, after a morning's tramp, down in some place about Dock Square, and was told to step to Temple Place. Nor was that all. He might as well have asked me to catch a hummingbird, toast a salamander, or call on the man in the moon as find a doctor at home at the busiest hour of the day. It was a blow. But weariness had extinguished enthusiasm, and resignation clothed me as a garment. I sent Darby for Joan and doggedly paddled off, feeling that mud was my native element, and quite sure that the evening papers would announce the appearance of the Wandering Jew in feminine habiliments.

"Is Dr. H. in?"

"No, mum, he ain't."

Of course he wasn't. I knew that before I asked, and, considering it all in the light of a hollow mockery, added:

"When will he probably return?"

If the damsel had said "ten tonight," I should have felt a grim satisfaction in the fulfillment of my own dark prophecy; but she said, "At two, mum," and I felt it a personal insult.

"I'll call then. Tell him my business is important." With which mysteriously delivered message I departed, hoping that I left her consumed with curiosity, for mud rendered me an object of interest.

By way of resting myself, I crossed the Common for the third time, bespoke the carriage, got some lunch, packed my purchases, smoothed my plumage, and was back again as the clock struck two. The doctor hadn't come yet; and I was morally certain that he would not till, having waited till the last minute, I was driven to buy a ticket and, five minutes after the irrevocable deed was done, he would be at my service, with all manner of helpful documents and directions. Everything goes by contraries with me. So, having made up my mind to be disappointed, of course I wasn't; for, presently, in walked Dr. H., and no sooner had he heard my errand and glanced at my credentials than he said with the most engaging readiness:

"I will give you the order with pleasure, madam."

Words cannot express how soothing and delightful it was to find at last somebody who could do what I wanted without sending me from Dan to Beersheba for a dozen other bodies to do something else first. Peace descended like oil upon the ruffled waters of my being as I sat listening to the busy scratch of his pen; and when he turned about, giving me not only the order but a paper of directions wherewith to smooth away all difficulties between Boston and Washington, I felt as did poor Christian when the Evangelist gave him the scroll on the safe side of the Slough of Despond. I've no doubt many dismal nurses have inflicted themselves upon the worthy gentleman since then, but I am sure none have been more kindly helped, or are more grateful, than T. P., for that short interview added another to the many pleasant associations that already surround his name.

Feeling myself no longer a "Martha Struggles," but a comfortable young woman with plain sailing before her and the worst of the voyage well over, I once more presented myself to the valuable McK. The order was read, and certain printed papers, necessary to be filled out, were given a young gentleman—no, I prefer to say boy, with a scornful emphasis upon the word, as the only means of revenge now left me. This boy, instead of doing his duty with the diligence so charming in the

young, loitered and lounged, in a manner which proved his
education to have been sadly neglected in the—

"How doth the little busy bee,"

direction. He stared at me, gaped out of the window, ate
peanuts, and gossiped with his neighbors—boys, like himself,
and all penned in a row, like colts at a cattle show. I don't
imagine he knew the anguish he was inflicting; for it was
nearly three, the train left at five, and I had my ticket to get,
my dinner to eat, my blessed sister to see, and the depot to
reach, if I didn't die of apoplexy. Meanwhile, Patience certainly had her perfect work that day, and I hope she enjoyed
the job more than I did. Having waited some twenty minutes,
it pleased this reprehensible boy to make various marks and
blots on my documents, toss them to a venerable creature of
sixteen, who delivered them to me with such paternal directions that it only needed a pat on the head and an encouraging
"Now run home to your ma, little girl, and mind the crossings,
my dear," to make the illusion quite perfect.

Why I was sent to a steamboat office for car tickets is not
for me to say, though I went as meekly as I should have gone
to the probate court, if sent. A fat, easy gentleman gave me
several bits of paper with coupons attached, with a warning
not to separate them, which instantly inspired me with a
yearning to pluck them apart and see what came of it. But remembering through what fear and tribulation I had obtained
them, I curbed Satan's promptings, and clutching my prize as
if it were my pass to the Elysian fields, I hurried home. Dinner
was rapidly consumed; Joan enlightened, comforted, and
kissed; the dearest of apple-faced cousins hugged; the kindest
of apple-faced cousins' fathers subjected to the same process;
and I mounted the ambulance, baggage wagon, or anything
you please but hack, and drove away, too tired to feel excited,
sorry, or glad.

CHAPTER II

A FORWARD MOVEMENT

As travelers like to give their own impressions of a journey, though every inch of the way may have been described a half a dozen times before, I add some of the notes made by the way, hoping that they will amuse the reader and convince the skeptical that such a being as Nurse Periwinkle does exist, that she really did go to Washington, and that these "Sketches" are not romance.

New York Train—Seven P.M.—Spinning along to take the boat at New London. Very comfortable; munch gingerbread, and Mrs. C.'s fine pear, which deserves honorable mention, because my first loneliness was comforted by it, and pleasant recollections of both kindly sender and bearer. Look much at Dr. H.'s paper of directions—put my tickets in every conceivable place, that they may be get-at-able, and finish by losing them entirely. Suffer agonies till a compassionate neighbor pokes them out of a crack with his penknife. Put them in the inmost corner of my purse, that in the deepest recesses of my pocket, pile a collection of miscellaneous articles atop, and pin up the whole. Just get composed, feeling that I've done my best to keep them safely, when the Conductor appears and I'm forced to rout them all out again, exposing my precautions and getting into a flutter at keeping the man waiting. Finally, fasten them on the seat before me and keep one eye steadily upon the yellow torments till I forget all about them in chat with the gentleman who shares my seat. Having heard complaints of the absurd way in which American women become images of petrified propriety if addressed by strangers, when traveling alone, the inborn perversity of my nature causes me to assume an entirely opposite style of deportment; and finding my companion hails from Little Athens, is acquainted with several of my three hundred and sixty-five cousins, and in every way a respectable and respectful member of society, I put my bashfulness in my pocket and plunge into a long conversation on the war, the weather, music, Carlyle, skating, genius, hoops, and the immortality of the soul.

Ten P.M.—Very sleepy. Nothing to be seen outside but darkness made visible; nothing inside but every variety of bunch into which the human form can be twisted, rolled, or "massed," as Miss Prescott says of her jewels. Every man's legs sprawl drowsily; every woman's head (but mine) nods till it finally settles on somebody's shoulder, a new proof of the truth of the everlasting oak-and-vine simile; children fret; lovers whisper; old folks snore; and somebody privately imbibes brandy when the lamps go out. The penetrating perfume rouses the multitude, causing some to start up like war horses at the smell of powder. When the lamps are relighted, everyone laughs, sniffs, and looks inquiringly at his neighbor—everyone but a stout gentleman, who, with well-gloved hands folded upon his broadcloth rotundity, sleeps on impressively. Had he been innocent, he would have waked up, for to slumber in that babelike manner, with a car full of giggling, staring, sniffing humanity, was simply preposterous. Public suspicion was down upon him at once. I doubt if the appearance of a flat black bottle with a label would have settled the matter more effectually than did the overdignified and profound repose of this shortsighted being. His moral neck cloth, virtuous boots, and pious attitude availed him nothing, and it was well he kept his eyes shut, for "Humbug!" twinkled at him from every windowpane, brass nail, and human eye around him.

Eleven P.M.—In the boat *City of Boston,* escorted thither by my car acquaintance and deposited in the cabin. Trying to look as if the greater portion of my life had been passed on board boats, but painfully conscious that I don't know the first thing. So sit bolt upright, and stare about me till I hear one lady say to another, "We must secure our berths at once"— whereupon I dart at one and, while leisurely taking off my cloak, wait to discover what the second move may be. Several ladies draw the curtains that hang in a semicircle before each nest—instantly I whisk mine smartly together and then peep out to see what next. Gradually, on hooks above the blue and yellow drapery, appear the coats and bonnets of my neighbors, while their boots and shoes, in every imaginable attitude, assert themselves below, as if their owners had committed suicide in a body. A violent creaking, scrambling, and fussing causes the fact that people are going regularly to bed to dawn upon my mind. Of course they are; and so am I—but pause at the seventh pin, remembering that as I was born to be drowned, an eligible opportunity now presents itself; and having twice escaped a watery grave, the third immersion will certainly extinguish my vital spark. The boat is new, but if it ever intends to blow up, spring a leak, catch afire, or be run into, it will do the deed tonight because I'm here to fulfill my destiny. With tragic calmness I resign myself, replace my pins, lash my purse and papers together with my handkerchief, examine the saving circumference of my hoop, and look about me for any means of deliverance when the moist moment shall arrive; for I've no intention of folding my hands and bubbling to death without an energetic splashing first. Barrels, hen coops, portable settees, and life preservers do not adorn the cabin, as they should; and roving wildly to and fro, my eye sees no ray of hope till it falls upon a plump old lady, devoutly reading in the cabin Bible, and a voluminous nightcap. I remember that at the swimming school fat girls always floated best, and in an instant my plan is laid. At the first alarm I firmly attach myself to the plump lady, and cling to her through fire and water, for I feel that my old enemy, the cramp, will seize me by the foot if I attempt to swim; and, though I can hardly expect to reach Jersey City with myself and my baggage in as good condition as I hoped, I might manage to get picked up by holding to my fat friend; if not, it will be a comfort to feel that I've made an effort and shall die in good society. Poor dear woman! How little she dreamed, as she read and rocked, with her cap in a high state of starch and her feet comfortably cooking at the register, what fell designs were hovering about her, and how intently a small but determined eye watched her, till it suddenly closed.

Sleep got the better of fear to such an extent that my boots appeared to gape, and my bonnet nodded on its peg, before I gave in. Having piled my cloak, bag, rubbers, books, and umbrella on the lower shelf, I drowsily swarmed onto the upper one, tumbling down a few times and excoriating the knobby portions of my frame in the act. A very brief nap on the upper roost was enough to set me gasping as if a dozen feather beds and the whole boat were laid over me. Out I turned, and after a series of convulsions, which caused my neighbor to ask if I wanted the stewardess, I managed to get my luggage up and myself down. But even in the lower berth, my rest was not unbroken; for various articles kept dropping off the little shelf at the bottom of the bed, and every time I flew up, thinking my hour had come, I bumped my head severely against the little shelf at the top, evidently put there for that express purpose. At last, after listening to the swash of the waves outside, wondering if the machinery usually creaked in that way, and watching a knothole in the side of my berth, sure that death would creep in there as soon as I took my eye from it, I dropped asleep and dreamed of muffins.

Five A.M.—On deck, trying to wake up and enjoy an east wind and a morning fog and a twilight sort of view of something on the shore. Rapidly achieve my purpose and do enjoy every moment as we go rushing through the Sound, with steamboats passing up and down, lights dancing on the shore, mist wreaths slowly furling off, and a pale pink sky above us as the sun comes up.

Seven A.M.—In the cars, at Jersey City. Much fuss with tickets, which one man scribbles over, another snips, and a third "makes note on." Partake of refreshment in the gloom of a very large and dirty depot. Think that my sandwiches would be more relishing without so strong a flavor of napkin and my gingerbread more easy of consumption if it had not been pulverized by being sat upon. People act as if early traveling didn't agree with them. Children scream and scamper; men smoke and growl; women shiver and fret; porters swear; great truck horses pace up and down with loads of baggage; and everyone seems to get into the wrong car and come tumbling out again. One man, with three children, a dog, a bird cage, and several bundles, puts himself and his possessions into every possible place where a man, three children, dog, bird cage, and bundles could be got, and is satisfied with none of them. I follow their movements with an interest that is really exhausting and, as they vanish, hope for rest, but don't get it. A strong-minded woman, with a tumbler in her hand and no cloak or shawl on, comes rushing through the car, talking loudly to a small porter, who lugs a folding bed after her and looks as if life were a burden to him.

"You promised to have it ready. It is not ready. It must be a car with a water jar, the windows must be shut, the fire must be kept up, the blinds must be down. No, this won't do. I shall go through the whole train and suit myself, for you promised to have it ready. It is not ready," etc., all through again, like a hand organ. She haunted the cars, the depot, the office and baggage room, with her bed, her tumbler, and her tongue, till the train started; and a sense of fervent gratitude filled my soul when I found that she and her unknown invalid were not to share our car.

Philadelphia.—An old place, full of Dutch women, in "bellus top" bonnets, selling vegetables in long, open markets. Everyone seems to be scrubbing their white steps. All the houses look like tidy jails, with their outside shutters. Several have crape on the door handles, and many have flags flying from roof or balcony. Few men appear, and the women seem to do the business, which perhaps accounts for its being so well done. Pass fine buildings, but don't know what they are. Would like to stop and see my native city, for, having left it at the tender age of two, my recollections are not vivid.

Baltimore.—A big, dirty, shippy, shiftless place, full of goats, geese, colored people, and coal, at least the part of it I see. Pass near the spot where the riot took place, and feel as if I should enjoy throwing a stone at somebody, hard. Find a guard at the ferry, the depot, and here and there along the road. A camp whitens one hillside, and a cavalry training school, or whatever it should be called, is a very interesting sight, with quantities of horses and riders galloping, marching, leaping, and skirmishing over all manner of breakneck places. A party of English people get in—the men with sandy hair and red whiskers, all trimmed alike, to a hair; rough gray coats; very rosy, clean faces; and a fine, full way of speaking, which is particularly agreeable after our slipshod American gabble. The two ladies wear funny velvet fur-trimmed hoods; are done up, like compact bundles, in tartan shawls; and look as if bent on seeing everything thoroughly. The devotion of one elderly John Bull to his red-nosed spouse was really beautiful to behold. She was plain and cross, and fussy and stupid, but J. B., Esq., read no papers when she was awake, turned no cold shoulder when she wished to sleep, and cheerfully said "Yes, me dear" to every wish or want the wife of his bosom expressed. I quite warmed to the excellent man and asked a question or two as the only means of expressing my goodwill. He answered very civilly, but evidently hadn't been used to being addressed by strange women in public conveyances; and Mrs. B. fixed her green eyes upon me, as if she thought me a forward hussy, or whatever is good English for a presuming young woman. The pair left their friends before we reached Washington; and the last I saw of them was a vision of a large plaid lady stalking grimly away on the arm of a rosy, stout gentleman loaded with rugs, bags, and books, but still devoted, still smiling, and waving a hearty "Fare ye well! We'll meet ye at Willard's on Chusday."

Soon after their departure we had an accident, for no long

journey in America would be complete without one. A coupling iron broke, and after leaving the last car behind us, we waited for it to come up, which it did, with a crash that knocked everyone forward on their faces and caused several old ladies to screech dismally. Hats flew off, bonnets were flattened, the stove skipped, the lamps fell down, the water jar turned a somersault, and the wheel just over which I sat received some damage. Of course it became necessary for all the men to get out and stand about in everybody's way while repairs were made, and for the women to wrestle their heads out of the windows, asking ninety-nine foolish questions to one sensible one. A few wise females seized this favorable moment to better their seats, well knowing that few men can face the wooden stare with which they regard the former possessors of the places they have invaded.

The country through which we passed did not seem so very unlike that which I had left, except that it was more level and less wintry. In summertime the wide fields would have shown me new sights and the wayside hedges blossomed with new flowers. Now everything was sere and sodden, and a general air of shiftlessness prevailed, which would have caused a New England farmer much disgust and a strong desire to "buckle to" and "right up" things. Dreary little houses with chimneys built outside, with clay and rough sticks piled crosswise, as we used to build cob towers, stood in barren-looking fields, with cow, pig, or mule lounging about the door. We often passed colored people, looking as if they had come out of a picture book or off the stage, but not at all the sort of people I'd been accustomed to see at the North.

Wayside encampments made the fields and lanes gay with blue coats and the glitter of buttons. Military washes flapped and fluttered on the fences; pots were steaming in the open air, all sorts of tableaux seen through the openings of tents; and everywhere the boys threw up their caps and cut capers as we passed.

Washington.—It was dark when we arrived, and but for the presence of another friendly gentleman, I should have yielded myself a helpless prey to the first overpowering hackman who insisted that I wanted to go just where I didn't. Putting me into the conveyance I belonged in, my escort added to the obligation by pointing out the objects of interest which we passed in our long drive. Though I'd often been told that Washington was a spacious place, its visible magnitude quite took my breath away, and of course I quoted Randolph's expression, "a city of magnificent distances," as I suppose everyone does when they see it. The Capitol was so like the pictures that hang opposite the staring Father of His Country in boardinghouses and hotels that it did not impress me, except to recall the time when I was sure that Cinderella went to housekeeping in just such a place after she had married the inflammable Prince, though even at that early period I had my doubts as to the wisdom of a match whose foundation was of glass.

The White House was lighted up, and carriages were rolling in and out of the great gate. I stared hard at the famous East Room and would have liked a peep through the crack of the door. My old gentleman was indefatigable in his attentions, and I said "Splendid!" to everything he pointed out, though I suspect I often admired the wrong place and missed the right. Pennsylvania Avenue, with its bustle, lights, music, and military, made me feel as if I'd crossed the water and landed somewhere in Carnival time. Coming to less noticeable parts of the city, my companion fell silent, and I meditated upon the perfection which Art had attained in America—having just passed a bronze statue of some hero, who looked like a black Methodist minister, in a cocked hat, above the waist and a tipsy squire below, while his horse stood like an opera dancer, on one leg, in a high but somewhat remarkable wind, which blew his mane one way and his massive tail the other.

"Hurly-burly House, ma'am!" called a voice, startling me from my reverie, as we stopped before a great pile of buildings, with a flag flying before it, sentinels at the door, and a very trying quantity of men lounging about. My heart beat rather faster than usual, and it suddenly struck me that I was very far from home. But I descended with dignity, wondering whether I should be stopped for want of a countersign and forced to pass the night in the street. Marching boldly up the steps, I found that no form was necessary; for the men fell back, the guards touched their caps, a boy opened the door, and, as it closed behind me, I felt that I was fairly started and Nurse Periwinkle's mission was begun.

CHAPTER III

A DAY

"They've come! They've come! Hurry up, ladies—you're wanted."

"Who have come? The rebels?"

This sudden summons in the gray dawn was somewhat startling to a three days' nurse like myself, and as the thundering knock came at our door, I sprang up in my bed, prepared—

> "To gird my woman's form,
> And on the ramparts die,"

if necessary. But my roommate took it more coolly and, as she began a rapid toilet, answered my bewildered question:

"Bless you, no, child. It's the wounded from Fredericksburg. Forty ambulances are at the door, and we shall have our hands full in fifteen minutes."

"What shall we have to do?"

"Wash, dress, feed, warm, and nurse them for the next three months, I daresay. Eighty beds are ready, and we were getting impatient for the men to come. Now you will begin to see hospital life in earnest, for you won't probably find time to sit down all day and may think yourself fortunate if you get to bed by midnight. Come to me in the ballroom when you are ready. The worst cases are always carried there, and I shall need your help."

So saying, the energetic little woman twirled her hair into a button at the back of her head, in a "cleared for action" sort of style, and vanished, wrestling her way into a feminine kind of pea jacket as she went.

I am free to confess that I had a realizing sense of the fact that my hospital bed was not a bed of roses just then, or the prospect before me one of unmingled rapture. My three days' experiences had begun with a death and, owing to the defalcation of another nurse, a somewhat abrupt plunge into the superintendence of a ward containing forty beds, where I spent my shining hours washing faces, serving rations, giving medicine, and sitting in a very hard chair, with pneumonia on one side, diphtheria on the other, five typhoids on the opposite, and a dozen dilapidated patriots, hopping, lying, and lounging about, all staring more or less at the new "nuss," who suffered untold agonies, but concealed them under as matronly an aspect as a spinster could assume, and blundered through her trying labors with a Spartan firmness, which I hope they appreciated, but am afraid they didn't. Having a taste for "ghastliness," I had rather longed for the wounded to arrive; for rheumatism wasn't heroic, neither was liver complaint or measles. Even fever had lost its charms, since "bathing burning brows" had been used up in romances, real and ideal. But when I peeped into the dusky street lined with what I at first had innocently called market carts, now unloading their sad freight at our door, I recalled sundry reminiscences I had heard from nurses of longer standing, my ardor experienced a sudden chill, and I indulged in a most unpatriotic wish that I was safe at home again, with a quiet day before me and no necessity for being hustled up, as if I were a hen and had only to hop off my roost, give my plumage a peck, and be ready for action. A second bang at the door sent this recreant desire to the right about as a little woolly head popped in and Joey (a six-year-old contraband) announced:

"Miss Blank is jes' wild fer ye and says fly round right away. They's comin' in, I tell yer, heaps on 'em—one was took out dead, and I see him—ky, warn't he a goner!"

With which cheerful intelligence the imp scuttled away,

singing like a blackbird, and I followed, feeling that Richard was *not* himself again and wouldn't be for a long time to come.

The first thing I met was a regiment of the vilest odors that ever assaulted the human nose and took it by storm. Cologne, with its seven-and-seventy evil savors, was a posy bed to it, and the worst of this affliction was, everyone had assured me that it was a chronic weakness of all hospitals and I must bear it. I did, armed with lavender water, with which I so besprinkled myself and premises that like my friend Sairy, I was soon known among my patients as "the nurse with the bottle." Having been run over by three excited surgeons, bumped against by migratory coal hods, water pails, and small boys, nearly scalded by an avalanche of newly filled teapots, and hopelessly entangled in a knot of colored sisters coming to wash, I progressed by slow stages upstairs and down till the main hall was reached, and I paused to take breath and a survey. There they were, "our brave boys," as the papers justly call them, for cowards could hardly have been so riddled with shot and shell, so torn and shattered, nor have borne suffering for which we have no name, with an uncomplaining fortitude, which made one glad to cherish each as a brother. In they came, some on stretchers, some in men's arms, some feebly staggering along propped on rude crutches, and one lay stark and still with covered face as a comrade gave his name to be recorded before they carried him away to the dead house. All was hurry and confusion. The hall was full of these wrecks of humanity, for the most exhausted could not reach a bed till duly ticketed and registered. The walls were lined with rows of such as could sit, the floor covered with the more disabled, the steps and doorways filled with helpers and lookers-on. The sound of many feet and voices made that usually quiet hour as noisy as noon, and in the midst of it all, the matron's motherly face brought more comfort to many a poor soul than the cordial drafts she administered or the cheery words that welcomed all, making of the hospital a home.

The sight of several stretchers, each with its legless, armless, or desperately wounded occupant, entering my ward admonished me that I was there to work, not to wonder or weep. So I corked up my feelings and returned to the path of duty, which was rather "a hard road to travel" just then. The house had been a hotel before hospitals were needed, and many of the doors still bore their old names; some not so inappropriate as might be imagined, for my ward was in truth a *ballroom,* if gunshot wounds could christen it. Forty beds were prepared, many already tenanted by tired men who fell down anywhere and drowsed till the smell of food roused them. Around the great stove was gathered the dreariest group I ever saw— ragged, gaunt, and pale, mud to the knees, with bloody bandages untouched since put on days before; many bundled up in blankets, coats being lost or useless; and all wearing that disheartened look which proclaimed defeat more plainly than any telegram of the Burnside blunder. I pitied them so much I dared not speak to them, though, remembering all they had been through since the rout at Fredericksburg, I yearned to serve the dreariest of them all. Presently Miss Blank tore me from my refuge behind piles of one-sleeved shirts, odd socks, bandages, and lint; put basin, sponge, towels, and a block of brown soap into my hands, with these appalling directions:

"Come, my dear, begin to wash as fast as you can. Tell them to take off socks, coats, and shirts, scrub them well, put on clean shirts, and the attendants will finish them off and lay them in bed."

If she had requested me to shave them all or dance a hornpipe on the stove funnel, I should have been less staggered; but to scrub some dozen lords of creation at a moment's notice was really—really— However, there was no time for nonsense, and having resolved, when I came, to do everything I was bid, I drowned my scruples in my washbowl, clutched my soap manfully, and, assuming a businesslike air, made a dab at the first dirty specimen I saw, bent on performing my task *vi et armis* if necessary. I chanced to light on a withered old Irishman, wounded in the head, which caused that portion of his frame to be tastefully laid out like a garden, the bandages

being the walks, his hair the shrubbery. He was so overpowered by the honor of having a lady wash him, as he expressed
it, that he did nothing but roll up his eyes and bless me in an
irresistible style which was too much for my sense of the ludicrous. So we laughed together, and when I knelt down to take
off his shoes, he "flopped" also and wouldn't hear of my touching "them dirty craters. May your bed above be aisy, darlin',
for the day's work ye are doon! Whoosh! There ye are, and
bedad, it's hard tellin' which is the dirtiest, the fut or the
shoe." It was; and if he hadn't been to the fore, I should have
gone on pulling, under the impression that the "fut" was a
boot, for trousers, socks, shoes, and legs were a mass of mud.
This comical tableau produced a general grin, at which propitious beginning I took heart and scrubbed away like any tidy
parent on a Saturday night. Some of them took the performance like sleepy children, leaning their tired heads against
me as I worked. Others looked grimly scandalized, and several
of the roughest colored like bashful girls. One wore a soiled
little bag about his neck, and as I moved it to bathe his
wounded breast, I said:

"Your talisman didn't save you, did it?"

"Well, I reckon it did, marm, for that shot would a gone a
couple a inches deeper but for my old mammy's camphor bag,"
answered the cheerful philosopher.

Another, with a gunshot wound through the cheek, asked
for a looking glass and, when I brought one, regarded his
swollen face with a dolorous expression as he muttered:

"I vow to gosh, that's too bad! I warn't a bad-looking chap
before, and now I'm done for. Won't there be a thunderin'
scar? And what on earth will Josephine Skinner say?"

He looked up at me with his one eye so appealingly that I
controlled my risibles and assured him that if Josephine was a
girl of sense, she would admire the honorable scar as a lasting
proof that he had faced the enemy, for all women thought a
wound the best decoration a brave soldier could wear. I hope
Miss Skinner verified the good opinion I so rashly expressed of
her, but I shall never know.

The next scrubbee was a nice-looking lad with a curly brown mane and a budding trace of gingerbread over the lip, which he called his beard and defended stoutly when the barber jocosely suggested its immolation. He lay on a bed, with one leg gone and the right arm so shattered that it must evidently follow. Yet the little Sergeant was as merry as if his afflictions were not worth lamenting over, and when a drop or two of salt water mingled with my suds at the sight of this strong young body so marred and maimed, the boy looked up with a brave smile, though there was a little quiver of the lips, as he said:

"Now, don't you fret yourself about me, miss. I'm first-rate here, for it's nuts to lie still on this bed after knocking about in those confounded ambulances that shake what there is left of a fellow to jelly. I never was in one of these places before and think this cleaning up a jolly thing for us, though I'm afraid it isn't for you ladies."

"Is this your first battle, Sergeant?"

"No, miss, I've been in six scrimmages, and never got a scratch till this last one, but it's done the business pretty thoroughly for me, I should say. Lord! What a scramble there'll be for arms and legs when we old boys come out of our graves on the Judgment Day. Wonder if we shall get our own again? If we do, my leg will have to tramp from Fredericksburg, my arm from here, I suppose, and meet my body wherever it may be."

The fancy seemed to tickle him mightily; for he laughed blithely, and so did I, which, no doubt, caused the new nurse to be regarded as a light-minded sinner by the chaplain, who roamed vaguely about, informing the men that they were all worms, corrupt of heart, with perishable bodies and souls only to be saved by a diligent perusal of certain tracts, and other equally cheering bits of spiritual consolation, when spirituous ditto would have been preferred.

"I say, Mrs.!" called a voice behind me, and, turning, I saw a rough Michigander, with an arm blown off at the shoulder and two or three bullets still in him—as he afterwards mentioned, as carelessly as if gentlemen were in the habit of carrying such trifles about with them. I went to him, and while administering a dose of soap and water, he whispered irefully:

"That redheaded devil over yonder is a reb, damn him! You'll agree to that, I bet. He's got shet of a foot, or he'd a cut like the rest of the lot. Don't you wash him nor feed him, but jest let him holler till he's tired. It's a blasted shame to fetch them fellers in here alongside of us, and so I'll tell the chap that bosses this concern. Cuss me if I don't."

I regret to say that I did not deliver a moral sermon upon the duty of forgiving our enemies and the sin of profanity then and there but, being a red-hot abolitionist, stared fixedly at the tall rebel, who was a copperhead in every sense of the word, and privately resolved to put soap in his eyes, rub his nose the wrong way, and excoriate his cuticle generally if I had the washing of him.

My amiable intentions, however, were frustrated; for when I approached, with as Christian an expression as my principles would allow, and asked the question—"Shall I try to make you more comfortable, sir?"—all I got for my pains was a gruff—

"No, I'll do it myself."

"Here's your Southern chivalry, with a witness," thought I, dumping the basin down before him, thereby quenching a strong desire to give him a summary baptism in return for his ungraciousness; for my angry passions rose at this rebuff, in a way that would have scandalized good Dr. Watts. He was a disappointment in all respects (the rebel, not the blessed doctor), for he was neither fiendish, romantic, pathetic, nor anything interesting, but a long, fat man with a head like a burning bush and a perfectly expressionless face. So I could hate him without the slightest drawback, and ignored his existence from that day forth. One redeeming trait he certainly did possess, as the floor speedily testified; for his ablutions were so vigorously performed that his bed soon stood like an isolated island in a sea of soapsuds and he resembled a dripping merman suffering from the loss of a fin. If cleanliness is a near neighbor to godliness, then was the big rebel the godliest man in my ward that day.

Having done up our human wash and laid it out to dry, the second syllable of our version of the word "warfare" was enacted with much success. Great trays of bread, meat, soup, and coffee appeared, and both nurses and attendants turned waiters, serving bountiful rations to all who could eat. I can call my pinafore to testify to my goodwill in the work, for in ten minutes it was reduced to a perambulating bill of fare, presenting samples of all the refreshments going or gone. It was a lively scene, the long room lined with rows of beds, each filled by an occupant, whom water, shears, and clean raiment had transformed from a dismal ragamuffin into a recumbent hero with a cropped head. To and fro rushed matrons, maids, and convalescent "boys," skirmishing with knives and forks; retreating with empty plates; marching and countermarching with unvaried success, while the clash of busy spoons made most inspiring music for the charge of our Light Brigade:

> "Beds to the front of them,
> Beds to the right of them,
> Beds to the left of them,
>   Nobody blundered.
> Beamed at by hungry souls,
> Screamed at with brimming bowls,
> Steamed at by army rolls,
>   Buttered and sundered.
> With coffee not cannon plied,
> Each must be satisfied,
> Whether they lived or died;
>   All the men wondered."

Very welcome seemed the generous meal after a week of suffering, exposure, and short commons. Soon the brown faces began to smile as food, warmth, and rest did their pleasant work, and the grateful "Thankee's" were followed by more

graphic accounts of the battle and retreat than any paid reporter could have given us. Curious contrasts of the tragic and
comic met one everywhere, and some touching as well as ludicrous episodes might have been recorded that day. A six-foot
New Hampshire man, with a leg broken and perforated by a
piece of shell so large that, had I not seen the wound, I should
have regarded the story as a Munchausenism, beckoned me to
come and help him, as he could not sit up and both his bed
and beard were getting plentifully anointed with soup. As I
fed my big nestling with corresponding mouthfuls, I asked him
how he felt during the battle.

"Well, 'twas my fust, you see, so I ain't ashamed to say I
was a trifle flustered in the beginnin', there was such an all-
fired racket; for ef there's anything I do spleen agin, it's noise.
But when my mate, Eph Sylvester, caved with a bullet through
his head, I got mad and pitched in, licketty-cut. Our part of
the fight didn't last long. So a lot of us larked round Fredericksburg and give some of them houses a pretty consid'able of
a rummage till we was ordered out of the mess. Some of our
fellows cut like time, but I warn't a-goin' to run for nobody.
And fust thing I knew, a shell bust right in front of us, and I
keeled over, feelin' as if I was blowed higher'n a kite. I sung
out and the boys come back for me, double quick, but the way
they chucked me over them fences was a caution, I tell you.
Next day I was most as black as that darky yonder, lickin'
plates on the sly. This is bully coffee, ain't it? Give us another
pull at it, and I'll be obleeged to you."

I did, and as the last gulp subsided, he said, with a rub of
his old handkerchief over eyes as well as mouth:

"Look a here, I've got a pair a earbobs and a handkercher
pin I'm a-goin' to give you, if you'll have them, for you're the
very moral o' Lizy Sylvester, poor Eph's wife. That's why I sig-
naled you to come over here. They ain't much, I guess, but
they'll do to memorize the rebs by."

Burrowing under his pillow, he produced a little bundle of
what he called "truck," and gallantly presented me with a pair
of earrings, each representing a cluster of corpulent grapes,

and the pin a basket of astonishing fruit, the whole large and coppery enough for a small warming pan. Feeling delicate about depriving him of such valuable relics, I accepted the ear-rings alone and was obliged to depart somewhat abruptly when my friend stuck the warming pan in the bosom of his nightgown, viewing it with much complacency and, perhaps, some tender memory, in that rough heart of his, for the com-rade he had lost.

Observing that the man next him had left his meal un-touched, I offered the same service I had performed for his neighbor, but he shook his head.

"Thank you, ma'am. I don't think I'll ever eat again, for I'm shot in the stomach. But I'd like a drink of water, if you ain't too busy."

I rushed away, but the water pails were gone to be refilled, and it was some time before they reappeared. I did not forget my patient patient, meanwhile, and with the first mugful, hur-ried back to him. He seemed asleep, but something in the tired white face caused me to listen at his lips for a breath. None came. I touched his forehead. It was cold, and then I knew that while he waited, a better nurse than I had given him a cooler draft and healed him with a touch. I laid the sheet over the quiet sleeper, whom no noise could now disturb, and half an hour later, the bed was empty. It seemed a poor requital for all he had sacrificed and suffered—that hospital bed, lonely even in a crowd—for there was no familiar face for him to look his last upon, no friendly voice to say good-bye, no hand to lead him gently down into the Valley of the Shadow, and he vanished, like a drop in that red sea upon whose shores so many women stand lamenting. For a moment I felt bitterly in-dignant at this seeming carelessness of the value of life, the sanctity of death; then consoled myself with the thought that when the great muster roll was called, these nameless men might be promoted above many whose tall monuments record the barren honors they have won.

All having eaten, drunk, and rested, the surgeons began their rounds, and I took my first lesson in the art of dressing wounds. It wasn't a festive scene by any means, for Dr. P., whose aide I constituted myself, fell to work with a vigor which soon convinced me that I was a weaker vessel, though nothing would have induced me to confess it then. He had served in the Crimea, and seemed to regard a dilapidated body very much as I should have regarded a damaged garment; and, turning up his cuffs, whipped out a very unpleasant-looking housewife, cutting, sawing, patching, and piecing with the enthusiasm of an accomplished surgical seamstress; explaining the process, in scientific terms, to the patient meantime, which, of course, was immensely cheering and comfortable. There was an uncanny sort of fascination in watching him as he peered and probed into the mechanism of those wonderful bodies, whose mysteries he understood so well. The more intricate the wound, the better he liked it. A poor private, with both legs off, and shot through the lungs, possessed more attractions for him than a dozen generals slightly scratched in some "masterly retreat"; and had anyone appeared in small pieces, requesting to be put together again, he would have considered it a special dispensation.

The amputations were reserved till the morrow, and the merciful magic of ether was not thought necessary that day, so the poor souls had to bear their pains as best they might. It is all very well to talk of the patience of woman—and far be it from me to pluck that feather from her cap, for, heaven knows, she isn't allowed to wear many—but the patient endurance of these men under trials of the flesh was truly wonderful. Their fortitude seemed contagious, and scarcely a cry escaped them, though I often longed to groan for them when pride kept their white lips shut, while great drops stood upon their foreheads and the bed shook with the irrepressible tremor of their tortured bodies. One or two Irishmen anathematized the doctors with the frankness of their nation and ordered the Virgin to stand by them, as if she had been the wedded Biddy to whom they could administer the poker if she didn't. But as a general thing, the work went on in silence, broken only by some quiet request for roller, instruments, or plaster, a sigh from the patient, or a sympathizing murmur from the nurse.

It was long past noon before these repairs were even partially made; and having got the bodies of my boys into something like order, the next task was to minister to their minds by writing letters to the anxious souls at home, answering questions, reading papers, taking possession of money and valuables; for the Eighth Commandment was reduced to a very fragmentary condition, both by the blacks and whites who ornamented our hospital with their presence. Pocketbooks, purses, miniatures, and watches were sealed up, labeled, and handed over to the matron till such times as the owners thereof were ready to depart homeward or campward again. The letters dictated to me and revised by me that afternoon would have made an excellent chapter for some future history of the war; for, like that which Thackeray's "Ensign Spooney" wrote his mother just before Waterloo, they were "full of affection, pluck, and bad spelling," nearly all giving lively accounts of the battle and ending with a somewhat sudden plunge from patriotism to provender, desiring "Marm," "Mary Ann," or "Aunt Peters" to send along some pies, pickles, sweet stuff, and apples, "to yourn in haste," Joe, Sam, or Ned, as the case might be.

My little Sergeant insisted on trying to scribble something with his left hand and patiently accomplished some half dozen lines of hieroglyphics, which he gave me to fold and direct, with a boyish blush that rendered a glimpse of "My dearest Jane" unnecessary to assure me that the heroic lad had been more successful in the service of Commander-in-Chief Cupid than that of General Mars; and a charming little romance blossomed instanter in Nurse Periwinkle's romantic fancy, though no further confidences were made that day, for Sergeant fell asleep and, judging from his tranquil face, visited his absent sweetheart in the pleasant land of dreams.

At five o'clock a great bell rang, and the attendants flew, not to arms but to their trays, to bring up supper when a second uproar announced that it was ready. The newcomers woke at the sound, and I presently discovered that it took a very bad wound to incapacitate the defenders of the faith for the consumption of their rations. The amount that some of them sequestered was amazing; but when I suggested the probability of a famine hereafter to the matron, that motherly lady cried out: "Bless their hearts, why shouldn't they eat? It's their only amusement. So fill everyone, and if there's not enough ready tonight, I'll lend my share to the Lord by giving it to the boys." And whipping up her coffeepot and plate of toast, she gladdened the eyes and stomachs of two or three dissatisfied heroes by serving them with a liberal hand, and I haven't the slightest doubt that having cast her bread upon the waters, it came back buttered, as another largehearted old lady was wont to say.

Then came the doctor's evening visit; the administration of medicines; washing feverish faces; smoothing tumbled beds; wetting wounds; singing lullabies; and preparations for the night. By eleven the last labor of love was done, the last good night spoken; and if any needed a reward for that day's work, they surely received it in the silent eloquence of those long lines of faces, showing pale and peaceful in the shaded rooms, as we quitted them, followed by grateful glances that lighted us to bed, where rest, the sweetest, made our pillows soft, while Night and Nature took our places, filling that great house of pain with the healing miracles of Sleep and his diviner brother, Death.

CHAPTER IV

A NIGHT

Being fond of the night side of nature, I was soon promoted to the post of night nurse, with every facility for indulging in my favorite pastime of "owling." My colleague, a black-eyed widow, relieved me at dawn, we two taking care of the ward between us, like the immortal Sairy and Betsy, "turn and turn about." I usually found my boys in the jolliest state of mind their condition allowed, for it was a known fact that Nurse Periwinkle objected to blue devils and entertained a belief that he who laughed most was surest of recovery. At the beginning of my reign, dumps and dismals prevailed. The nurses looked anxious and tired, the men gloomy or sad; and a general "Hark! from the tombs a doleful sound" style of conversation seemed to be the fashion—a state of things which caused one coming from a merry, social New England town to feel as if she had got into an exhausted receiver—and the instinct of self-preservation, to say nothing of a philanthropic desire to serve the race, caused a speedy change in Ward No. 1.

More flattering than the most gracefully turned compliment, more grateful than the most admiring glance, was the sight of those rows of faces, all strange to me a little while ago, now lighting up with smiles of welcome as I came among them, enjoying that moment heartily, with a womanly pride in their regard, a motherly affection for them all. The evenings were spent in reading aloud, writing letters, waiting on and amusing the men, going the rounds with Dr. P. as he made his second daily survey, dressing my dozen wounds afresh, giving last doses, and making them cozy for the long hours to come till the nine o'clock bell rang, the gas was turned down, the day nurses went off duty, the night watch came on, and my nocturnal adventure began.

My ward was now divided into three rooms, and under favor of the matron I had managed to sort out the patients in such a way that I had what I called my "duty room," my "pleasure room," and my "pathetic room," and worked for each in a different way. One I visited armed with a dressing tray, full of rollers, plasters, and pins; another, with books, flowers, games, and gossip; a third, with teapots, lullabies, consolation, and sometimes a shroud.

Wherever the sickest or most helpless man chanced to be, there I held my watch, often visiting the other rooms to see that the general watchman of the ward did his duty by the fires and the wounds, the latter needing constant wetting. Not only on this account did I meander, but also to get fresher air than the close rooms afforded; for, owing to the stupidity of that mysterious "somebody" who does all the damage in the world, the windows had been carefully nailed down above, and the lower sashes could only be raised in the mildest weather, for the men lay just below. I had suggested a summary smashing of a few panes here and there when frequent appeals to headquarters had proved unavailing and daily orders to lazy attendants had come to nothing. No one seconded the motion, however, and the nails were far beyond my reach; for, though belonging to the sisterhood of "ministering angels," I had no wings and might as well have asked for Jacob's ladder as a pair of steps, in that charitable chaos.

One of the harmless ghosts who bore me company during the haunted hours was Dan, the watchman, whom I regarded with a certain awe; for, though so much together, I never fairly saw his face and, but for his legs, should never have recognized him, as we seldom met by day. These legs were remarkable, as was his whole figure, for his body was short, rotund, and done up in a big jacket and a muffler. His beard hid the lower part of his face, his hat brim the upper, and all I ever discovered was a pair of sleepy eyes and a very mild voice. But the legs!—very long, very thin, very crooked and feeble, looking like gray sausages in their tight coverings, without a ray of peg-toppishness about them, and finished off with a pair of expansive green cloth shoes, very like Chinese junks with the sails down. This figure, gliding noiselessly about the dimly lighted rooms, was strongly suggestive of the spirit of a beer barrel mounted on corkscrews, haunting the old hotel in search of its lost mates, emptied and staved in long ago.

Another goblin who frequently appeared to me was the attendant of the "pathetic room," who, being a faithful soul, was often up to tend two or three men, weak and wandering as babies after the fever had gone. The amiable creature beguiled the watches of the night by brewing jorums of a fearful beverage, which he called coffee and insisted on sharing with me, coming in with a great bowl of something like mud soup, scalding hot, guiltless of cream, rich in an all-pervading flavor of molasses, scorch, and tin pot. Such an amount of goodwill and neighborly kindness also went into the mess that I never could find the heart to refuse, but always received it with thanks, sipped it with hypocritical relish while he remained, and whipped it into the slop jar the instant he departed, thereby gratifying him, securing one rousing laugh in the doziest hour of the night, and no one was the worse for the transaction but the pigs. Whether they were "cut off untimely in their sins" or not, I carefully abstained from inquiring.

It was a strange life—asleep half the day, exploring Washington the other half, and all night hovering, like a massive cherubim in a red rigolette, over the slumbering sons of man. I liked it and found many things to amuse, instruct, and interest me. The snores alone were quite a study, varying from the mild sniff to the stentorian snort, which startled the echoes and hoisted the performer erect to accuse his neighbor of the deed, magnanimously forgive him, and, wrapping the drapery of his couch about him, lie down to vocal slumber. After listening for a week to this band of wind instruments, I indulged in the belief that I could recognize each by the snore alone, and was tempted to join the chorus by breaking out with John Brown's favorite hymn:

"Blow ye the trumpet, blow!"

I would have given much to have possessed the art of sketching, for many of the faces became wonderfully interesting when unconscious. Some grew stern and grim, the men evidently dreaming of war, as they gave orders, groaned over their wounds, or damned the rebels vigorously; some grew sad and infinitely pathetic, as if the pain borne silently all day revenged itself by now betraying what the man's pride had concealed so well. Often the roughest grew young and pleasant when sleep smoothed the hard lines away, letting the real nature assert itself. Many almost seemed to speak, and I learned to know these men better by night than through any intercourse by day. Sometimes they disappointed me, for faces that looked merry and good in the light grew bad and sly when the shadows came; and though they made no confidences in words, I read their lives, leaving them to wonder at the change of manner this midnight magic wrought in their nurse. A few talked busily; one drummer boy sang sweetly, though no persuasions could win a note from him by day; and several depended on being told what they had talked of in the morning. Even my constitutionals in the chilly halls possessed a certain charm, for the house was never still. Sentinels tramped around it all night long, their muskets glittering in the wintry moonlight as they walked, or stood before the doors, straight and silent as figures of stone, causing one to conjure up romantic visions of guarded forts, sudden surprises, and daring deeds; for in these war times the humdrum life of Yankeedom has vanished, and the most prosaic feel some thrill of that excitement which stirs the nation's heart and makes its capital a camp of hospitals. Wandering up and down these lower halls,

I often heard cries from above, steps hurrying to and fro, saw surgeons passing up or men coming down carrying a stretcher, where lay a long white figure, whose face was shrouded and whose fight was done. Sometimes I stopped to watch the passers in the street, the moonlight shining on the spire opposite, or the gleam of some vessel floating, like a white-winged sea gull, down the broad Potomac, whose fullest flow can never wash away the red stain of the land.

The night whose events I have a fancy to record opened with a little comedy, and closed with a great tragedy; for a virtuous and useful life untimely ended is always tragical to those who see not as God sees. My headquarters were beside the bed of a New Jersey boy, crazed by the horrors of that dreadful Saturday. A slight wound in the knee brought him there, but his mind had suffered more than his body. Some string of that delicate machine was overstrained, and for days he had been reliving in imagination the scenes he could not forget, till his distress broke out in incoherent ravings, pitiful to hear. As I sat by him, endeavoring to soothe his poor distracted brain by the constant touch of wet hands over his hot forehead, he lay cheering his comrades on, hurrying them back, then counting them as they fell around him, often clutching my arm to drag me from the vicinity of a bursting shell, or covering up his head to screen himself from a shower of shot—his face brilliant with fever, his eyes restless, his head never still, every muscle strained and rigid—while an incessant stream of defiant shouts, whispered warnings, and broken laments poured from his lips with that forceful bewilderment which makes such wanderings so hard to overhear.

It was past eleven, and my patient was slowly wearying himself into fitful intervals of quietude, when in one of these pauses a curious sound arrested my attention. Looking over my shoulder, I saw a one-legged phantom hopping nimbly down the room and, going to meet it, recognized a certain Pennsylvania gentleman whose wound fever had taken a turn for the worse and, depriving him of the few wits a drunken campaign had left him, set him literally tripping on the light, fantastic toe "toward home," as he blandly informed me, touching the military cap which formed a striking contrast to the severe simplicity of the rest of his decidedly *undress* uniform. When sane, the least movement produced a roar of pain or a volley of oaths. But the departure of reason seemed to have wrought an agreeable change, both in the man and his manners; for, balancing himself on one leg, like a meditative stork, he plunged into an animated discussion of the war, the President, lager beer, and Enfield rifles, regardless of any suggestions of mine as to the propriety of returning to bed, lest he be court-martialed for desertion.

Anything more supremely ridiculous can hardly be imagined than this figure, scantily draped in white, its one foot covered with a big blue sock, a dingy cap set rakingly askew on its shaven head, and placid satisfaction beaming in its broad red face as it flourished a mug in one hand, an old boot in the other, calling them canteen and knapsack, while it skipped and fluttered in the most unearthly fashion. What to do with the creature I didn't know. Dan was absent, and if I went to find him, the perambulator might festoon himself out of the window, set his toga on fire, or do some of his neighbors a mischief. The attendant of the room was sleeping like a near relative of the celebrated Seven, and nothing short of pins would rouse him; for he had been out that day, and whiskey asserted its supremacy in balmy whiffs. Still declaiming in a fine flow of eloquence, the demented gentleman hopped on, blind and deaf to my graspings and entreaties; and I was about to slam the door in his face and run for help when a second and saner phantom, "all in white," came to the rescue, in the likeness of a big Prussian, who spoke no English, but divined the crisis and put an end to it by bundling the lively monoped into his bed, like a baby, with an authoritative command to "stay put," which received added weight from being delivered in an odd conglomeration of French and German, accompanied by warning wags of a head decorated with a yellow cotton nightcap, rendered most imposing by a tassel like a bellpull. Rather exhausted by his excursion, the member from

Pennsylvania subsided, and after an irrepressible laugh together, my Prussian ally and myself were returning to our places when the echo of a sob caused us to glance along the beds. It came from one in the corner—such a little bed!—and such a tearful little face looked up at us as we stopped beside it! The twelve-year-old drummer boy was not singing now, but sobbing, with a manly effort all the while to stifle the distressful sounds that would break out.

"What is it, Teddy?" I asked, as he rubbed the tears away and checked himself in the middle of a great sob to answer plaintively:

"I've got a chill, ma'am, but I ain't cryin' for that, 'cause I'm used to it. I dreamed Kit was here, and when I waked up, he wasn't, and I couldn't help it, then."

The boy came in with the rest, and the man who was taken dead from the ambulance was the Kit he mourned. Well he might; for when the wounded were brought from Fredericksburg, the child lay in one of the camps thereabout, and this good friend, though sorely hurt himself, would not leave him to the exposure and neglect of such a time and place, but wrapping him in his own blanket, carried him in his arms to the transport, tended him during the passage, and only yielded up his charge when Death met him at the door of the hospital which promised care and comfort for the boy. For ten days Teddy had shivered or burned with fever and ague, pining the while for Kit and refusing to be comforted, because he had not been able to thank him for the generous protection, which perhaps had cost the giver's life. The vivid dream had wrung the childish heart with a fresh pang, and when I tried the solace fitted for his years, the remorseful fear that haunted him found vent in a fresh burst of tears as he looked at the wasted hands I was endeavoring to warm:

"Oh, if I'd only been as thin when Kit carried me as I am now, maybe he wouldn't have died. But I was heavy, he was hurt worser than we knew, and so it killed him—and I didn't see him to say good-bye."

This thought had troubled him in secret, and my assurances that his friend would probably have died at all events hardly assuaged the bitterness of his regretful grief.

At this juncture the delirious man began to shout; the one-legged rose up in his bed, as if preparing for another dart; Teddy bewailed himself more piteously than before; and if ever a woman was at her wit's end, that distracted female was Nurse Periwinkle during the space of two or three minutes, as she vibrated between the three beds, like an agitated pendulum. Like a most opportune reinforcement, Dan, the bandy, appeared and devoted himself to the lively party, leaving me free to return to my post; for the Prussian, with a nod and a smile, took the lad away to his own bed and lulled him to sleep with a soothing murmur, like a mammoth humble-bee. I liked that in Fritz, and if he ever wondered afterward at the dainties which sometimes found their way into his rations, or the extra comforts of his bed, he might have found a solution of the mystery in sundry persons' knowledge of the fatherly action of that night.

Hardly was I settled again, when the inevitable bowl appeared and its bearer delivered a message I had expected, yet dreaded to receive:

"John is going, ma'am, and wants to see you, if you can come."

"The moment this boy is asleep. Tell him so, and let me know if I am in danger of being too late."

My Ganymede departed, and while I quieted poor Shaw, I thought of John. He came in a day or two after the others, and one evening, when I entered my "pathetic room," I found a lately emptied bed occupied by a large, fair man with a fine face and the serenest eyes I ever met. One of the earlier comers had often spoken of a friend, who had remained behind, that those apparently worse wounded than himself might reach a shelter first. It seemed a David-and-Jonathan sort of friendship. The man fretted for his mate and was never tired of praising John—his courage, sobriety, self-denial, and unfailing kindliness of heart—always winding up with: "He's an out-an'-out fine feller, ma'am. You see if he ain't."

I had some curiosity to behold this piece of excellence and, when he came, watched him for a night or two before I made friends with him. For, to tell the truth, I was a little afraid of the stately-looking man, whose bed had to be lengthened to accommodate his commanding stature, who seldom spoke, uttered no complaint, asked no sympathy, but tranquilly observed what went on about him; and as he lay high upon his pillows, no picture of dying statesman or warrior was ever fuller of real dignity than this Virginia blacksmith. A most attractive face he had, framed in brown hair and beard, comely featured and full of vigor, as yet unsubdued by pain, thoughtful and often beautifully mild while watching the afflictions of others, as if entirely forgetful of his own. His mouth was grave and firm, with plenty of will and courage in its lines, but a smile could make it as sweet as any woman's; and his eyes were child's eyes, looking one fairly in the face with a clear, straightforward glance, which promised well for such as placed their faith in him. He seemed to cling to life, as if it were rich in duties and delights and he had learned the secret of content. The only time I saw his composure disturbed was when my surgeon brought another to examine John, who scrutinized their faces with an anxious look, asking of the elder: "Do you think I shall pull through, sir?" "I hope so, my man." And as the two passed on, John's eye still followed them, with an intentness which would have won a clearer answer from them, had they seen it. A momentary shadow flitted over his face; then came the usual serenity, as if in that brief eclipse he had acknowledged the existence of some hard possibility and, asking nothing yet hoping all things, left the issue in God's hands, with that submission which is true piety.

The next night, as I went my rounds with Dr. P., I happened to ask which man in the room probably suffered most, and to my great surprise, he glanced at John:

"Every breath he draws is like a stab, for the ball pierced the left lung, broke a rib, and did no end of damage here and there. So the poor lad can find neither forgetfulness nor ease, because he must lie on his wounded back or suffocate. It will be a hard struggle, and a long one, for he possesses great vitality. But even his temperate life can't save him. I wish it could."

"You don't mean he must die, doctor?"

"Bless you, there's not the slightest hope for him, and you'd better tell him so before long. Women have a way of doing such things comfortably, so I leave it to you. He won't last more than a day or two, at furthest."

I could have sat down on the spot and cried heartily if I had not learned the wisdom of bottling up one's tears for leisure moments. Such an end seemed very hard for such a man, when half a dozen worn-out, worthless bodies around him were gathering up the remnants of wasted lives, to linger on for years perhaps, burdens to others, daily reproaches to themselves. The army needed men like John, earnest, brave, and faithful, fighting for liberty and justice with both heart and hand, true soldiers of the Lord. I could not give him up so soon, nor think with any patience of so excellent a nature robbed of its fulfillment and blundered into eternity by the rashness or stupidity of those at whose hands so many lives may be required. It was an easy thing for Dr. P. to say, "Tell him he must die," but a cruelly hard thing to do, and by no means as "comfortable" as he politely suggested. I had not the heart to do it then and privately indulged the hope that some change for the better might take place, in spite of gloomy prophecies, so rendering my task unnecessary. A few minutes later, as I came in again, with fresh rollers, I saw John sitting erect, with no one to support him, while the surgeon dressed his back. I had never hitherto seen it done; for, having simpler wounds to attend to and knowing the fidelity of the attendant, I had left John to him, thinking it might be more agreeable and safe, for both strength and experience were needed in his case. I had forgotten that the strong man might long for the gentle tendance of a woman's hands, the sympathetic magnetism of a woman's presence, as well as the feebler souls about him. The doctor's words caused me to reproach myself with neglect, not of any real duty perhaps, but of those little cares and kindnesses that solace homesick spirits and make the heavy hours pass easier. John looked lonely and forsaken just then, as he sat with bent head, hands folded on his knee, and no outward sign of suffering till, looking nearer, I saw great tears roll down and drop upon the floor. It was a new sight there; for though I had seen many suffer, some swore, some groaned, most endured silently, but none wept. Yet it did not seem weak, only very touching. And straightway my fear vanished, my heart opened wide and took him in, as, gathering the bent head in my arms, as freely as if he had been a little child, I said, "Let me help you bear it, John."

Never on any human countenance have I seen so swift and beautiful a look of gratitude, surprise, and comfort as that which answered me more eloquently than the whispered—

"Thank you, ma'am, this is right good! This is what I wanted!"

"Then why not ask for it before?"

"I didn't like to be a trouble. You seemed so busy, and I could manage to get on alone."

"You shall not want it anymore, John."

Nor did he. For now I understood the wistful look that sometimes followed me as I went out after a brief pause beside his bed, or merely a passing nod, while busied with those who seemed to need me more than he, because more urgent in their demands. Now I knew that to him, as to so many, I was the poor substitute for mother, wife, or sister, and in his eyes no stranger, but a friend who hitherto had seemed neglectful, for in his modesty he had never guessed the truth. This was changed now; and through the tedious operation of probing, bathing, and dressing his wounds, he leaned against me, holding my hand fast, and if pain wrung further tears from him, no one saw them fall but me. When he was laid down again, I hovered about him in a remorseful state of mind that would not let me rest till I had bathed his face, brushed his bonny brown hair, set all things smooth about him, and laid a knot of heath and heliotrope on his clean pillow. While doing this, he watched me with the satisfied

expression I so liked to see; and, when I offered the little
nosegay, held it carefully in his great hand, smoothed a ruffled
leaf or two, surveyed and smelled it with an air of genuine delight, and lay contentedly regarding the glimmer of the sunshine on the green. Although the manliest man among my
forty, he said, "Yes, ma'am," like a little boy, received suggestions for his comfort with the quick smile that brightened his
whole face; and now and then, as I stood tidying the table by
his bed, I felt him softly touch my gown, as if to assure himself
that I was there. Anything more natural and frank I never
saw, and found this brave John as bashful as brave, yet full of
excellencies and fine aspirations, which, having no power to
express themselves in words, seemed to have bloomed into his
character and made him what he was.

After that night, an hour of each evening that remained to
me was devoted to his ease or pleasure. He could not talk
much, for breath was precious, and he spoke in whispers. But
from occasional conversations I gleaned scraps of private history which only added to the affection and respect I felt for
him. Once he asked me to write a letter, and as I settled pen
and paper, I said with an irrepressible glimmer of feminine
curiosity: "Shall it be addressed to wife or mother, John?"

"Neither, ma'am. I've got no wife and will write to Mother
myself when I get better. Did you think I was married because
of this?" he asked, touching a plain ring he wore and often
turned thoughtfully on his finger when he lay alone.

"Partly that, but more from a settled sort of look you have,
a look which young men seldom get until they marry."

"I don't know that, but I'm not so very young, ma'am,
thirty in May, and have been what you might call settled this
ten years, for Mother's a widow. I'm the oldest child she has,
and it wouldn't do for me to marry until Lizzy has a home of
her own and Laurie's learned his trade. For we're not rich, and
I must be father to the children and husband to the dear old
woman, if I can."

"No doubt but you are both, John. Yet how came you to go
to war if you felt so? Wasn't enlisting as bad as marrying?"

"No, ma'am, not as I see it, for one is helping my neighbor, the other pleasing myself. I went because I couldn't help it. I didn't want the glory or the pay. I wanted the right thing done, and people kept saying the men who were in earnest ought to fight. I was in earnest—the Lord knows!—but I held off as long as I could, not knowing which was my duty. Mother saw the case, gave me her ring to keep me steady, and said 'Go.' So I went."

A short story and a simple one, but the man and the mother were portrayed better than pages of fine writing could have done it.

"Do you ever regret that you came, when you lie here suffering so much?"

"Never, ma'am. I haven't helped a great deal, but I've shown I was willing to give my life, and perhaps I've got to. But I don't blame anybody, and if it was to do over again, I'd do it. I'm a little sorry I wasn't wounded in front. It looks cowardly to be hit in the back, but I obeyed orders, and it don't matter in the end, I know."

Poor John! It did not matter now, except that a shot in front might have spared the long agony in store for him. He seemed to read the thought that troubled me, as he spoke so hopefully when there was no hope, for he suddenly added:

"This is my first battle. Do they think it's going to be my last?"

"I'm afraid they do, John."

It was the hardest question I had ever been called upon to answer—doubly hard with those clear eyes fixed on mine, forcing a truthful answer by their own truth. He seemed a little startled at first, pondered over the fateful fact a moment, then shook his head, with a glance at the broad chest and muscular limbs stretched out before him:

"I'm not afraid, but it's difficult to believe all at once. I'm so strong it don't seem possible for such a little wound to kill me."

Merry Mercutio's dying words glanced through my memory as he spoke: "'Tis not so deep as a well, nor so wide as a church door, but 'tis enough." And John would have said the same, could he have seen the ominous black holes between his shoulders. He never had and, seeing the ghastly sights about him, could not believe his own wound more fatal than these, for all the suffering it caused him.

"Shall I write to your mother, now?" I asked, thinking that these sudden tidings might change all plans and purposes. But they did not, for the man received the order of the Divine Commander to march with the same unquestioning obedience with which the soldier had received that of the human one, doubtless remembering that the first led him to life and the last to death.

"No, ma'am. To Laurie just the same. He'll break it to her best, and I'll add a line to her myself when you get done."

So I wrote the letter which he dictated, finding it better than any I had sent. For, though here and there a little un-grammatical or inelegant, each sentence came to me briefly worded, but most expressive, full of excellent counsel to the boy, tenderly bequeathing "Mother and Lizzy" to his care and bidding him good-bye in words the sadder for their simplicity. He added a few lines, with steady hand, and as I sealed it, said with a patient sort of sigh: "I hope the answer will come in time for me to see it"; then, turning away his face, laid the flowers against his lips, as if to hide some quiver of emotion at the thought of such a sudden sundering of all the dear home ties.

These things had happened two days before. Now John was dying and the letter had not come. I had been summoned to many deathbeds in my life, but to none that made my heart ache as it did then, since my mother called me to watch the departure of a spirit akin to this in its gentleness and patient strength. As I went in, John stretched out both hands:

"I knew you'd come! I guess I'm moving on, ma'am."

He was, and so rapidly that even while he spoke, over his face I saw the gray veil falling that no human hand can lift. I sat down by him, wiped the drops from his forehead, stirred the air about him with the slow wave of a fan, and waited to help him die. He stood in sore need of help—and I could do so little; for as the doctor had foretold, the strong body rebelled against death and fought every inch of the way, forcing him to draw each breath with a spasm and clench his hands with an imploring look, as if he asked, "How long must I endure this and be still!" For hours he suffered dumbly, without a moment's respite or a moment's murmuring. His limbs grew cold, his face damp, his lips white, and again and again, he tore the covering off his breast, as if the lightest weight added to his agony. Yet through it all, his eyes never lost their perfect serenity, and the man's soul seemed to sit therein, undaunted by the ills that vexed his flesh.

One by one, the men woke, and around the room appeared a circle of pale faces and watchful eyes, full of awe and pity, for, though a stranger, John was beloved by all. Each man there had wondered at his patience, respected his piety, admired his fortitude, and now lamented his hard death, for the influence of an upright nature had made itself deeply felt, even in one little week. Presently the Jonathan who so loved this comely David came creeping from his bed for a last look and word. The kind soul was full of trouble, as the choke in his voice, the grasp of his hand, betrayed. But there were no tears, and the farewell of the friends was the more touching for its brevity.

"Old boy, how are you?" faltered the one.

"'Most through, thank heaven!" whispered the other.

"Can I say or do anything for you anywheres?"

"Take my things home, and tell them that I did my best."

"I will! I will!"

"Good-bye, Ned."

"Good-bye, John, good-bye!"

They kissed each other, tenderly as women, and so parted, for poor Ned could not stay to see his comrade die. For a little while, there was no sound in the room but the drip of water from a stump or two, and John's distressful gasps as he slowly breathed his life away. I thought him nearly gone and had just laid down the fan, believing its help to be no longer needed,

when suddenly he rose up in his bed and cried out with a bitter cry that broke the silence, sharply startling everyone with
its agonized appeal:

"For God's sake, give me air!"

It was the only cry pain or death had wrung from him, the
only boon he had asked; and none of us could grant it, for all
the airs that blew were useless now. Dan flung up the window.
The first red streak of dawn was warming the gray east, a her-
ald of the coming sun. John saw it and, with the love of light
which lingers in us to the end, seemed to read in it a sign of
hope of help, for over his whole face there broke that mysterious expression, brighter than any smile, which often comes to
eyes that look their last. He laid himself gently down and,
stretching out his strong right arm, as if to grasp and bring the
blessed air to his lips in a fuller flow, lapsed into a merciful
unconsciousness, which assured us that for him suffering was
forever past. He died then, for though the heavy breaths still
tore their way up for a little longer, they were but the waves
of an ebbing tide that beat unfelt against the wreck, which an
immortal voyager had deserted with a smile. He never spoke
again, but to the end held my hand close, so close that when
he was asleep at last, I could not draw it away. Dan helped
me, warning me as he did so that it was unsafe for dead
and living flesh to lie so long together. But though my hand
was strangely cold and stiff and four white marks remained
across its back, even when warmth and color had returned
elsewhere, I could not but be glad that through its touch the
presence of human sympathy, perhaps, had lightened that
hard hour.

When they had made him ready for the grave, John lay in
state for half an hour, a thing which seldom happened in that
busy place; but a universal sentiment of reverence and affection seemed to fill the hearts of all who had known or heard
of him; and when the rumor of his death went through the
house, always astir, many came to see him, and I felt a tender
sort of pride in my lost patient; for he looked a most heroic
figure, lying there stately and still as the statue of some young

knight asleep upon his tomb. The lovely expression which so often beautifies dead faces soon replaced the marks of pain, and I longed for those who loved him best to see him when half an hour's acquaintance with Death had made them friends. As we stood looking at him, the ward master handed me a letter, saying it had been forgotten the night before. It was John's letter, come just an hour too late to gladden the eyes that had longed and looked for it so eagerly. Yet he had it, for after I had cut some brown locks for his mother and taken off the ring to send her, telling how well the talisman had done its work, I kissed this good son for her sake and laid the letter in his hand, still folded as when I drew my own away, feeling that its place was there, and making myself happy with the thought that even in his solitary place in the "Government Lot," he would not be without some token of the love which makes life beautiful and outlives death. Then I left him, glad to have known so genuine a man and carrying with me an enduring memory of the brave Virginia blacksmith, as he lay serenely waiting for the dawn of that long day which knows no night.

CHAPTER V

OFF DUTY

"My dear girl, we shall have you sick in your bed unless you keep yourself warm and quiet for a few days. Widow Wadman can take care of the ward alone, now the men are so comfortable, and have her vacation when you are about again. Now, do be prudent in time, and don't let me have to add a Periwinkle to my bouquet of patients."

This advice was delivered in a paternal manner by the youngest surgeon in the hospital, a kindhearted little gentleman, who seemed to consider me a frail young blossom that needed much cherishing, instead of a tough old spinster who had been knocking about the world for thirty years. At the time I write of, he discovered me sitting on the stairs, with a nice cloud of unwholesome steam rising from the washroom; a party of January breezes disporting themselves in the halls; and perfumes, by no means from "Araby the blest," keeping them company; while I enjoyed a fit of coughing, which caused my head to spin in a way that made the application of a cool banister both necessary and agreeable as I waited for the frolicsome wind to restore the breath I'd lost, cheering myself meantime with a secret conviction that pneumonia was waiting for me around the corner. This piece of advice had been offered by several persons for a week, and refused by me with the obstinacy with which my sex is so richly gifted. But the last few hours had developed several surprising internal and external phenomena, which impressed upon me the fact that if I didn't make a masterly retreat very soon, I should tumble down somewhere and have to be borne ignominiously from the field. My head felt like a cannonball; my feet had a tendency to cleave to the floor; the walls at times undulated in a most disagreeable manner; people looked unnaturally big; and the "very bottles on the mankle shelf" appeared to dance derisively before my eyes. Taking these things into consideration while blinking stupidly at Dr. Z., I resolved to retire gracefully, if I must. So with a valedictory to my boys, a private lecture to Mrs. Wadman, and a fervent wish that I could take off my body and work in my soul, I mournfully ascended to my apartment, and Nurse P. was reported off duty.

For the benefit of any ardent damsel whose patriotic fancy may have surrounded hospital life with a halo of charms, I will briefly describe the bower to which I retired in a somewhat ruinous condition. It was well ventilated, for five panes of glass had suffered compound fractures, which all the surgeons and nurses had failed to heal. The two windows were draped with sheets, the church hospital opposite being a brick-and-mortar Argus and the female mind cherishing a prejudice in favor of retiracy during the nightcapped periods of existence. A bare floor supported two narrow iron beds, spread with thin mattresses like plasters, furnished with pillows in the last stages of consumption. In a fireplace, guiltless of shovel, tongs, andirons, or grate, burned a log, inch by inch, being too long to go on all at once. So while the fire blazed away at one end, I did the same at the other as I tripped over it a dozen times a day and flew up to poke it a dozen times at night. A mirror (let us be elegant!) of the dimensions of a muffin, and about as reflective, hung over a tin basin, blue pitcher, and a brace of yellow mugs. Two invalid tables, ditto chairs, wandered here and there, and the closet contained a varied collection of bonnets, bottles, bags, boots, bread and butter, boxes and bugs. The closet was a regular bluebeard cupboard to me. I always opened it with fear and trembling, owing to rats, and shut it in anguish of spirit; for time and space were not to be had, and chaos reigned along with the rats. Our chimneypiece was decorated with a flatiron, a Bible, a candle minus stick, a lavender bottle, a new tin pan, so brilliant that it served nicely for a pier glass, and such of the portly black bugs as preferred a warmer climate than the rubbish hole afforded. Two arks, commonly called trunks, lurked behind the door, containing the worldly goods of the twain who laughed and cried, slept and scrambled, in this refuge; while from the whitewashed walls above either bed looked down the pictured faces of those whose memory can make for us—

"One little room an everywhere."

For a day or two I managed to appear at meals; for the human grub must eat till the butterfly is ready to break loose, and no one had time to come up two flights while it was possible for me to come down. Far be it from me to add another affliction or reproach to that enduring man, the steward; for, compared with his predecessor, he was a horn of plenty. But— I put it to any candid mind—is not the following bill of fare susceptible of improvement without plunging the nation madly into debt? The three meals were "pretty much of a muchness" and consisted of beef, evidently put down for the men of '76; pork, just in from the street; army bread, composed of sawdust and saleratus; butter, salt as if churned by Lot's wife; stewed blackberries, so much like preserved cockroaches that only those devoid of imagination could partake thereof with relish; coffee, mild and muddy; tea, three dried huckleberry leaves to a quart of water—flavored with lime— also animated and unconscious of any approach to clearness. Variety being the spice of life, a small pinch of the article would have been appreciated by the hungry, hardworking sisterhood, one of whom, though accustomed to plain fare, soon found herself reduced to bread and water, having an inborn repugnance to the fat of the land and the salt of the earth.

Another peculiarity of these hospital meals was the rapidity with which the edibles vanished, and the impossibility of get-

ting a drop or crumb after the usual time. At the first ring of
the bell a general stampede took place. Some twenty hungry
souls rushed to the dining room, swept over the table like a
swarm of locusts, and left no fragment for any tardy creature
who arrived fifteen minutes late. Thinking it of more importance that the patients should be well and comfortably fed, I
took my time about my own meals for the first day or two
after I came, but was speedily enlightened by Isaac, the black
waiter, who bore with me a few times and then informed me,
looking as stern as fate:

"I say, mam, ef you comes so late, you can't have no vittles—'cause I'm 'bleeged fer ter git things ready fer de doctors
'mazin' spry arter you nusses and folks is done. De gen'lemen
don't kere fer ter wait, no more does I. So you jes' please ter
come at de time, and dere won't be no frettin' nowheres."

It was a new sensation to stand looking at a full table,
painfully conscious of one of the vacuums which Nature ab-
hors, and receive orders to right about face, without partaking
of the nourishment which your inner woman clamorously demanded. The doctors always fared better than we, and for a
moment a desperate impulse prompted me to give them a hint
by walking off with the mutton or confiscating the pie. But
Ike's eye was on me, and to my shame be it spoken, I walked
meekly away, went dinnerless that day, and that evening went
to market, laying in a small stock of crackers, cheese, and apples, that my boys might not be neglected, nor myself obliged
to bolt solid and liquid dyspepsias, or starve. This plan would
have succeeded admirably had not the evil star under which I
was born been in the ascendant during that month and cast its
malign influences even into my "'umble" larder; for the rats
had their dessert off my cheese, the bugs set up housekeeping
in my cracker bag, and the apples, like all worldly riches, took
to themselves wings and flew away; whither no man could
tell, though certain black imps might have thrown light upon
the matter, had not the plaintiff in the case been loath to add
another to the many trials of long-suffering Africa. After this
failure I resigned myself to fate and, remembering that bread

was called the staff of life, leaned pretty exclusively upon it. But it proved a broken reed, and I came to the ground after a few weeks of prison fare, varied by an occasional potato or surreptitious sip of milk.

Very soon after leaving the care of my ward, I discovered that I had no appetite, and cut the bread-and-butter interests almost entirely, trying the exercise-and-sun cure instead. Flattering myself that I had plenty of time and could see all that was to be seen, so far as a lone lorn female could venture in a city one half of whose male population seemed to be taking the other half to the guardhouse—every morning I took a brisk run in one direction or another, for the January days were as mild as spring. A rollicking north wind and occasional snowstorm would have been more to my taste, for the one would have braced and refreshed tired body and soul, the other have purified the air and spread a clean coverlet over the bed wherein the capital of these United States appeared to be dozing pretty soundly just then.

One of these trips was to the Armory Hospital, the neatness, comfort, and convenience of which makes it an honor to its presiding genius and arouses all the covetous propensities of such nurses as came from other hospitals to visit it.

The long, clean, warm, and airy wards, built barrack fashion, with the nurse's room at the end, were fully appreciated by Nurse Periwinkle, whose ward and private bower were cold, dirty, inconvenient, upstairs and downstairs, and in everybody's chamber. At the Armory, in Ward K, I found a cheery, bright-eyed, white-aproned little lady reading at her post near the stove—matting under her feet; a draft of fresh air flowing in above her head; a table full of trays, glasses, and such matters on one side, a large, well-stocked medicine chest on the other; and all her duty seemed to be going about now and then to give doses, issue orders, which well-trained attendants executed, and pet, advise, or comfort Tom, Dick, or Harry, as she found best. As I watched the proceedings, I recalled my own tribulations and contrasted the two hospitals in a way that would have caused my summary dismissal, could it have been reported at headquarters. Here, order, method, common sense, and liberality reigned and ruled in a style that did one's heart good to see. At the Hurly-burly Hotel, disorder, discomfort, bad management, and no visible head reduced things to a condition which I despair of describing. The circumlocution fashion prevailed, forms and fusses tormented our souls, and unnecessary strictness in one place was counterbalanced by unpardonable laxity in another. Here is a sample: I am dressing Sam Dammer's shoulder and, having cleansed the wound, look about for some strips of adhesive plaster to hold on the little square of wet linen which is to cover the gunshot wound; the case is not in the tray; Frank, the sleepy, half-sick attendant, knows nothing of it; we rummage high and low; Sam is tired and fumes; Frank dawdles and yawns; the men advise and laugh at the flurry; I feel like a boiling teakettle with the lid ready to fly off and damage somebody.

"Go and borrow some from the next ward, and spend the rest of the day in finding ours," I finally command. A pause; then Frank scuffles back with the message: "Miss Peppercorn ain't got none and says you ain't no business to lose your own duds and go borrowin' other folkses." I say nothing for fear of saying too much, but fly to the surgery. Mr. Toddypestle informs me that I can't have anything without an order from the surgeon of my ward. Great heavens! Where is he? And away I rush, up and down, here and there, till at last I find him, in a state of bliss over a complicated amputation, in the fourth story. I make my demand; he answers, "In five minutes," and works away, with his head upside down, as he ties an artery, saws a bone, or does a little needlework, with a visible relish and very sanguinary pair of hands. The five minutes grow to fifteen, and Frank appears, with the remark that "Dammer wants to know what in thunder you are keeping him there with his finger on a wet rag for?" Dr. P. tears himself away long enough to scribble the order, with which I plunge downward to the surgery again, find the door locked, and while hammering away on it, am told that two friends are waiting to see me in the hall. The matron being away, her parlor is locked, and there is nowhere to see my guests but in my own room, and no time to enjoy them till the plaster is found. I settle this matter and circulate through the house to find Toddypestle, who has no right to leave the surgery till night. He is discovered in the dead house, smoking a cigar and very much the worse for his researches among the spirituous preparations that fill the surgery shelves. He is inclined to be gallant and puts the finishing blow to the fire of my wrath; for the teakettle lid flies off, and driving him before me to his post, I fling down the order, take what I choose, and, leaving the absurd incapable kissing his hand to me, depart, feeling as Grandma Riglesty is reported to have done when she vainly sought for chips in Bimleck Jackwood's "shifless paster."

I find Dammer a well-acted charade of his own name, and just as I get him done, struggling the while with a burning desire to clap an adhesive strip across his mouth, full of heaven-defying oaths, Frank takes up his boot to put it on and exclaims:

"I'm blest ef here ain't that case now! I recollect seeing it pitch in this mornin', but forgot all about it till my heel went smash inter it. Here, ma'am, ketch hold on it, and give the boys a sheet on't all round, 'gainst it tumbles inter t'other boot next time yer want it."

If a look could annihilate, Francis Saucebox would have ceased to exist. But it couldn't; therefore, he yet lives, to aggravate some unhappy woman's soul and wax fat in some equally congenial situation.

Now, while I'm freeing my mind, I should like to enter my protest against employing convalescents as attendants, instead of strong, properly trained, and cheerful men. How it may be in other places I cannot say, but here it was a source of constant trouble and confusion, these feeble, ignorant men trying to sweep, scrub, lift, and wait upon their sicker comrades. One, with a diseased heart, was expected to run up and down stairs, carry heavy trays, and move helpless men. He tried it and grew rapidly worse than when he first came, and when he was ordered out to march away to the convalescent hospital, fell in a sort of fit before he turned the corner, and was brought back to die. Another, hurt by a fall from his horse, endeavored to do his duty, but failed entirely, and the wrath of the ward master fell upon the nurse, who must either scrub the rooms herself or take the lecture; for the boy looked stout and well, and the master never happened to see him turn white with pain or hear him groan in his sleep when an involuntary motion strained his poor back. Constant complaints were being made of incompetent attendants, and some dozen women did double duty and then were blamed for breaking down. If any hospital director fancies this a good and economical arrangement, allow one used-up nurse to tell him it isn't, and beg him to spare the sisterhood, who sometimes, in their sympathy, forget that they are mortal and run the risk of being made immortal, sooner than is agreeable to their partial friends.

Another of my few rambles took me to the Senate Chamber, hoping to hear and see if this large machine was run any better than some small ones I knew of. I was too late, and found the Speaker's chair occupied by a colored gentleman of ten, while two others were "on their legs," having a hot debate on the cornball question as they gathered the wastepaper strewn about the floor into bags; and several white members played leapfrog over the desks, a much wholesomer relaxation than some of the older senators indulge in, I fancy. Finding the coast clear, I likewise gamboled up and down, from gallery to gallery; sat in Sumner's chair and cudgeled an imaginary Brooks within an inch of his life; examined Wilson's books in the coolest possible manner; warmed my feet at one of the national registers; read people's names on scattered envelopes and pocketed a castaway autograph or two; watched the somewhat unparliamentary proceedings going on about me and wondered who in the world all the sedate gentlemen were who kept popping out of odd doors here and there, like respectable jacks-in-the-box. Then I wandered over the "palatial residence" of Mrs. Columbia and examined its many beauties, though I can't say I thought her a tidy housekeeper, and didn't admire her taste in pictures, for the eye of this humble individual soon wearied of expiring patriots, who all appeared to be quitting their earthly tabernacles in convulsions, ruffled shirts, and a whirl of torn banners, bombshells, and buff and blue arms and legs. The statuary also was massive and concrete, but rather wearying to examine; for the colossal ladies and gentlemen carried no cards of introduction in face or figure. So whether the meditative party in a kilt, with well-developed legs, shoes like army slippers, and a ponderous nose, was Columbus, Cato, or Cockelorum Tibby the tragedian was more than I could tell. Several robust ladies attracted me, as I felt particularly "wimbly" myself, as old countrywomen say. But which was America and which Pocahontas was a mystery, for all affected much looseness of costume, dishevelment of hair, swords, arrows, lances, scales, and other ornaments quite passé with damsels of our day, whose effigies should go down to posterity armed with fans, crochet needles, riding whips, and parasols, with here and there one holding pen or pencil, rolling pin or broom. The Statue of Liberty I recognized at once, for it had no pedestal as yet, but stood flat in the mud, with Young America most symbolically making dirt pies and chip forts in its shadow. But high above the squabbling little throng and their petty plans, the sun shone full on Liberty's broad forehead, and in her hand some summer bird had built its nest. I accepted the good omen then, and on the first of January, the Emancipation Act gave the statue a nobler and more enduring pedestal than any marble or granite ever carved and quarried by human hands.

One trip to Georgetown Heights, where cedars sighed overhead, dead leaves rustled underfoot, pleasant paths led up and down, and a brook wound like a silver snake by the blackened ruins of some French minister's house, through the poor gardens of the black washerwomen who congregated there, and, passing the cemetery with a murmurous lullaby, rolled away to pay its little tribute to the river. This breezy run was the last I took; for on the morrow came rain and wind, and confinement soon proved a powerful reinforcement to the enemy, who was quietly preparing to spring a mine and blow me five hundred miles from the position I had taken in what I called my Chickahominy Swamp.

Shut up in my room, with no voice, spirits, or books, that week was not a holiday by any means. Finding meals a humbug, I stopped away altogether, trusting that if this sparrow was of any worth, the Lord would not let it fall to the ground. Like a flock of friendly ravens, my sister nurses fed me, not only with food for the body, but kind words for the mind; and soon, from being half starved, I found myself so beteaed and betoasted, petted and served, that I was quite "in the lap of luxury," in spite of cough, headache, a painful consciousness of my pleura, and a realizing sense of bones in the human frame. From the pleasant house on the hill, the home in the heart of Washington, and the Willard caravansary came friends new and old, with bottles, baskets, carriages, and invitations for the invalid; and daily our Florence Nightingale climbed the steep stairs, stealing a moment from her busy life, to watch over the stranger, of whom she was as thoughtfully tender as any mother. Long may she wave! Whatever others may think or say, Nurse Periwinkle is forever grateful; and among her relics of that Washington defeat, none is more valued than the little book which appeared on her pillow one dreary day, for the "D.D." written in it means to her far more than "Doctor of Divinity."

Being forbidden to meddle with fleshly arms and legs, I solaced myself by mending cotton ones and, as I sat sewing at my window, watched the moving panorama that passed below, amusing myself with taking notes of the most striking figures in it. Long trains of army wagons kept up a perpetual rumble from morning till night; ambulances rattled to and fro with busy surgeons, nurses taking an airing, or convalescents going in parties to be fitted to artificial limbs. Strings of sorry-looking horses passed, saying as plainly as dumb creatures could, "Why in a city full of them is there no *horse*pital for us?" Often a cart came by, with several rough coffins in it and no mourners following; barouches with invalid officers rolled around the corner, and carriageloads of pretty children, with black coachmen, footmen, and maids. The women who took their walks abroad were so extinguished in three-story bonnets, with overhanging balconies of flowers, that their charms were obscured; and all I can say of them is that they dressed in the worst possible taste and walked like ducks.

The men did the picturesque, and did it so well that Washington looked like a mammoth masquerade. Spanish hats, scarlet-lined riding cloaks, swords and sashes, high boots and bright spurs, beards and mustaches, which made plain faces comely, and comely faces heroic. These vanities of the flesh transformed our butchers, bakers, and candlestick makers into gallant riders of gaily caparisoned horses, much handsomer than themselves; and dozens of such figures were constantly prancing by, with private prickings of spurs, for the benefit of the perambulating flower bed. Some of these gentlemen affected painfully tight uniforms and little caps, kept on by some new law of gravitation, as they covered only the bridge of the nose, yet never fell off. The men looked like stuffed fowls and rode as if the safety of the nation depended on their speed alone. The fattest, grayest officers dressed most and ambled statelily along, with orderlies behind, trying to look as if they didn't know the stout party in front and doing much caracoling on their own account.

The mules were my especial delight; and an hour's study of a constant succession of them introduced me to many of their characteristics, for six of these odd little beasts drew each army wagon and went hopping like frogs through the stream of mud that gently rolled along the street. The coquettish mule had small feet, a nicely trimmed tassel of a tail, perked-up ears, and seemed much given to little tosses of the head, affected skips and prances, and if he wore the bells or were bedizened with a bit of finery, put on as many airs as any belle. The moral mule was a stout, hardworking creature, always tugging with all his might, often pulling away after the rest had stopped, laboring under the conscientious delusion that food for the entire army depended upon his private exertions. I respected this style of mule and, had I possessed a juicy cabbage, would have pressed it upon him, with thanks for his excellent example. The historical mule was a melodramatic quadruped, prone to startling humanity by erratic leaps and wild plunges, much shaking of his stubborn head and lashing-out of his vicious heels, now and then falling flat and apparently dying à la Forrest: a gasp—a squirm—a flop and so on till the street was well blocked up, the drivers all swearing like demons in bad hats, and the chief actor's circulation decidedly quickened by every variety of kick, cuff, jerk, and haul. When the last breath seemed to have left his body and "doctors were in vain," a sudden resurrection took place; and if ever a mule laughed with scornful triumph, that was the beast, as he leisurely rose, gave a comfortable shake, and, calmly regarding the excited crowd, seemed to say—"A hit! A decided hit! For the stupidest of animals has bamboozled a dozen men. Now, then, what are *you* stopping the way for?" The pathetic mule was, perhaps, the most interesting of all; for though he always seemed to be the smallest, thinnest, weakest of the six, the postilion, with big boots, long-tailed coat, and heavy whip, was sure to bestride this one, who struggled feebly along, head down, coat muddy and rough, eye spiritless and sad, his very tail a mortified stump, and the whole beast a picture of meek misery, fit to touch a heart of stone. The jovial mule was a roly-poly, happy-go-lucky little piece of horseflesh, taking everything easily, from cudgeling to caressing, strolling along with a roguish twinkle of the eye, and, if the thing were possible, would have had his hands in his pockets and whistled as he went. If there ever chanced to be an apple core, a stray turnip, or wisp of hay in the gutter, this Mark Tapley was sure to find it, and none of his mates seemed to begrudge him his bite. I suspected this fellow was the peacemaker, confidant, and friend of all the others, for he had a sort of "Cheer up, old boy, I'll pull you through" look, which was exceedingly engaging.

Pigs also possessed attractions for me, never having had an

opportunity of observing their graces of mind and manner till I came to Washington, whose porcine citizens appeared to enjoy a larger liberty than many of its human ones. Stout, sedate-looking pigs hurried by each morning to their places of business, with a preoccupied air and sonorous greeting to their friends. Genteel pigs, with an extra curl to their tails, promenaded in pairs, lunching here and there, like gentlemen of leisure. Rowdy pigs pushed the passersby off the sidewalk; tipsy pigs hiccuped their version of "We won't go home till morning" from the gutter; and delicate young pigs tripped daintily through the mud, as if, like "Mrs. Peerybingle," they plumed themselves upon their ankles and kept themselves particularly neat in point of stockings. Maternal pigs with their interesting families strolled by in the sun, and often the pink, babylike squealers lay down for a nap, with a trust in Providence worthy of human imitation.

But more interesting than officers, ladies, mules, or pigs were my colored brothers and sisters, because so unlike the respectable members of society I'd known in moral Boston.

Here was the genuine article—no, not the genuine article at all, we must go to Africa for that—but the sort of creatures generations of slavery have made them: obsequious, trickish, lazy, and ignorant, yet kindhearted, merry-tempered, quick to feel and accept the least token of the brotherly love which is slowly teaching the white hand to grasp the black in this great struggle for the liberty of both the races.

Having been warned not to be too rampant on the subject of slavery, as secesh* principles flourished even under the respectable nose of Father Abraham, I had endeavored to walk discreetly and curb my unruly member, looking about me with all my eyes the while and saving up the result of my observations for future use. I had not been there a week before the neglected, devil-may-care expression in many of the faces about me seemed an urgent appeal to leave nursing white bodies and take some care for these black souls. Much as the

* secessionist

lazy boys and saucy girls tormented me, I liked them and found that any show of interest or friendliness brought out the better traits which live in the most degraded and forsaken of us all. I liked their cheerfulness, for the dreariest old hag, who scrubbed all day in that pestilential steam, gossiped and grinned all the way out when night set her free from drudgery. The girls romped with their dusky sweethearts or tossed their babies with the tender pride that makes mother-love a beautifier to the homeliest face. The men and boys sang and whistled all day long; and often, as I held my watch, the silence of the night was sweetly broken by some chorus from the street, full of real melody, whether the song was of heaven or of hoecakes; and as I listened, I felt that we never should doubt nor despair concerning a race which, through such griefs and wrongs, still clings to this good gift and seems to solace with it the patient hearts that wait and watch and hope until the end.

I expected to have to defend myself from accusations of a prejudice against color, but was surprised to find things just the other way, and daily shocked some neighbor by treating the blacks as I did the whites. The men *would* swear at the "darkies," would put two g's into "Negro" and scoff at the idea of any good coming from such trash. The nurses were willing to be served by the colored people, but seldom thanked them, never praised, and scarcely recognized them in the street— whereat the blood of two generations of abolitionists waxed hot in my veins and, at the first opportunity, proclaimed itself and asserted the right of free speech as doggedly as the irrepressible Folsom herself.

Happening to catch up a funny little black baby, who was toddling about the nurses' kitchen one day when I went down to make a mess for some of my men, a Virginia woman standing by elevated her most prominent feature with a sniff of disapprobation, exclaiming:

"Gracious, Miss P.! How can you? I've been here six months and never so much as touched the little toad with a poker."

"More shame for you, ma'am," responded Miss P., and with

the natural perversity of a Yankee, followed up the blow by kissing "the toad" with ardor. His face was providentially as clean and shiny as if his mama had just polished it up with a corner of her apron and a drop from the teakettle spout, like old Aunt Chloe. This rash act, and the antislavery lecture that followed, while one hand stirred gruel for sick America and the other hugged baby Africa, did not produce the cheering result which I fondly expected; for my comrade henceforth regarded me as a dangerous fanatic, and my protégé nearly came to his death by insisting on swarming upstairs to my room on all occasions and being walked on like a little black spider.

I waited for New Year's Day with more eagerness than I had ever known before, and though it brought me no gift, I felt rich in the act of justice so tardily performed toward some of those about me. As the bells rang midnight, I electrified my roommate by dancing out of bed, throwing up the window, and flapping my handkerchief with a feeble cheer in answer to the shout of a group of colored men in the street below. All night they tooted and tramped, fired crackers, sang "Glory, Hallelujah," and took comfort, poor souls, in their own way. The sky was clear, the moon shone benignly, a mild wind blew across the river, and all good omens seemed to usher in the dawn of the day whose noontide cannot now be long in coming. If the colored people had taken hands and danced around the White House, with a few cheers for the much abused gentleman who has immortalized himself by one just act, no President could have had a finer levee, or one to be prouder of.

While these sights and sounds were going on without, curious scenes were passing within, and I was learning that one of the best methods of fitting oneself to be a nurse in a hospital is to be a patient there. For then only can one wholly realize what the men suffer and sigh for; how acts of kindness touch and win; how much or little we are to those about us; and for the first time really see that in coming there we have taken our lives in our hands and may have to pay dearly for a brief experience. Everyone was very kind; the attendants of my ward often came up to report progress, to fill my woodbox or bring messages and presents from my boys. The nurses took many steps with those tired feet of theirs, and several came each evening to chat over my fire and make things cosy for the night. The doctors paid daily visits, tapped at my lungs to see if pneumonia was within, left doses without names, and went away, leaving me as ignorant and much more uncomfortable than when they came. Hours began to get confused; people looked odd; queer faces haunted the room; and the nights were one long fight with weariness and pain. Letters from home grew anxious; the doctors lifted their eyebrows and nodded ominously; friends said, "Don't stay," and an internal rebellion seconded the advice. But the three months were not out, and the idea of giving up so soon was proclaiming a defeat before I was fairly routed. So to all "Don't stays" I opposed "I wills," till one fine morning a gray-headed gentleman rose like a welcome ghost on my hearth; and at the sight of him my resolution melted away, my heart turned traitor to my boys, and when he said, "Come home," I answered, "Yes, Father"; and so ended my career as an army nurse.

I never shall regret the going, though a sharp tussle with typhoid, ten dollars, and a wig are all the visible results of the experiment; for one may live and learn much in a month. A good fit of illness proves the value of health, real danger tries one's mettle, and self-sacrifice sweetens character. Let no one who sincerely desires to help the work on in this way delay going through any fear; for the worth of life lies in the experiences that fill it, and this is one which cannot be forgotten. All that is best and bravest in the hearts of men and women comes out in scenes like these; and though a hospital is a rough school, its lessons are both stern and salutary; and the humblest of pupils there, in proportion to his faithfulness, learns a deeper faith in God and in himself. I, for one, would return tomorrow, on the "up again and take another" principle, if I could; for the amount of pleasure and profit I got out of that month compensates for all after pangs; and though a sadly womanish feeling, I take some satisfaction in the thought that if I could not lay my head on the altar of my country, I have my hair; and that is more than handsome Helen did for her dead husband when she sacrificed only the ends of her ringlets on his urn. Therefore, I close this little chapter of hospital experiences with the regret that they were no better worth recording, and add the poetical gem with which I console myself for the untimely demise of "Nurse Periwinkle":

> Oh, lay her in a little pit,
> With a marble stone to cover it;
> And carve thereon a gruel spoon,
> To show a "nuss" has died too soon.

CHAPTER VI

A POSTSCRIPT

My dear S.:—As inquiries like your own have come to me from various friendly readers of the "Sketches," I will answer them en masse and in printed form, as a sort of postscript to what has gone before. One of these questions was "Are there no services by hospital deathbeds or on Sundays?"

In most hospitals, I hope, there are; in ours, the men died and were carried away with as little ceremony as on a battle-field. The first event of this kind which I witnessed was so very brief, and bare of anything like reverence, sorrow, or pious consolation, that I heartily agreed with the bluntly expressed opinion of a Maine man lying next his comrade, who died with no visible help near him but a compassionate woman and a tenderhearted Irishman, who dropped upon his knees and told his beads, with Catholic fervor, for the good of his Protestant brother's parting soul:

"If, after gettin' all the hard knocks, we are left to die this way, with nothing but a Paddy's prayers to help us, I guess Christians are rather scarce round Washington."

I thought so, too, but though Miss Blank, one of my mates, anxious that souls should be ministered to as well as bodies, spoke more than once to the chaplain, nothing ever came of it. Unlike another shepherd, whose earnest piety weekly purified the Senate Chamber, this man did not feed as well as fold his flock, nor make himself a human symbol of the Divine Samaritan, who never passes by on the other side.

I have since learned that our noncommital chaplain had been a professor in some Southern college; and though he maintained that he had no secesh proclivities, I can testify that he seceded from his ministerial duties—I may say, ske-daddled—for, being one of his own words, it is as appropriate as inelegant. He read Emerson, quoted Carlyle, and tried to be a chaplain, but judging from his success, I am afraid he still hankered after the hominy pots of Rebeldom.

Occasionally, on a Sunday afternoon, such of the nurses, officers, attendants, and patients as could avail themselves of it were gathered in the ballroom for an hour's service, of which the singing was the better part. To me it seemed that if ever strong, wise, and loving words were needed, it was then; if ever mortal man had living texts before his eyes to illustrate and illuminate his thought, it was there; and if ever hearts were prompted to devoutest self-abnegation, it was in the work which brought us to anything but a Chapel of Ease. But some spiritual paralysis seemed to have befallen our pastor; for though many faces turned toward him, full of the dumb hunger that often comes to men when suffering or danger brings them nearer to the heart of things, they were offered the chaff of divinity, and its wheat was left for less needy gleaners, who knew where to look. Even the fine old Bible sto-ries, which may be made as lifelike as any history of our day by a vivid fancy and pictorial diction, were robbed of all their charms by dry explanations and literal applications, instead of being useful and pleasant lessons to those men, whom weak-ness had rendered as docile as children in a father's hands.

I watched the listless countenances all about me, while a mild Daniel was moralizing in a den of utterly uninteresting lions; while Shadrach, Meshach, and Abednego were leisurely passing through the fiery furnace, where, I sadly feared, some of us sincerely wished they had remained as permanencies; while the Temple of Solomon was laboriously erected with minute descriptions of the process and any quantity of bells and pomegranates on the raiment of the priests. Listless they were at the beginning, and listless at the end; but the instant some stirring old hymn was given out, sleepy eyes brightened, lounging figures sat erect, and many a poor lad rose up in his bed or stretched an eager hand for the book, while all broke out with a heartiness that proved that somewhere at the core of even the most abandoned, there still glowed some remnant of the native piety that flows in music from the heart of every little child. Even the big rebel joined, and boomed away in a thunderous bass, singing—

"Salvation! let the echoes fly,"

as energetically as if he felt the need of a speedy execution of the command.

That was the pleasantest moment of the hour, for then it seemed a homelike and happy spot—the groups of men looking over one another's shoulders as they sang, the few silent figures in the beds, here and there a woman noiselessly performing some necessary duty and singing as she worked, while in the armchair standing in the midst, I placed, for my own satisfaction, the imaginary likeness of a certain faithful pastor, who took all outcasts by the hand, smote the devil in whatever guise he came, and comforted the indigent in spirit with the best wisdom of a great and tender heart, which still speaks to us from its Italian grave. With that addition, my picture was complete; and I often longed to take a veritable sketch of a hospital Sunday, for despite its drawbacks, consisting of continued labor, the want of proper books, the barren preaching that bore no fruit, this day was never like the other six.

True to their home training, our New England boys did their best to make it what it should be. With many, there was much reading of Testaments, humming over of favorite hymns, and looking at such books as I could cull from a miscellaneous library. Some lay idle, slept, or gossiped; yet when I came to them for a quiet evening chat, they often talked freely and well of themselves; would blunder out some timid hope that their troubles might "do 'em good and keep 'em stiddy"; would choke a little as they said good night and turned their faces to the wall to think of mother, wife, or home, these human ties seeming to be the most vital religion which they yet knew. I observed that some of them did not wear their caps on this day, though at other times they clung to them like Quakers, wearing them in bed, putting them on to read the paper, eat an apple, or write a letter, as if, like a new sort of Samson, their strength lay not in their hair, but in their hats. Many read no novels, swore less, were more silent, orderly, and cheerful, as if the Lord were an invisible ward master who went his rounds but once a week and must find all things at their best. I liked all this in the poor, rough boys and could have found it in my heart to put down sponge and teapot and preach a little sermon then and there, while home-sickness and pain had made these natures soft, that some good seed might be cast therein to blossom and bear fruit here or hereafter.

Regarding the admission of friends to nurse their sick, I can only say, it was not allowed at Hurly-burly House, though one indomitable parent took my ward by storm and held her position, in spite of doctors, matron, and Nurse Periwinkle. Though it was against the rules, though the culprit was an acid, frostbitten female, though the young man would have done quite as well without her anxious fussiness and the whole roomful been much more comfortable, there was something so irresistible in this persistent devotion that no one had the heart to oust her from her post. She slept on the floor without uttering a complaint; bore jokes somewhat of the rudest; fared scantily, though her basket was daily filled with luxuries for her boy; and tended that petulant personage with a never-failing patience beautiful to see.

I feel a glow of moral rectitude in saying this of her; for, though a perfect pelican to her young, she pecked and cackled (I don't know that pelicans usually express their emotions in that manner) most obstreperously when others invaded her premises; and led me a weary life, with "George's tea rusks," "George's footbath," "George's measles," and "George's mother," till, after a sharp passage of arms and tongues with the matron, she wrathfully packed up her rusks, her son, and herself and departed in an ambulance, scolding to the very last.

This is the comic side of the matter. The serious one is harder to describe, for the presence, however brief, of relations and friends by the bedsides of the dead or dying is always a trial to the bystanders. They are not near enough to know how best to comfort, yet too near to turn their backs upon the sorrow that finds its only solace in listening to recitals of last words, breathed into nurse's ears, or receiving the tender legacies of love and longing bequeathed through them.

To me, the saddest sight I saw in that sad place was the spectacle of a gray-haired father, sitting hour after hour by his son dying from the poison of his wound: the old father hale and hearty; the young son past all help, though one could scarcely believe it, for the subtle fever, burning his strength away, flushed his cheeks with color, filled his eyes with luster, and lent a mournful mockery of health to face and figure, making the poor lad comelier in death than in life. His bed was not in my ward, but I was often in and out; and for a day or two, the pair were much together, saying little but looking much. The old man tried to busy himself with book or pen, that his presence might not be a burden; and once, when he sat writing, to the anxious mother at home doubtless, I saw the son's eyes fixed upon his face, with a look of mingled resignation and regret, as if endeavoring to teach himself to say cheerfully the long good-bye. And again, when the son slept, the father watched him as he had himself been watched, and though no feature of his grave countenance changed, the rough hand smoothing the lock of hair upon the pillow and the bowed attitude of the gray head were more pathetic than the loudest lamentations. The son died, and the father took home the pale relic of the life he gave, offering a little money to the nurse as the only visible return it was in his power to make her, for, though very grateful, he was poor. Of course she did not take it, but found a richer compensation in the old man's earnest declaration:

"My boy couldn't have been better cared for if he'd been at home, and God will reward you for it, though I can't."

My own experiences of this sort began when my first man died. He had scarcely been removed when his wife came in. Her eye went straight to the well-known bed; it was empty; and feeling yet not believing the hard truth, she cried out, with a look I never shall forget:

"Why, where's Emanuel?"

I had never seen her before, did not know her relationship to the man whom I had only nursed for a day, and was about to tell her he was gone, when McGee, the tenderhearted Irishman before mentioned, brushed by me with a cheerful "It's shifted to a better bed he is, Mrs. Connel. Come out, dear, till I show ye"; and taking her gently by the arm, he led her to the matron, who broke the heavy tidings to the wife and comforted the widow.

Another day, running up to my room for a breath of fresh air and a five minutes' rest after a disagreeable task, I found a stout young woman sitting on my bed, wearing the miserable look which I had learned to know by that time. Seeing her reminded me that I had heard of someone's dying in the night and his sister's arriving in the morning. This must be she, I thought. I pitied her with all my heart. What could I say or do? Words always seem impertinent at such times; I did not know the man; the woman was neither interesting in herself nor graceful in her grief; yet, having known a sister's sorrow myself, I could not leave her alone with her trouble in that strange place, without a word. So, feeling heartsick, homesick, and not knowing what else to do, I just put my arms about her and began to cry in a very helpless but hearty way; for as I seldom indulge in this moist luxury, I like to enjoy it with all my might when I do.

It so happened I could not have done a better thing; for though not a word was spoken, each felt the other's sympathy, and in the silence our handkerchiefs were more eloquent than words. She soon sobbed herself quiet, and leaving her on my bed, I went back to work, feeling much refreshed by the shower, though I'd forgotten to rest and had washed my face instead of my hands. I mention this successful experiment as a receipt proved and approved, for the use of any nurse who may find herself called upon to minister to these wounds of the heart. They will find it more efficacious than cups of tea, smelling bottles, psalms, or sermons, for a friendly touch and a companionable cry unite the consolations of all the rest for womankind and, if genuine, will be found a sovereign cure for the first sharp pang so many suffer in these heavy times.

I am gratified to find that my little Sergeant has found favor in several quarters, and gladly respond to sundry calls for news of him, though my personal knowledge ended five months ago. Next to my good John—I hope the grass is green above him, far away there in Virginia!—I placed the Sergeant on my list of worthy boys; and many a jovial chat have I enjoyed with the merry-hearted lad, who had a fancy for fun, when his poor arm was dressed. While Dr. P. poked and strapped, I brushed the remains of the Sergeant's brown mane—shorn sorely against his will—and gossiped with all my might, the boy making odd faces, exclamations, and appeals when nerves got the better of nonsense, as they sometimes did:

"I'd rather laugh than cry, when I must sing out anyhow, so just say that bit from Dickens again, please, and I'll stand it like a man." He did; for "Mrs. Cluppins," "Chadband," and "Sam Weller" always helped him through, thereby causing me to lay another offering of love and admiration on the shrine of the god of my idolatry, though he does wear too much jewelry and talk slang.

The Sergeant also originated, I believe, the fashion of calling his neighbors by their afflictions instead of their names, and I was rather taken aback by hearing them bandy remarks of this sort, with perfect good humor and much enjoyment of the new game.

"Hallo, old Fits is off again!" "How are you, Rheumatiz?" "Will you trade apples, Ribs?" "I say, Miss P., may I give Typhus a drink of this?" "Look here, No Toes, lend us a stamp, there's a good feller," etc. He himself was christened "Baby B." because he tended his arm on a little pillow and called it his infant.

Very fussy about his grub was Sergeant B., and much trotting of attendants was necessary when he partook of nourishment. Anything more irresistibly wheedlesome I never saw, and constantly found myself indulging him, like the most weak-minded parent, merely for the pleasure of seeing his brown eyes twinkle, his merry mouth break into a smile, and his one hand execute a jaunty little salute that was entirely captivating. I am afraid that Nurse P. damaged her dignity frolicking with this persuasive young gentleman, though done for his well-being. But "boys will be boys" is perfectly applicable to the case; for in spite of years, sex, and the "prunes-and-prisms" doctrine laid down for our use, I have a fellow feeling for lads and always owed Fate a grudge because I wasn't a lord of creation instead of a lady.

Since I left, I have heard from a reliable source that my Sergeant has gone home; therefore, the small romance that budded the first day I saw him has blossomed into its second chapter; and I now imagine "dearest Jane" filling my place, tending the wounds I tended, brushing the curly jungle I brushed, loving the excellent little youth I loved, and eventually walking altarward with the Sergeant stumping gallantly at her side. If she doesn't do all this, and no end more, I'll never forgive her, and sincerely pray to the guardian saint of lovers that "Baby B." may prosper in his wooing and his name be long in the land.

One of the lively episodes of hospital life is the frequent marching away of such as are well enough to rejoin their regiments or betake themselves to some convalescent camp. The ward master comes to the door of each room that is to be thinned, reads off a list of names, bids their owners look sharp and be ready when called for; and as he vanishes, the rooms fall into an indescribable state of topsy-turviness as the boys begin to black their boots, brighten spurs if they have them, overhaul knapsacks, make presents; are fitted out with needfuls, and—well, why not?—kissed sometimes, as they say, good-bye; for in all human probability we shall never meet again, and a woman's heart yearns over anything that has clung to her for help and comfort. I never liked these breakings-up of my little household, though my short stay showed me but three. I was immensely gratified by the handshakes I got, for their somewhat painful cordiality assured me that I had not tried in vain. The big Prussian rumbled out his unintelligible adieux, with a grateful face and a premonitory smooth of his yellow mustache, but got no farther, for someone else stepped up with a large brown hand extended and this recommendation of our very faulty establishment:

"We're off, ma'am, and I'm powerful sorry, for I'd no idea a 'orspittle was such a jolly place. Hope I'll git another ball somewheres easy, so I'll come back and be took care on again. Mean, ain't it?"

I didn't think so, but the doctrine of inglorious ease was not the right one to preach up, so I tried to look shocked, failed signally, and consoled myself by giving him the fat pincushion he had admired as the "cutest little machine a-goin'." Then they fell into line in front of the house, looking rather wan and feeble, some of them, but trying to step out smartly and march in good order, though half the knapsacks were carried by the guard and several leaned on sticks instead of shouldering guns. All looked up and smiled, or waved their hands and touched their caps, as they passed under our windows down the long street, and so away, some to their homes in this world and some to that in the next; and for the rest of the day I felt like Rachel mourning for her children when I saw the empty beds and missed the familiar faces.

You ask if nurses are obliged to witness amputations and such matters as a part of their duty. I think not, unless they wish, for the patient is under the effects of ether and needs no care but such as the surgeons can best give. Our work begins afterward, when the poor soul comes to himself, sick, faint, and wandering, full of strange pains and confused visions, of disagreeable sensations and sights. Then we must soothe and sustain, tend and watch, preaching and practicing patience, till sleep and time have restored courage and self-control.

I witnessed several operations; for the height of my ambition was to go to the front after a battle, and feeling that the sooner I inured myself to trying sights, the more useful I should be. Several of my mates shrank from such things, for though the spirit was wholly willing, the flesh was inconveniently weak. One funereal lady came to try her powers as a nurse; but, a brief conversation eliciting the facts that she fainted at the sight of blood, was afraid to watch alone, couldn't possibly take care of delirious persons, was nervous about infections and unable to bear much fatigue, she was mildly dismissed. I hope she found her sphere, but fancy a comfortable bandbox on a high shelf would best meet the requirements of her case.

Dr. Z. suggested that I should witness a dissection. But I never accepted his invitations, thinking that my nerves belonged to the living, not to the dead, and I had better finish my education as a nurse before I began that of a surgeon. But I never met the little man skipping through the hall, with oddly shaped cases in his hand and an absorbed expression of countenance, without being sure that a select party of surgeons were at work in the dead house, which idea was a rather trying one, when I knew the subject was some person whom I had nursed and cared for.

But this must not lead anyone to suppose that the surgeons were willfully hard or cruel, though one of them remorsefully confided to me that he feared his profession blunted his sensibilities and, perhaps, rendered him indifferent to the sight of pain.

I am inclined to think that in some cases it does; for, though a capital surgeon and a kindly man, Dr. P., through long acquaintance with many of the ills flesh is heir to, had acquired a somewhat trying habit of regarding a man and his wound as separate institutions, and seemed rather annoyed that the former should express any opinion upon the latter or claim any right in it while under his care. He had a way of twitching off a bandage and giving a limb a comprehensive sort of clutch, which, though no doubt entirely scientific, was rather startling than soothing, and highly objectionable as a means of preparing nerves for any fresh trial. He also expected the patient to assist in small operations, as he considered them, and to restrain all demonstrations during the process.

"Here, my man, just hold it this way while I look into it a bit," he said one day to Fitz G., putting a wounded arm into the keeping of a sound one and proceeding to poke about among bits of bone and visible muscles in a red and black chasm made by some infernal machine of the shot or shell description. Poor Fitz held on like grim Death, ashamed to show fear before a woman, till it grew more than he could bear in silence; and after a few smothered groans, he looked at me imploringly, as if he said, "I wouldn't, ma'am, if I could help it," and fainted quietly away.

Dr. P. looked up, gave a compassionate sort of cluck, and poked away more busily than ever, with a nod at me and a brief "Never mind; be so good as to hold this till I finish."

I obeyed, cherishing the while a strong desire to insinuate a few of his own disagreeable knives and scissors into him and see how he liked it. A very disrespectful and ridiculous fancy, of course; for he was doing all that could be done, and the arm prospered finely in his hands. But the human mind is prone to prejudice; and though a personable man, speaking French like a born "Parley voo" and whipping off legs like an animated guillotine, I must confess to a sense of relief when he was ordered elsewhere, and suspect that several of the men would have faced a rebel battery with less trepidation than they did Dr. P. when he came briskly in on his morning round.

As if to give us the pleasures of contrast, Dr. Z. succeeded him, who, I think, suffered more in giving pain than did his patients in enduring it; for he often paused to ask, "Do I hurt you?" and seeing his solicitude, the boys invariably answered, "Not much, go ahead, doctor," though the lips that uttered this amiable fib might be white with pain as they spoke. Over the dressing of some of the wounds, we used to carry on conversations upon subjects foreign to the work in hand, that the patient might forget himself in the charms of our discourse. Christmas Eve was spent in this way—the doctor strapping the little Sergeant's arm, I holding the lamp, while all three laughed and talked, as if anywhere but in a hospital ward, except when the chat was broken by a long-drawn "Oh!" from "Baby B.," an abrupt request from the doctor to "Hold the lamp a little higher, please," or an encouraging "'Most through, Sergeant" from Nurse P.

The chief surgeon, Dr. O., I was told, refused the higher salary, greater honor, and less labor of an appointment to the officers' hospital around the corner, that he might serve the poor fellows at Hurly-burly House, or go to the front, working there day and night among the horrors that succeed the glories of a battle. I liked that so much that the quiet, brown-eyed doctor was my especial admiration, and, when my own turn came, had more faith in him than in all the rest put together, although he did advise me to go home and authorize the consumption of blue pills.

Speaking of the surgeons reminds me that, having found all manner of fault, it becomes me to celebrate the redeeming feature of Hurly-burly House. I had been prepared by the accounts of others to expect much humiliation of spirit from the surgeons and to be treated by them like a doormat, a worm, or any other meek and lowly article whose mission it is to be put down and walked upon—nurses being considered as mere servants, receiving the lowest pay, and, it's my private opinion, doing the hardest work of any part of the army, except the mules. Great, therefore, was my surprise when I found myself treated with the utmost courtesy and kindness. Very soon my carefully prepared meekness was laid upon the shelf, and going from one extreme to the other, I more than once expressed a difference of opinion regarding sundry messes it was my painful duty to administer.

As eight of us nurses chanced to be off duty at once, we had an excellent opportunity of trying the virtues of these gentlemen, and I am bound to say they stood the test admirably, as far as my personal observation went. Dr. O.'s stethoscope was unremitting in its attentions; Dr. S. brought his buttons into my room twice a day, with the regularity of a medical clock; while Dr. Z. filled my table with neat little bottles, which I never emptied, prescribed Browning, bedewed me with cologne, and kept my fire going, as if, like the candles in St. Peter's, it must never be permitted to die out. Waking one cold night, with the certainty that my last spark had pined away and died and consequently hours of coughing were in store for me, I was much amazed to see a ruddy light dancing on the wall, a jolly blaze roaring up the chimney, and, down upon his knees before it, Dr. Z., whittling shavings. I ought to have risen up and thanked him on the spot; but knowing that he was one of those who like to do good by stealth, I only peeped at him as if he were a friendly ghost, till, having made things as cozy as the most motherly of nurses could have done, he crept away, leaving me to feel, as somebody says, "as if angels were a-watching of me in my sleep," though that species of wildfowl do not usually descend in broadcloth and glasses. I afterwards discovered that he split the wood himself on that cool January midnight and went about making or mending fires for the poor old ladies in their dismal dens, thus causing himself to be felt a bright and shining light in more ways than one. I never thanked him as I ought; therefore, I publicly make a note of it and further aggravate that modest M.D. by saying that if this was not being the best of doctors and the gentlest of gentlemen, I shall be happy to see any improvement upon it.

To such as wish to know where these scenes took place, I must respectfully decline to answer, for Hurly-burly House has ceased to exist as a hospital. So let it rest, with all its sins upon its head—perhaps I should say chimney top. When the nurses felt ill, the doctors departed, and the patients got well, I believe the concern gently faded from existence or was merged into some other and better establishment, where I hope the washing of three hundred sick people is done out of

the house, the food is eatable, and mortal women are not expected to possess an angelic exemption from all wants and the
endurance of truck horses.

Since the appearance of these hasty "Sketches," I have
heard from several of my comrades at the hospital, and their
approval assures me that I have not let sympathy and fancy
run away with me, as that lively team is apt to do when harnessed to a pen. As no two persons see the same thing with
the same eyes, my view of hospital life must be taken through
my glass and held for what it is worth. Certainly, nothing was
set down in malice, and to the serious-minded party who objected to a tone of levity in some portions of the "Sketches," I
can only say that it is a part of my religion to look well after
the cheerfulnesses of life and let the dismals shift for themselves, believing with good Sir Thomas More that it is wise to
"be merrie in God."

The next hospital I enter will, I hope, be one for the colored regiments, as they seem to be proving their right to the
admiration and kind offices of their white relations, who owe
them so large a debt, a little part of which I shall be so proud
to pay.

Yours,
With a firm faith
In the good time coming,
Tribulation Periwinkle

THE HOSPITAL LAMP

It was a very dull lamp, the only one that burned in that sad place. The others were extinguished as the bell rang nine, and this central one was lowered till it became a pale star in the twilight of the room. All night it burned above the motley sleepers, showing the sights only to be seen in a hospital ward; and all night one pair of eyes seemed to watch it, with a wistful constancy which caused me to wonder what thought or purpose was illuminated by that feeble ray.

Wearied with a long watch by a fever patient's bed, I took advantage of the heavy sleep that fell upon him, to rest and refresh myself by pacing noiselessly up and down the aisle, on either side of which stretched the long rows of beds covered with gray army blankets and looking in the dusk as narrow, dark, and still as new-made graves. On one of these beds lay the watcher of the light—a rough, dark man, with keen eyes and a mane of long black hair, which he never would have cut, although it caused him to be christened "Absalom Tonser" by his mates. Stern and silent was this Hunt, showing a grim sort of fortitude and patience under great suffering, which won respect but not affection, for he also possessed gruff manners and a decidedly "let me alone" expression of countenance. Very short answers were all any questioner received, and an absent "Thanky, ma'am" was the only acknowledgment of the daily cares it was my duty to bestow upon him.

Though the most ungracious and unpromising of all my

boys, that one habit of his made him interesting to me, and for several days I had been taking reconnaissance and preparing to steal a march upon him, fancying that he had something on his mind and would be the easier for telling it. By day he slept much, or appeared to do so, for, turning his face to the wall, he drew his long hair over his eyes and either shut out the world entirely or viewed it stealthily from behind that screen. But at night, when the room was still and no one stirring but myself, he emerged from his covert, folded his arms under his head, and lay staring fixedly at the light, as if it had some irresistible fascination for him. He took no heed of me, and I seldom spoke; but while apparently unmindful of him, I watched the varying expression of his face, sometimes gloomy and despondent, sometimes restless and eager, but of late grave and steady, as if the dull lamp had shed a comfortable gleam upon some anxious thought of his. His face wore that expression then, and as I paused to wet the stump of the leg left at Fredericksburg, I could not resist speaking to him, though I only put the question often asked:

"Are you in pain, Hunt?"

He slowly turned his glance from the lamp to me, paused a moment to recall and comprehend the half-heard words, then answered with his usual brevity:

"Not more'n common."

"Doesn't the light trouble you?"

"No, ma'am, I like it."

"I am afraid it keeps you awake. Your bed can be turned, or the lamp shaded, if it is so."

"Don't put out the light or move me anywheres. I'm easiest so."

He spoke eagerly, and curious to discover the cause of his whim, I said:

"But you don't sleep, and you need all that you can get."

"Time enough for that, by and by. I get something better'n sleep these times."

"What are you so busy about all night, when the other men are dreaming?"

"Thinking, ma'am."

"Well, don't think too much; and if there is anything you wish to have written or attended to, remember I am here, and glad to do it for you."

"Thank ye, ma'am. I guess I shall have to study this out single-handed. If I can't, I'll let you know."

Still hoping to win the confidence which sooner or later was pretty sure to be bestowed, I dropped that subject and took up another, which usually proved an agreeable one to the boys, because so full of personal interest, anxiety, or pride.

"Your wound is getting on bravely. Do you know Dr. Cutter says you won't have to lose the knee joint after all, you have kept so quiet and been so patient."

There was a flash of pleasure in Hunt's face, but he seemed more intent upon some happier fact than the preservation of the joint, the loss of which would have entailed greater suffering, danger, and helplessness. "He thinks it's owing to my being still and so on, does he?" was all the answer Hunt made me.

"Yes, he says that when you came, he was afraid you were going to have a bad time of it, because your leg was not well amputated and you were a restless, excitable person. But you very pleasantly disappointed him, and here you are, doing well, thanks to your self-control, or to the subject that seems to absorb your mind and keep your thoughts from your wound."

He drew a long breath, gave a satisfied little nod, and said as if to himself:

"I guess the thinking did it."

Seeing signs of promise in the half smile that seemed to break out against his will, and the nod so strongly suggestive of contentment and relief, I pursued the propitious topic.

"I like to hear the men tell about their wounds, but you never told me how you lost your leg."

"Shouldn't think that sort of thing would be interesting to a lady."

He looked gratified, for all his gruff way of speaking, and I replied with as much enthusiasm as a very drowsy voice and countenance could express.

"It *is* very interesting to me, and as we are the only wakeful ones, let us have a sociable little chat about it."

"I ain't much given to that kind of thing, by nature or by grace neither. Must be lonesome here for you, though."

He seemed to add the last sentence as if to atone for the bluntness of the preceding one and looked as if he would like to be sociable, if he only knew how.

"Yes, it is lonely sometimes. But you can make it pleasanter by talking a little, and perhaps the sound of your own voice and the cool trickle of the water will make you sleepy after a while."

"Don't the water make your hands dreadful cold, ma'am?" he asked as I began on a fresh basinful.

It did, but I could have clapped them both warm again at that speech, for it was the first sign of friendliness the man had ever shown. I only gave the big sponge a grateful squeeze, however, and answered soberly:

"I rather like to splash about in this way, particularly if I have stories told me at the same time."

"There isn't much to tell, anyway," he began, after a pause of recollection. "You've heard enough about our battle to know how things were, so I needn't stop for that. We were doing our best after we got over the bridge, when there came a shell and scattered half a dozen of us pretty lively. I was pitched flat, but I didn't feel hurt—only mad—and jumped up to hit 'em again, but just tumbled over with an awful wrench and a still-awfuller feeling that both my legs were gone."

"Did no one stop to help you?"

"Too busy for that, ma'am. The boys can't stop to pick up their mates when there are rebs ahead to be knocked down. I knew there was no more fighting for me, and just laid still with the balls singing round me, wondering where they'd hit next."

"How did you feel?"

"Dreadful busy, at first, for everything I'd ever said, seen, or done seemed to go spinning through my head, till I got so dizzy trying to keep my wits stiddy that I lost 'em altogether. I didn't find 'em again till somebody laid hold of me. Two of our boys were lugging me along back, but they had to dodge behind walls and cut up and down, for the scrimmage was going on all round us. One of 'em was hit in the side, the other in the face, but not bad, and they managed to get me into a little rayvine sort of a place, out of danger. There I begged 'em to lay me down and let me be, for I couldn't go any farther. Believed I was bleeding to death, rapid. But it wasn't hard, and I only wanted to drop off easy, if I could."

"Did you want to die, Hunt?"

"Didn't much care then."

An unconscious emphasis on the "then" caused me to ask:

"But you do now?"

"Well, I ain't quite ready yet." As he spoke, his eye went back to the light, as if from force of habit, and the anxious, thoughtful look disturbed the composure of his face for a moment. He seemed to forget his story, so I brought him back to it.

"They didn't leave you there, I hope?"

"No, ma'am, for just as they were at their wits' end what to do with me, we come upon a surgeon lurking there, either to watch the fight or to hide. Don't know which, and never found out who he was or where he come from. There he was, anyway, looking scared enough, and, when he saw us, would have cut and run if Tom Hyde, one of the chaps carrying me, hadn't made him stop and take a look at me. My leg was smashed and ought to come off right away, he said. 'Do it, then,' says Tom. He was one of your rough-and-readys, Tom was, but underneath as kind as a—well—as a woman."

I made my best bow over the basin in return for the compliment and the odd, half-shy, half-grateful look that accompanied it. At which demonstration Hunt showed symptoms of a desire to wrap himself up in his hair again, but thought better of it and went on.

"The surgeon was young and scared and out of sorts every way, and said he couldn't do it, hadn't got his things, and so on. 'Yes, you have, so out with 'em,' says Tom, rapping on a case he sees in the chap's breast pocket. 'Can't without bandages,' he says next. 'Here they are, and more where they come from,' says Tom; and shedding his coat, off come his shirtsleeves, and was stripped up in a jiffy. 'I must have help,' says the surgeon, still dawdling round, and me groaning my life out at his feet. 'Here's help—lots of it,' says Tom, taking my head on his arm, while Joel Parkes tied up his bleeding face and stood ready to lend a hand. Seeing no way out of it, the surgeon turned up his cuffs and went at me as if I'd done it a-purpose to spite him. Good Lord, but that was awful!"

The mere memory of it made him quiver and shut his eyes, as if he felt again the sharp agony of shattered bones, rent flesh, and pitiless knife.

"Never mind that part of the story, Hunt. Tell how you got comfortable again, and forget the rest of it."

"I don't want to forget it," he said decidedly. "It's part of the concern and makes things easier now. I didn't know a man could bear so much and live. It's bad enough when done well, with chloroform and everything handy. But laying on the wet ground with nothing right and a beast of a surgeon hackin' away at you, it's torment, and no mistake. It seemed as if he was cutting my heart out, and I never could have stood it if it hadn't been for Tom. He held me close and steady, but he cried like a baby the whole time, and that did me good. Can't say why, but it did. As for Joel, he gave out altogether and went off for help, seeing as he hadn't pluck enough to stay, though he'd fight till he couldn't see. I'll never forget that place if I live to be a hundred! Seems as if I could see the very grass I tore up, the muddy brook they laid me by, the high bank with Joel creeping up it, Tom's face wet and white, the surgeon with his red hands, swearing to himself as he worked, and all the while such a roar of guns in my ears I hardly heard myself crying out for someone to shoot me and put me out of my misery."

"How did you get to the hospital?" I asked, anxious that he should neither sadden nor excite himself by reliving in imagination the horrors of that hour.

"Don't know, ma'am. There came a time when I couldn't bear any more, and what happened till I got over the river again is more than I can tell. I didn't mind matters much for a day or two, and the first thing that brought me round was being put aboard the transport to come up here. I was packed in with a lot of poor fellows and was beginning to wish I'd stayed queer, so I shouldn't care where I was, when I heard Tom's voice saying, 'Never mind, boys, put me down any-wheres, and see to the others first. I can wait.' That set me up. I sung out, and they stowed him alongside of me. It was so dark down there I couldn't see his face. But his voice and ways were just as hearty as ever, and he kept up my spirits wonderful all that day. I was pretty weak and kept dozing off, but whenever I woke, I always felt for Tom, and Tom was always there. He told me that when Joel came back with help, I was taken off to the field hospital and he went back for another go at the rebs, but got a ball in his throat and was in rather a bad way, but guessed he'd weather it. He couldn't lay down, but sat leaning back with his hand on my pillar where I could find it easy, and talked to me all he could, for he hadn't much voice left and there was a dismal groaning all round us. Ain't you tired, ma'am?"

"No, indeed, do finish, if you are not sleepy." He showed an inclination to stop there, but I wanted the rest, and seeing the sincerity of my desire, he gravely finished his little story.

"That was a long, dark day, not like any I'd ever seen be-fore, for somehow I seemed out of the world and done with. Come night, I felt so weak and cold I thought I was 'most over Jordan, so I gave my watch to Tom as a keepsake and told him to say good-bye to the boys for me. I hadn't any folks of my own. Tom had—wife, children, father, mother, brothers and sisters, and lots of friends everywhere. I, thinking of this, said it was lucky it was me that was going, not him, for no one would care. 'That isn't all,' says he; 'are you ready to go, Charley?' I hadn't thought of that, not being pious, and living a wild, rough-and-tumble sort of a life. 'Are you?' says I, feel-ing scared all of a sudden. 'Hope so,' says he; 'anyway, I've tried to be, and that tells, Charley—that tells in the end.' I didn't say any more, but dropped off to sleep, wishing I was Tom. In the morning, as soon as ever I woke, I looked around to thank him, for a great piece of his blanket was over me. There he was, sitting as I left him, his hand on my pillar, his face turned toward me so quiet looking and so happy I couldn't believe he was gone. But he was, and for all he left so many to miss him, I couldn't help feeling that he was the one to go, for I—"

Hunt stopped abruptly, laid his arm across his face, and said no more for several minutes. I, too, was silent, reproaching myself for the injustice I had done him, when underneath his forbidding exterior he hid so much of the genuine tenderness which few men are without. Now I had found the clue to these wakeful hours of his and the love he bore the lamp whose little flame had lighted him to a clearer knowledge of himself, bringing from the painful present the promise of a nobler future. He seemed so unconscious of the revelation he had made to me, and so slow to speak of that which lay nearest to him, that I made no comment on it then, except to ask for the confirmation of my thought:

"And when you lie here looking at the light, you are thinking of that good friend, Tom?"

"Yes, ma'am, and trying to be ready."

As if fearing to betray emotion, he made his mouth grimmer than ever when he spoke, but involuntarily his eyes turned to the lamp shining above them in the gloom, and as he looked, his steady gaze flickered suddenly as two lesser lights were reflected in those softened eyes of his. I knew what was coming, and softly laying a clean, cool napkin on his wound, I went away, that nothing should disturb the precious moment that had come to him.

Half an hour later, as I went down the room in search of water for lips too parched to syllable the word, I glanced at Hunt. He was fast asleep, one cheek pillowed on his hand, and in his rough brown face the tranquil expression of a tired child. It was a sight that made the light flicker before my eyes also as I went back to my watch, feeling sure that for this man peace would come out of war and the flame kindled in the darkness of a transport, fed by the pale glimmer of a hospital lamp, would not die out, but brighten this life for him and make him "ready" for the life to come.

PREFACE

TO *HOSPITAL SKETCHES* (1869)*

These sketches, taken from letters hastily written in the few leisure moments of a very busy life, make no pretension to literary merit, but are simply a brief record of one person's hospital experience. As such, they are republished, with their many faults but partially amended, lest in retouching they should lose whatever force or freshness the inspiration of the time may have given them.

To those who have objected to a "tone of levity" in some portions of the sketches, I desire to say that the wish to make the best of everything and send home cheerful reports even from that saddest of scenes, an army hospital, probably produced the impression of levity upon those who have never known the sharp contrasts of the tragic and comic in such a life.

That Nurse Periwinkle gave no account of her religious services, thereby showing a "sad want of Christian experience," can only be explained by the fact that it would have as soon

---

* *Hospital Sketches* (1863) was reprinted in *Hospital Sketches and Camp and Fireside Stories,* published by Roberts Brothers in 1869. The 1869 text is almost identical to the original. Although most of the changes are minor and amendatory, some are textually significant and were made apparently at the behest of Alcott's publisher. She wrote in her journal on February 1, 1868, "Arranged 'Hospital Sketches and War Stories' for a book. By taking out all Biblical allusions and softening all allusions to rebs., the book may be made 'quite perfect,' I am told. Anything to suit customers."

occurred to her to print the letters written for the men, their penitent confidences, or their dying messages as to mention the prayers she prayed, the hymns she sang, the sacred words she read, while the "Christian experience" she was receiving then and there was far too deep and earnest to be recorded in a newspaper.

The unexpected favor with which the little book was greeted, and the desire for a new edition, increase the author's regret that it is not more worthy such a kind reception.

L. M. A.
Concord, Massachusetts
March 1869

LETTERS FROM THE MOUNTAINS

I

Dear Commonwealth: *Following my usual fashion, I took notes by the way, and having copied my hieroglyphics from the cindery paper on which they were written, I forward them according to agreement.*

Boston, eight A.M.—All aboard, fare paid, trunks checked, bag stowed, and composure pervading my being generally. On viewing the scene I come to the conclusion that the infant population is taking its walks abroad, for no less than a dozen sprightly specimens pervade the car and howl in concert. A young mama with nurse and patriotic baby staggering under a small drum and big cockade sit opposite. Papa comes to say good-bye, baby plucks him by the nose and dots moist kisses all over his countenance, beats the drum and the paternal head indiscriminately, flattens the cockade by standing on his own head, and airs the soles of his shoes by waving them convulsively in the face of the world. Papa beams with tender pride, mama cries "The darling!" and nurse regards the multitude triumphantly, as if defying them to produce another such gem. Brown spinster turns up her nose and thanks her stars she has no encumbrances but a pie which has a tendency to betray itself by dancing out of the paper on the floor.

In front of me sits a fat Irishwoman with four children, all of a size, all dirty, all crying, and all with pocket handkerchiefs of the largest proportions and brilliantly illustrated. The fat parent and four babes try to cram into one seat, but arms and legs boil over the sides in all directions and the tender martyrs wail dolefully. Brown spinster relents, offers half her seat to the most distracted infant, and strews ginger nuts among them with a liberal hand. Unpleasant man laughs; spinster becomes a fine crimson and sniffs with dignified disapprobation. Irish parent says, "Thank ye kindly, mam," wipes her hot face, hunches her limp baby under her shawl, and informs the company that she is going to Dover to meet "the father kilt in a factory," after which she devotes herself to her offspring, one of whom needs a "Whist Dinnis, stop still, ye bad boy" every two minutes.

Farther down, several young families prey upon the public and swarm about the seats till "Patience on a monument" is entirely eclipsed by—Spinster in a baby car.

The rest of my companions are dandified young men with as many hats and canes and as great a profusion of wristband as Mr. Toots; young ladies in full dress with as many weak novels as a circulating library; old gentlemen shrouded in groves of newspapers; old ladies in rusty black or snuff color going to see their "darters toe the east'ard"; and oily workmen simmering in corners. The scenery without is flat and dispirited, as if the world wanted to bathe its feet and go to bed with a sick headache.

Portland, one P.M.—Large place, built in the topsy-turvy style of architecture. Inhabitants appear to lead the lives of flies, for all the streets that are not violently up are violently down, with steps, bridges, and balconies in all manner of places which they are not usually expected to adorn. Streets seem to be composed of hogsheads, lumber, coal, children, and dirt, in equal proportions. A new sort of livery stable strikes my eye, the sign whereof is "Towboats to let." Likewise, a strong fragrance of rum pervades the air, and every man's face is crocky. Wait half an hour at the depot, have a private interview with the baggage master, who says, "You're all right ma'am," when I know I'm all wrong, but can do nothing but clutch my checks and not patronize the public dinner table. Absorb my pie, hoping it will be easier of carriage this way than the other, and leave the ark-born snaps to harder times. Dart at the cars as soon as they appear, and am swiftly whisked into new scenes and experiences.

Two P.M.—Getting very warm. First one eye and then the other is rendered useless by cinders, so I try to go to sleep. Don't succeed; feel very cross; think we are going perilously fast; predict smashery and meditate upon immortality of the soul. Hear odd names called out and see comical sights at the depots. "Cluck!"—or what sounds like it—shouts the red-nosed conductor. I look out, see a group of women all talking at once like a flock of excited hens, so I infer that this unusual fact gives rise to the name—may be wrong. Pass a great river, ought to know its name, but don't, geography being defective.

Biddeford is made forever famous by my partaking of bananas at its station and leaving the skins to go down to posterity as a relic and proof of the actual passage of Miss P. Stout young lady in blue flies at thin young lady in pink and kisses her rapturously, to the intense interest of six young men, who break the Tenth Commandment and envy her. Old man hugs dry little woman and roars, "Why, sister Fletcher, I'm proper glad to see yer!" and other affecting sights refresh the eye.

Kennebunk.—Classical name! Little boys and girls appear with pretty birch-bark pottles of red raspberries. I am lured into buying one by a most enticing little damsel, but presently come to the conclusion that beauty is not always its "own excuse for being," for while I daintily pick the berries off the top of the charming little basket, the juice is gently meandering over my raiment, whereat I fling my purchase out of the window and spurn the next small vendor of such delusive wares with as much decision as if he offered "a cup of cold poison."

Falmouth.—Landscape getting knobby, like a pie under whose green crust the apple asserts itself. Simile suggested by a dyspeptic consciousness of my own long-cherished and too hastily devoured turnover. A shrill boy has pervaded the car ever since leaving Portland, shouting, "Papers, corn, books, water, lozenges, sandwiches, oranges," and other unattractive mental and corporeal refreshments. He often vanishes, as I fondly believe forever, but in five minutes he is back again, shriller than before, with some new abomination, and I finally believe that he must be the ghost of some lad killed on the road, who haunts the cars and so avenges himself on the corporation for having made a corpse of him.

Empire Station.—Very small, of course, having a big name. Very warm. Decide to patronize the shrill boy next time he comes around with ice tinkling in his tray of tumblers. The longing for him seems to lay him like a spell, for he appears no more; and I gasp for water and the noisy ghost in vain.

Mechanic Falls.—Landscape knobbier than ever. See acres of burned stumps, looking as if Nature's mouth needed a dentist. Feel like a rusty jackknife and as if I'd been shut up so long I should creak when opened. Ask a snuff-taking lady if we are not coming among the mountains—"Law, no! Them are only hills and it's eighty mile to Gorrum." I am quenched and return to the prospect thinking that if these are "only hills," the mountains must be worth seeing and the town I live in the flattest of all pancakes.

Stare about me for eighty miles of wonderful scenery, and at six o'clock stop before a hotel as if riding in my own carriage. The hotel is a convenient impertinence up there among the everlasting hills, and I'm disgusted with it while I enjoy its comforts, for romance and rain don't agree as well as one could desire.

Cousin Will appears as I descend. He embraces me, says "How are you?" takes my checks, and has me on the piazza before I can get my breath and set my bonnet straight. Cousin Laura greets me cordially, a comely porter whips up a massive trunk in either hand, and we ascend to my bower in a procession of four. Find the room large and cozy, with a fresh breeze waiting to kiss me as I enter, books ready on the table, flowers nodding from a rustic vase, and Mount Carter, the Imp, and Moriah looking in at the window with a sunshining welcome. Will makes an inaugural address and departs; Laura does the honors and talks while I assume a clean bib and tucker. Then we sit on the piazza, and I look about me, feeling excessively new and trying not to show it.

English gentlemen in blue flannel, white shoes, and Skye terrier "face trimmings" varying in shades like Bottom's collection—"Your straw-colored beard, your orange tawny, your French-crown-color beard, your perfect yellow"—smoked and read as if cigars and newspapers were the only ties that bound them to life. A Montreal family covered the lawn with French maids, bare-legged children, dogs, and toys. Ladies sewed and criticized their friends with the charming frankness of their sex. Parties came and went. Amazonian damsels trotted by in agonizing habits and muffin hats. Five bridal pairs mooned about in corners, conscious that Mrs. Grundy's eye was upon them; for all the brides were in a chronic state of blush, and the grooms appeared embarrassed by their arms and legs.

Two of these pairs were particularly interesting to me from the strong contrasts they afforded. One couple were from the lower ranks, for even in democratic America, society is nothing but a ridiculous staircase. The man was in the "spread-eagle" style and seemed bent on enjoying himself in the largest possible way; if he could have sat in a dozen chairs at once, hired the whole hotel, or had the word "Bridegroom" borne before him on a triumphal banner, I think it would have afforded him supreme delight and seemed but a neat and appropriate manner of glorifying "the mountainous me," whose importance really oppressed him. The only vent within his means was a dressing gown, which he not only wore all day and to all three meals, but went out in it, traveled in it for all I know, and flaunted it in the world's face with a lordly air, which, taken in connection with the style of the garment, was one too many for the rest of creation. It is a fact that this astonishing and independent article of attire was a deep blue with a buff trellis, over which a "red, red rose" flung its leaves and blossoms in reckless profusion. The man's back was broad, the skirts were long, and when he paced through the breezy halls, the effect was gorgeous in the extreme, being a curious conglomeration of perambulating parterre and Eastern rajah in full dress. The better quarter (she was nothing like a half) of this noble being was a coffee-colored and speechless young woman, apparently burdened with her trousseau, for Laura told me she had appeared in nine new gowns in three days, all rather startling in make and unbecoming as to color. A gooseberry-hued dress with a yard or two of gold chain festooned about the waist thereof, an impractical handkerchief, and a "let us be genteel or die" air were the points which first arrested my attention. She observed my interest, doubtless pitied my gray gown and single state, and from that moment seemed to dress, act, and "my dear" her lord for my sole aggravation. If she enjoyed it half as much as I did, she did not labor in vain, and "my fondest wishes are gratified," as actors say in their benefit speeches.

The other couple were so surprisingly young, I should have thought them a pair of affectionate twins but for the little girl's rapturous contemplation of her wedding ring with its diamond guard and the little boy's no less rapturous contemplation and introduction of "my wife." An elder sister appeared to have the care of them and to regard them with infinite pride, as if, having made the match, she had nothing left to do but to follow them about and enjoy the work of her hands. Everybody laughed at them, yet liked to see them, and a very pretty little picture they made. For the bride wore her hair in a curling crop, the groom a roundabout blue jacket à la Shelley; and both being comely, gay, and madly in love with each other, they caused quite a sensation as they went walking about under a half-grown umbrella like a pair of dolls eloped from a baby house.

After tea I went on a voyage of discovery. Found a dairy extending under half the house, saw two hundred pans of milk, half a dozen churns, and many dairymaids going to and fro with wooden tubs and pails on their heads quite in the picture-book fashion. The mistress of this lacteous realm was a jolly New Hampshire girl, enthusiastically fond of her work and proud to tell how many pans were "scum" each day and how many pounds of butter each "kag" held. Thirty cows, with a little German boy to herd them, came marching home from hilly pastures, following the tinkle of the bell the leader wore. A gang of Norwegians returned from work and, lying on the grass about the dairy door, smoked and talked in the language of some of Miss Bremer's heroes. It sounded like German with a few additional grunts and growls and a thunderous rumble when the speakers got excited. One of them sang a song, which was encored, though any tuneful bullfrog with a cold in his head could have done as well, I thought.

From this congenial society I was taken by cousin Will and, in company with Laura, ascended one of the mountain wagons which seem constructed upon the principle that once in, you are never to get out and, once out, you are never to get in; after which gymnastic feat we took a lovely drive along woody roads by pleasantly singing brooks, between wheat and barley fields, patches of grass ruffled by the wind and dark with cloudy shadows, or acres of purple and white potato flowers. Sheep, cows, and horses fed along the greenest hill-sides; hay making was going on in the broad meadows; the Androscoggin with its freight of logs rolled rapidly through the intervale; and all about stood the mountains green and grand. I enjoyed every moment, finding even cigar smoke, mosquitoes, and mud puddles glorified by the "evening purple," as Bettine calls it, and which exactly describes the twilight color of the hills.

We drove till moonrise and, coming home, found a band of music playing national airs in the valley and the dressing gown dancing with the gooseberry-colored ditto in a way that caused men's eyes to wink and women's mouths to pucker with suppressed merriment. The wedded babies sat on the upper balcony in the moonlight, very much as the doves had sat there in the sunshine, with first a bill and then a coo. We sat on the piazza, looking and listening, while Will and the Montreal lad made wonderful echoes with a four-foot tin horn, receiving musical good nights in return as mountain after mountain answered like a family circle, for the tones varied from the paternal bass of Mount Jefferson to the baby whisper of Paradise Hill at our feet.

I, too, will say good night and finish my scribble tomorrow.

II

Having promised to lie late and rest after my journey, of course I rose earlier than usual and, creeping through the quiet halls, paraded forth in search of adventures; for the idea of "doing" the mountains in the regular, everyday, guidebook style was not to be entertained for a moment by me. If there is anything I especially abominate, it is being trotted from place to place and ordered to go into ecstasies because everyone else does. I don't want admiration dragged out of me. I wish to give it when, where, and how I like, and have the privilege of turning up my nose at Niagara and adoring my own lazy Musketsquid, if I choose, for what is the use of living in a "land of the free" (which it isn't) if one cannot do as one likes? As sure as a person bores me with "Now, ain't you charmed?" "Isn't it splendid?" or "Don't it exceed your expectations?" a certain evil little demon who inhabits my being never fails to rap out a frigid "No!" and most ill-naturedly damp the amiable enthusiasm of my neighbor. Whereas if said neighbor has the gift of silence and levies no tax, I immediately contribute my best and do the rapturous with infinite relish.

Having been advised to take my first walk up the Glen Road, I marched away to the river in an exactly opposite direction, feasting on red raspberries by the way and filling my hat with a mountain nosegay of scarlet bunchberries, pale everlasting, dainty ferns, and blossoming—

"Grass with green flag half mast high";

made the acquaintance of sundry fine colts over a wall; received several hints concerning infant education from a venerable hen, a regular mother in Israel, to judge from the deference she received from her mates, and the number of her offspring, some twenty downy mites, so very young they looked like animated eggs with legs and heads. The devotion of this venerable biddy was beautiful to behold; for when a scoundrel in the likeness of a black and yellow cock-a-doodle had the meanness to peck at one of these innocents behind what he believed to be the safe shelter of a burdock leaf, the flash of wrath in that hen's eye was really "withering" as she seized the ruffian's lofty tail feathers in her beak; and though he basely fled, she hung on, allowing herself to be hustled over the grass with perilous and undignified speed till several of the neighboring chanticleers began to gurgle and strut suggestively. Then she let go and came proudly back, bearing a billful of the yellow plumage as trophies of the deed, and her maternal bosom heaving with the satisfaction of duties well performed. I could have applauded her and hissed the fallen foe, but feared to startle the young family, so continued my investigations, remembering that biddy-ology could be studied at any time, but mountains in the original could not.

My next discovery was an Indian tent, or wigwam, in which romantic but circumscribed abode were a man, his mother, wife, five children, and two dogs, all just from St. Francis, Canada. The man and wife, a pleasant-faced pair, were finishing off pretty baskets and fans for the day's sale. The mother, an evil, copper-colored old party with a scarred face, pipe, and moccasins, sat dyeing straw in one kettle and cooking some savage mess in another. Three roly-poly little girls lay in a heap, winking their heady black eyes at me and placidly munching lumps of cheese as if it were bread. A handsome boy, looking as dignified as a genuine Black Hawk chief, was making a birch canoe, often pausing to pull the string that rocked a little hammock wherein a fat brown baby was sleeping, with its hands tied down lest it should wake itself, and looking more like a plump mummy than a living child.

I bought a serious black-and-white fan and chatted with the father, who destroyed the effect of his fine face by chewing tobacco and telling me his name was Peter. The wife spoke no English but a soft, sweet-sounding language, half Canadian French, half Indian, and the old squaw grunted and "Ugh!"-ed like *The Last of the Mohicans.* All the children had colds, which rather diminished the romance of these native blossoms, pocket handkerchiefs not being included among their forest luxuries. I could not stay long, for the hotel gong roared "Breakfast!"—but as if painted on its smooth center, the fan will always recall the white wigwam on the knoll, the gray cliff behind, the rapid river below, the soft-voiced woman in the pointed doorway, and the ancient squaw's dark face thrown out like a bronze against the background of the man's red shirt, which gave the little picture the bit of color artists love.

After a breakfast made memorable by partaking of my first trout, which did not meet my expectations, though I broke a Pythagorean fast of twenty years' duration for the express purpose of enjoying this much bepraised delicacy, I devoted myself to the captivation of the dozen children, baiting my trap to catch sunbeams with pea-pod boats rich in rose-leaf sails, butterfly cages, and tissue-paper mansions for glowworms to illuminate at night. Very shy and coy at first were the little Montreal lasses. But presently confiding Bella, won by the promise of a vegetable man-of-war, came to lean upon my knee, and like a flock of lambs, the rest came trooping after, till even Pussy, the coyest of all, climbed into my lap, and a circle of black, blue, and brown eyes twinkled around me. A chorus of happy little voices oohed and aahed over the history of the immortal pigs and the Three Cakes, in which the tooth of time has made no breach.

Very flattering was the confidence and applause of these small personages, very pleasant their lively chat; and the happiest hour of all the day was the frolic in the sunshine full of morning mirth, and that best of influences, the innocent companionship of little children.

A trip to Willis's Gap was proposed, and the Gordon Clan, as I named the six pretty children and their little mates, with the addition of Will, Laura, and myself, went scrambling up a narrow gully, knee-deep in mossy mold, dead trees, and tangled vines, to the hilltop, where a clearing had been made, which gives a fine view of the blue peak of Mount Jefferson and adds much to the beauty of the prospect from below.

Everyone ran about, screamed, rasped their limbs, and cut capers, as if the mountains were made expressly for us to let off our steam upon. The boys swarmed up everything that was climbable, after imaginary squirrels, and came tumbling down again; the girls made birch panniers and filled them with flowers or fruit, thoughtful little Bella keeping hers for Mr. Hitchcock, the hotel keeper, lest "he shouldn't have enough for tea," she said. Laura went to sleep in the sun, like a lizard; Will roamed away into the wood; and for an hour I sat apparently ruminating like a cow, but in reality enjoying myself so thoroughly that I seemed soaked full of satisfaction like a beauty-loving sponge.

The mountains exceed my expectations in all respects, and I already love them heartily, for they seem to look down upon me like serene Titans, uttering a mute rebuke for all the petty follies and fusses I fret myself over. It is like beginning again; for people seem ashamed to go on in the foolish old way in such fine society, and feel as if they ought to turn poets, painters, philosophers, or at least their best and truest selves in honor of their grand hosts. Worldly folk grow simple, stiff ones turn jolly, sick ones breathe health, moody ones smile in spite of themselves, the old grow young, the young grow beautiful, and a general "Peace on earth, goodwill to man" atmosphere seems to influence all dwellers in these happy valleys.

As I sat aloft there, the mountains all about me seemed made of shaded velvet, so unbroken was the smooth sheet of verdure reaching to their tops—forests of maple, oak, and pine, where all manner of wild things live undisturbed, for many of these forests have never been explored—and there they stand as they were made, untouched by axes, untrodden by human feet. I never knew trees give such an impression before, but it is a strange and rather solemn sight, these unknown wildernesses living hundreds of years with their solitude unbroken and no little man to pry into their mysteries or shorten their beautiful lives. The hills are like a perpetual picture book whose leaves are turned by magic and whose colors never fade. No two hours are they alike, and each change seems lovelier than the last. In the morning the mist or scud rolls up their sides, hanging like white veils around their heads. All day the shadows of clouds float over them; at night they grow soft and smiling in the ruddy gold of sunset; then twilight darkens them till moonrise, when they stand out against the sky sharp and black, as if cut in marble.

Nature, the kind mother, seemed to have taken compassion upon her mighty children, adding the allurement of beauty to the majesty of strength, that when weary of their weird playmates, the whirlwind, thunderbolt, and avalanche, they might look down and feel themselves linked to humanity by the homesteads nestling confidingly at their feet, the villages like white flocks in the intervales, the pilgrims climbing up to make altars of them for offerings of reverence and love, so keeping their great hearts warm in spite of everlasting snow.

I settled it in my own mind that Carter was a feminine mountain, for, compared with the sterner, craggier mountains, it is green and graceful—capricious, too, as any pretty woman; one minute all smiles, the next all tears, seldom wearing the same costume long, yet beautiful in each and altogether a most fascinating piece of mountainhood (just pretend that last is a German word, and it will be all right). The Imp is Carter's grotesque son, and Mount Moriah her gossip, a quiet matronly mountain with less beauty and less caprice.

Speaking of costume reminds me of my own mishap in that line, and as a mortal weighing—excuse me if I don't mention how much over a hundred pounds—cannot, while the present laws of gravitation exist, be expected to remain long in the clouds, however enthusiastic one may be, I will descend to the grievances of a mundane woman. In spite of many warnings, I had spurned waterproof and rubbers and gone forth brave in new balmoral, boots, and hat, not to mention a dandelion-colored gown in a high state of starch. Thus regally arrayed, and more than usually comfortable in my mind, I sat innocently watching a pretty gray cloud come sailing up from the east, admiring its shadow on the green or purple fields below and thinking no evil till it came just over me. Then what did that scandalous vapor do but empty itself like a bucket right down upon our heads! It was really too pointed to be regarded as anything but a personal affront. I felt it so, and in high dudgeon streamed away home, bundling down the gully in mad haste, skimming over walls and brooks, and dodging cows, horses, and sheep in a way which caused the gentlemen on the piazza to offer audible bets which would win the race for shelter, myself or a mettlesome calf who joined in the steeple chase.

It was dreadfully humiliating to return in such an ignominious manner, with my drapery *more antique* than was agreeable, my feet swashing in my boots, and my hat—oh, my hat!—a wreck, a ruin, with rain dripping from its brim and ribbons of price, leaving livid green marks upon my agitated countenance. For the consolation of any sympathizing sister I will add that no bird, beetle, butterfly, worm, or other ornithological or entomological decoration fell a prey to the damp destroyer, as I do not affect the walking museum style. But the devastation was sufficiently extensive, as was the wrath, amiably masked by smiles till I reached my room in a state of heat, moisture, and internal powers of combustion that would have done honor to a steam engine.

Of course everyone soothed me by saying, "Didn't I tell you so?" and if a waterproof ever exulted or rubbers skipped derisively, mine would have performed those gratifying evolutions to my face. But like a pinafored angel, little Bella came to "'sist" me, as she said, and did so most effectually by mourning over the "downded hat." By the time I was reequipped and ready for another tramp, there was no tramp to be had; for as my blessed mother often says in domestic crises, "Just knock up a couple of pies," so the spirit of the hills seemed to have just knocked up a couple of clouds, and they were literally "pitching into" one another in a very lively manner. This rapid conjuration of wind, rain, thunder, and lightning was a surprising phenomenon to a native of Little Harmony, in which celebrated town even the elements conduct themselves in a decorous manner, owing to the great preponderance of mind over matter in which that sphinx's nest rejoices.

In less than an hour everything was changed from a sunny summer's morning to a gloomy, tempestuous squall, with an east wind howling like March, a fire looking and feeling as comfortable as in January, and everyone bundled up in shawls, jackets, and coats, as if the whole hotel had been whisked into another hemisphere like a castle in a pantomime. The gentlemen settled—as the heaviest particles always do, you know—at the bottom of the house in some subterranean den, where cigars, politics, and beverages might serve as nonconductors of lightning; and they were wise, for certainly nothing could be more unattractive to high powers of all kinds, unless they came as swift destroyers to the trio which do so much damage in this little world of ours. The women and children congregated in a large upper room, trying to amuse themselves, with the end of all things close at hand, apparently. Laura shivered by the fire like a chilly fairy in pink cambric; Mrs. A. entertained us with an enumeration of all her jewels and their respective prices; Mrs. B. related histories of the last illnesses and deaths of half a dozen friends, her bead headdress rattling impressively with the funereal wagging of her head; Mrs. G. sat among her babies like a full-blown rose in a nest of buds; the Misses D. played a crashing duet in opposition to the elements; three brides bereft of their lords roamed to and fro like lost sheep; and one individual ripped the trimming off a damp hat in mournful silence till a vivid flash caused her to fling down her scissors and cry out. A thunderclap followed, so sharp and startling the hills appeared to quake and "the crack of doom" ceased to be a vague idea. The brides shrieked, Mama G. gathered her flock closer, Mrs. B. paused with an abrupt "Lord bless us!" in the midst of Aunt Lavinia's erysipelas, and ignoring my late demonstrations, I coolly remarked, without picking up the scissors, however:

"That was very near."

A perfectly unnecessary observation from a person whose eyelashes had been nearly scorched off. But no utterance is lost upon the wise; for the thought of propinquity suggested danger, danger suggested measures for the safety of each number one, a universal cry of "Hoops?" arose, and with one impulse the perilous circumferences were hustled into bedrooms and under beds. Mrs. A. tore off her bracelets, in the firm conviction that all metals were conductors, and one of the brides precipitately departed to get rid of her teeth, I suspect, on the same principle. But the crowning tableau was prepared by Mrs. B., who, though already protected by silk, seated herself on a pillow in the middle of the room and, casting up her eyes, solemnly announced:

"Ladies, in the midst of life we are in death."

The next instant a second flash marred the impressiveness of the group by causing the excellent lady to fall flat upon her face.

Knowing that water, not fire, was to be my rock ahead through this life, though the latter element may be in the next, I amused myself by looking out of the window, hoop and all. But as the prospect consisted of a railroad, a horse block, and one despondent crow, I feel that no one will blame me that I was conscious of a sensation of delight when I beheld eight collegians approaching with knapsacks on their backs; guns, sticks, or fishing tackle in their hands; and more of their boots visible than is usually given to the public gaze; all of them wet as sponges and "jolly as sandboys"—whoever those individuals may be. Among a host of other weaknesses, I have one for collegians, especially freshmen. Seniors are apt to be too high-and-mighty, juniors priggish, sophs will do, but freshmen are "tip-top." I fancy 'tis because I both envy and pity them: envy because I always wanted to rollick through college, as it seems to be the fashion to do nowadays; pity because, like young bears, all their sorrows lie before them. There is something peculiarly agreeable in the frankness with which they glory in their promotion, the air with which they talk about "the men in my class," "our fellows," "our boat," and "our" possessions generally; the happy-go-lucky way in which they take everything, as if, having entered college, they had done all their country could expect and they had nothing to do for four years but enjoy themselves after the "horrid grind" and the tight squeeze it took to place them on such a pinnacle of honor.

As I saw the eight merry brown faces file in below and presently heard sixteen boots tramp by the door with an accompaniment of "By Joves," "What in thunder," and other expressions appropriate to students of classical lore, I bewailed my wrongs afresh, wishing that I too could be "one of our fellows," could wear a hat without any brim, tuck my trousers into my boots, and "lark" off whenever I liked—

"All in the blue unclouded weather,"

or otherwise—instead of being a martyr to haberdashery, smothered in coaches and cars, and handed about as gingerly as if I was labeled "Glass—this side up with care." There being no help for it, I went to my dinner, hoping to be regaled with freshmen, like an ogress, but the worthy lads dined elsewhere and kept their rooms while their clothes dried. The landlady said they were resting—and so they were, in a strictly collegiate fashion, for, having some knowledge of that species of warfare, I detected a "pillow fight" among other convulsions of nature, "u-pi-dee" choruses being chanted by the victors and one of the vanquished ejected through the window to the piazza roof, where he tranquilly finished his cigar, hatless and coatless, in the mizzle and then fought his way back again, like Horatius—

"In the brave days of old."

After tea they appeared, "clothed and in their right minds," so to speak, and also with company manners on, and consequently were not half as interesting as before, though they sang like a flock of blackbirds and danced till the gunpowder would have run out at the heels of their boots, as did the Joblinninnies and the Piccaninnies in the nursery legend, if that sort of sock was not out of fashion. They talked with everyone and anyone, flirted with all the young ladies, were mannish or boyish as they pleased; and though nobody knew them, they were "Hail fellow, well met" with every soul in or out of the house, from the bear to the babies.

I left them at eleven, still in full blast, and was roused about twelve by sounds as of someone putting bedroom furniture up the chimney and performing "The Wedding March" on the wall with boots. What new game was going on I cannot mention, but fell asleep comforting myself with my belief in metempsychosis; for, being sure that I was a horse or a cat in some former state, I felt equally sure that if I did my best, I might be a freshman in some future sphere where colleges exist. Before I was up next morning, the jovial eight were off to Mount Washington, whither I will follow them in my next.

III

"A fine day for the mountain, Mr. Hitchcock?"

"The best of the season, ma'am."

These two remarks are as much a part of the program as the mountain itself; for everyone starting on that memorable expedition firmly believes that the particular day they have chosen is the one perfect and propitious day of the three hundred and sixty-five, and jolly John Hitchcock is not the man to damp the soaring propensities and blithe prophecies of any guest under his capacious roof. Rain, wind, and fog seem utterly preposterous at six A.M. on a breezy July morning; the human mind refuses to believe in them, and even sage Uncle John, the weather-wise cobbler over the way, is considered a humbug when he shakes his head with a knowing cock of the eye and a slow "Wal, I do'no, it's a leetle dubersome. Shouldn't wonder if 'twas powerful squally bum by."

I indulged freely in these agreeable delusions as I stood on the steps of the Alpine House, taking my early draft of mountain air, which might be called oxygenated sweets, and set up a rivalry with the celebrated bitters. The Imp was pulling off his nightcap in honor of the ladies, for when one party leaves for Mount Washington, several other parties get up to see them do it, so the piazzas bloomed with pretty pink and white morning suits, relieved by gray and black masculine ditto, a sprinkling of newspapers, nurses, dogs, and jubilant children climbing everywhere like morning glories.

135

Six buckskin-colored horses and a vehicle very like a black sunbonnet trimmed with yellow stood before the door, and into it piled a merry company, eager for bears, landslides, whirlwinds, thunderbolts, and phenomena generally. Young ladies without hoops skimmed by, looking like limp ghosts of their former selves; old ladies compactly done up like plaid bundles going by some Arctic Express; men in every style of extraordinary cap, coat, and boots; small girls with hats tied down fore and aft; and youthful Izaak Waltons impaled themselves and attacked their friends with surreptitious fishing tackle, being haunted by visions of trout even at an altitude six thousand two hundred and eighty-five feet above the level of the sea. In they swarmed, the young folks laughing and joking, the old folks clacking and fussing, the whole thing looking like a modernized tableau of Noah's ark; for the dogs barked, the goats skipped, the doves fluttered, the bear sat up on end for a better view, Boniface beamed benignly, the "Doctor" skimmed to and fro for forgotten traps, and apple-faced Ira handed in men, women, children, guns, hammers, canes, camp stools, sketchbooks, spyglasses, bottles, baskets, cloaks, and umbrellas as gaily as if he hadn't been doing the same thing every day for six weeks. Abe the driver, not the President, finding his perch invaded by pretty girls, calmly subsided into a seat upon the small end of nothing whittled down. The buckskin pranced, the wagon swayed, everyone bawled, "Don't you wish you were going!" and away they went, veils streaming, hats waving, arms and legs in convulsions, and irrepressible boys bursting out into a patriotic—

"Hurrah for the red, white, and blue!"

If I had not been going also, I should have been much "tumbled up and down in my mind," as Bunyan says. Knowing that I was, I possessed my soul in patience till such time as it should please His Highness cousin Will to start, for, having been up and down so often that it's my private opinion he considers the mountain a neat little production of his own, he was not in such an eager state of mind as myself. Presently, around the corner swung our gallant grays and the "scramble cart," as I called the odd wagons that knock up hill and down dale with never a breakage, upset, or mishap. In we packed our wine bottles, cloaks, birch baskets, and precious selves with unusual care, for the elements are always all lying in wait to maltreat or try the mettle of the venturesome souls who invade these regions.

Off we drove, and in five minutes hotel, railroad, and civilization had entirely disappeared, and if anyone desired to see a wholly and heartily happy young woman, an eligible opportunity then occurred. It was the most eloquent hour of the day, for all was beautiful, all was fresh. Nothing was out of order, nothing disturbed eye or ear, and the world seemed to welcome us with its morning face. The road wound between forests full of the green gloom no artist has fully caught. Pines whispered, birches quivered, maples dropped hospitable shade across the way, and a little river foamed and sparkled by, carrying its melodious message from the mountains to the sea. Glimpses of hoary peaks broke on us now and then, dappled with shadows or half veiled in mists, floating and fading like incense smoke from censers, fit for a cathedral not built with hands. Leafy vistas opened temptingly on either side, berries blushed ripely in the grass, cowbells tinkled pleasantly along the hillsides, and that busy little farmer, the peabody bird, cried from tree to tree, "Sow your wheat, Peabody! Peabody! Peabody!" with such musical energy one ceased to wonder that fields were wrested from the forest to wave like green and golden breast knots on the bosoms of the hills.

Very soon the wonderful ascent began, and mile after mile we climbed up that smooth ladder—our modern beanstalk with a most friendly giant at the top—enjoying, as we went, the dissolving views the mountain gave us. Sometimes it was a glimpse into the primeval forest, where every tree was made beautiful in death by a pall of odorous Linnaea, every rock dressed in vines or sparkling with mica, and the ground knee-deep with the mold and moisture of a hundred seasons. Sometimes a little nook peopled with every brake and fern that loves the wood, and jubilant with mimic waterfalls plashing through the leaves as they tumbled over stone and slope, leaving fairy pools for birds to drink at. Sometimes we looked up granite walls that seemed to shut out the sky, then into gorges that sank sheer down a mile or more and turned the brain giddy with a glance. At one time we passed through a region weird as the "Blasted Heath," where many acres once visited by fire still kept the semblance of a forest, whose trees stood white and spectral as an army of skeletons bleached by years of sun and rain. As we entered it, the world seemed dead. Above us a waste of gray rock stretched for miles; below, a cloud hid the valley and sent its chilly breath into our faces; all about us stood the ghostly wood, mute and motionless, for there was no leaf to rustle, no bird to sing, no babble of water to break the awesome hush. But if that were death, there came a resurrection beautiful and swift, as if an angel rolled the stone away. The path, abruptly turning, shut out the dreary tract, the cloud swept by, the sun came dazzling athwart the granite boulders, the mountaintop rose clear before us, and a blithesome wind began to blow.

Hardly had we taken a long breath after this spectacle than a more wonderful one opened upon us; and let me tell you, it's not altogether an agreeable sensation to discover that neither eye, brain, mind, nor body is half large or strong enough to take in the magnitude and significance of all about you. We were now winding along the "Ledges," where the road, like a narrow balcony, suspends the traveler over a yawning gulf like Chaos come again, for earth, rocks, trees, water, mist, and snow were hurled pell-mell together, as if the Great Workman had left the fragments there when He finished the mountain and pronounced it "good." Anything more indescribably strange I never saw, and instinctively drew a little nearer my companions as my eye swept down the chasm, across the valley dark with untrodden forests, up the majestic range that undulated opposite, through gap after gap, each hazier than the last, out into the sea of blue that rolls around all the world.

When our journey first began, we had chattered, laughed, and sung, gradually growing stiller as we climbed, and our small gossip seemed impertinent; for the last mile we had been nearly silent because—

> "It is with feeling as with waters,
> The shallow murmur, but the deep are dumb."

Just here, however, seeing that Laura and I began to get choky, pale, and convulsive with excitement, cousin Will fell to talking, which was very provoking and very sensible of him, for at this height the rarefied air often produces queer sensations, such as shortness of breath, humming in the ears, and a general state of champagnity, if I may so express the pleasing but peculiar delusion that one is a young balloon out for a holiday.

He told us how several persons who had been up with him were affected at this spot: One lady wept copiously, one sang like a distracted nightingale, one fainted, and another yearned to take a leap at this jumping-off place and see what came of it.

I could understand their states, for in a few hours one finds oneself in such an entirely new world, one doesn't know how to behave. The intense silence almost frightened me, for we seemed to be in a region where nothing moved or made a sound, except the faint whisper of the wind. The clouds looked out of order, for they were often below us, often so near we looked into their misty depths or felt their soft embrace as they enveloped us and for a moment blotted out all sight and sound. The trees, too, were curious; for they grew smaller and smaller as we went, and the last miniature wood had something pathetic in it. The tiny trees were so like large ones in shape and age and, though so stunted, had a desperate sort of hardihood in clinging to the scanty soil, as if bent on living though all the elements forbid. I longed to bring away a two-foot patriarch to enjoy a green old age in some more sheltered spot; for I suspect the air has a bland influence which rouses all that is kindliest in us, and each pilgrim longs to leave some token of regard for their fine old host. We presently came to one of these memorials, called "Willis's Seat," a granite couch, shaped by nature and placed beside the road by a lover of Mount Washington so that others may enjoy a free seat at this grand panorama.

We rested here, and—oh, that I should have to mention such unromantic facts!—we ate our lunch and Will smoked a cigar. It is mournful to contemplate, but if people will breakfast on enthusiasm at five in the morning, drive eight miles, and adore all creation through every pore of their skin, they must eat or perish, and such scenery would glorify even a sausage, how much more a sandwich, constructed upon the best principles of art.

After this we went on again along the wonderful road that, like a serpent, seems to wind its way up in changeful coils from its ambush in the valley; looking backward as we climbed at the dangers so easily surmounted, forward at the apparently unattainable summit, and enjoying all the indescribable emotions that make this ascent—

"A thing to dream of, not to tell."

"This is the last stage, so don't look back till we are fairly up, because I want you to have it all in one grand burst and to hear what you'll say, Tot."

The remark was addressed to me, for, though not "a daughter of the gods" exactly, I am "divinely tall"—I wish I could add "divinely fair"—therefore, cousin Will considered "Tot" a peculiarly appropriate term of endearment. Being anxious to gratify him, I screened myself from temptation under a big umbrella and tried to condense the ideas simmering in my head into one satisfactory exclamation, but we were at our journey's end before the all-expressive word had been selected from my stock of adjectives.

Just before us, all the way up, had lumbered the big wagon with the buckskin horses, whose lines had certainly fallen in

pleasant places, but whose paths were decidedly not the paths
of peace. This groaning vehicle reached the summit first and
effectually blocked up the way, while its dozen or more occu-
pants debouched upon the small plateau which many feet
have worn bald upon the crown of Washington's venerable
pate. Out they tumbled, spread themselves, stared, and vented
the predominant sentiment of their variously affected minds
somewhat in this wise:

"Dear, how nice!"

"Emma, your hat is smashed as flat as a pancake! Is mine?"

"Oh, thunder! Ain't that a stunnin' prospect, though?"

"Hum, not bad to such as hav'n't seen Mont Blanc. *I* have."

"Wonder if they'll 'ave any porter at the 'ouse, 'Arry?"

"I'd like to know what that intervale would fetch cut up
into grass farms."

"Now, this don't meet my expectation a mite, Gusty."

"Lor', Cy! I'm sure it's the prettiest risin' I ever set eyes on."

"Ma, can we see our house in New York from here?"

"You dreadful boy! You've sat on the sandwiches and got
the mustard all over you!"

The last distracted exclamation was too much for me. The
sublime was overpowered by the ridiculous, and forgetting
that Will was waiting for my rapture, I broke into a fit of
laughter, exclaiming:

"Oh, Laura, isn't it as funny as a farce?"

Such a return for all his trouble was a shock from which
Will did not soon recover, though I remorsefully endeavored
to atone for it by rushing to the roof of the Tip-Top House and
nearly destroying my optic nerve by staring devotedly through
a telescope, crying "Superb!" "Splendid!" "Heavens, how fine!"
etc., though I give you my word I didn't see a thing. I was just
beginning to fear that I should acquire a chronic squint, when
a bell rang, someone shouted "Dinner!" and the crowd vanished from the roof like a flock of pigeons. If they had announced a suttee with myself to enact the devoted "widder,"
I couldn't have felt more disgusted, though an hour before
I should have clashed my cymbals for joy. But I dared not

express my feelings with the freedom so agreeable to me, having disappointed my escort once. So, seeing that it was etiquette to dine, I did the deed in the most thorough manner, first writhing into a crowded room built of rough stones and draped with white; next I wrote my name in a big book, with "Theophilus Smith, D.D." just above it and something that looked like "Nicklas Pfizmann, Heidelberg," below it; then struggled into a small closet where half a dozen ladies were madly endeavoring to prink with one little glass and a repulsive-looking brush. I had nothing to do, and nothing to do it with, if I had. But being told to go in, I went, that is, got my head and shoulders in, sneezed, and took them out again, saying briskly:

"Now I'm ready, Will."

And wholly unconscious of the hollow mockery of the thing, he bore me away to encounter struggle number four, which consisted in sitting between the mustardy boy and the red-bearded Nicklas, both of whom bolted tough beef, leathery pastry, and petrified potatoes in a way that filled me with respectful amazement; for I could only endeavor to look famished and hack away vigorously at the tempting viands on my plate.

We emerged at last, and leaving Will to do the honors to Laura, I went away to enjoy myself after my own heart. Choosing a secluded nook, I sat myself down in the shadow of a rock and sat there for an hour, I verily believe, without winking. Now, I hope no one expects a description of the indescribable, because if they do, they won't be gratified. I can only tell them that for an hour I was supremely happy, not because I was just then one of the most eminent women this side of the Rocky Mountains, but because I forgot my body, my cares, my fears, my fate, and seemed nothing but a spirit that, loving beauty, had found its fill for once. But I should as soon think of declaiming the Lord's Prayer on a steamboat landing, as a dramatic little pupil of mine once did, as of setting down what I thought, felt, and saw in any newspaper, even the respected and respectable *Commonwealth*.

The humane side of the affair they are very welcome to, for I very gladly turned to it when my eyes were ready to fall out of my head with gazing over hundreds of miles of sunny landscape and my head spun around with trying to imagine the lives these mountains led.

Slinging my panniers on either side, I strolled up and down, gathering russet mosses, purple heathlike bells, delicate white flowers, bits of stone, and other relics, while watching the continually changing groups about me. Universal free-and-easiness prevailed, for everybody spoke to everybody else as they sat, scrambled, or stood, as if the forms and fashions of the lower world had been left behind by general consent. Picturesque guides, with metal badges on their caps, gay jackets, and shrill calls to the files of horses they led, came and went along the paths that wound like white threads over the lower hills. A party of volunteers in the first flush of bravery and buttons drank healths, sang war songs, and had a mock combat. My charming freshmen were there, fresher and more charming than ever in spite of their tramp. Several old ladies hopped placidly from stone to stone like rheumatic robins, chirping as they went; geologists tapped and hammered, as if the mountain was a defective kettle and they intent on mending it; artists sketched and smoked; children romped; exhausted mamas dozed; two fine ladies in gauze bonnets and flounced gowns looked as comfortable and appropriate as wax dolls in Westminster Abbey. Lovers, of course, took advantage of the propitious hour; for I saw the "Oh, thunder!" youth laying violent siege to Emma, of the pancake hat, Nicklas excoriating himself in his efforts to destroy the velvety black spiders that haunted another damsel as ardently as himself, and our infantile couple kissing one another audibly under the inevitable little umbrella. As we had no less than six clergymen among us, it is a marvel to me why no one seized so excellent an occasion to be married then and there, in emulation of a certain romantic pair who were made one on "a misty, moisty morning" on the Island of Niagara.

The only service the reverend gentlemen performed was

that of calling upon the impromptu congregation to sit still while an indefatigable Mr. Somebody took pictures of the group. An impressive scene ensued, for, being requested to be mute and motionless, everyone was possessed with an unconquerable desire to giggle and squirm, while the operator implored, and one of the clergymen, in a voluminous white choker, commanded five-and-forty bodies to remain stiff and rigid, when their seats consisted of excessively sharp stones and a fierce sun was burning every individual nose to a fine copper color.

Three of the collegians sat behind Laura and me with Will, who, being as full of mischief as the youngest of them, told funny anecdotes, sotto voce, which the lads bore in convulsive silence till he reeled off a family joke about a reverend uncle who years ago took this jaunt with several companions when those now famous gentlemen were freshmen also—how in their ignorance they all partook copiously of bologna sausages, and being driven wild by the drought produced by that thirst-provoking viand, they had all rushed into a farmhouse and demanded milk, which they imbibed with such gusto that the good housewife held up her hands in blank amazement over the fourth emptied pan, exclaiming, "Sakes alive, gentlemen! Ain't you weaned yet?"

At which scandalous reminiscence the boys went off into a shout of such contagious merriment that everyone roared in concert and without the least idea why they were sending the echoes into hysterics.

Fortunately this outburst did not ruin the picture, though the dawn of that splendid laugh is visible in nearly every countenance, my own being perfectly unrecognizable, for I was nothing but a bottle of effervescent giggles with the cork ready to fly off in another minute. This work of art possesses great merits in my eyes for all that, because the commanding parson is preeminent, the Henglish 'Arry quite observable, and the little freshes as good as the originals, if not better.

After this jovial scene, Will tore us away in spite of our lamentations and prayers to be allowed to spend the night there, with the exciting possibility of having the roof blown off by some playful whirlwind, ourselves drenched, frozen, block-aded, or otherwise made famous in the annals of the Moun-tain. The drive down was the most perfect exemplification of the "trust in Providence and the other man" idea I ever knew, for we rattled along at a brisk trot over gullies with no appar-ent bottoms, through breakneck holes where not even a soft stone to fall upon was visible, and around sharp corners with all eternity on the other side of a low wall. This rate of speed and style of scenery caused the sensation of uncertainty—I won't say fear—to penetrate my being. A small pitch I could sustain, but to be spilled heels over head into chaos is not a sufficiently dignified exodus to suit my fancy. Therefore, I mildly proposed a short trip afoot in search of certain ficti-tious posies I professed to have seen on our way up and, by dexterous management, contrived to walk four miles of what seemed sure destruction in a carriage, with no fears to dis-turb, but birds, berries, and lovely views to make the walk memorable and a chorus of volunteers behind me to supply the social element. Will and Laura banged down and waited for me at the halfway spring, while I enjoyed my run, feeling like a very small bug creeping over a remarkably large apple, for it takes the vanities out of one amazingly to find oneself in such a place alone.

Being fairly mounted, my first experience was not to make me regret my past prudence; for, going down a steep slope, some essential part of the harness broke, and if we had had any but trained mountaineers like Lord Howe and Wood-chuck, my epitaph might have been condensed into the severe simplicity of the one word "Smashed." Finding ourselves sud-denly reduced to a somewhat perilous conglomeration of man, woman, horse, and wagon, Will took a survey and asked for a string, as men insist upon doing, as if women were a new sort of silkworm expressly created to produce any quantity and all varieties of cable, cord, and sewing cotton. Of course we had no string! And of course we indignantly demanded why, when he brought a hammer and nails, he hadn't had the forethought to add a clothesline. The question was unanswerable, except by that convenient refuge for perplexed Yankees, a whistle, which satisfactory response was instantly forthcoming.

Here was a situation for a romance, and mark how romantically it ended: three immortal souls—I should say mortal bodies—in imminent peril, halfway down that mighty mountain, the nearest house three miles off, harness unsafe, no string at hand, Will perplexed, Laura anxious, myself in secret anguish, though externally calm, quite calm, as the sequel will prove. Despair predominated, an impressive pause ensued, then the colossal intellect of Miss A. rose triumphantly above all obstacles of time, place, delicacy, and inconvenience; for with her usual decision of gesture and tone, she—I pause to collect myself for the disclosure—she plucked off a stout green—excuse me if I say—garter, briefly observing, "Tie up the strap and come on." It was done, and the verdant band which had bound the fragile limb of that inspired woman henceforth merits a place beside, and may be considered a fit mate to, that other ligature which an English Duchess made famous and which English matrons mention without a blush. History is requested to make a note of the later and sublimer act.

I think the effort sobered my spirits, for though the sunset drive homeward was delicious and the day an "epo" in my existence, foreboding fears would hover about the green knot, bobbing so picturesquely before my eyes, because Will was an inveterate joker and I predicted an undesirable publicity for that now doubly useful article of dress.

My fears proved true, for when Will came in from the stable, I saw from my window that he bore a trophy in his hand. A laugh from the piazza presently followed, and when I reluctantly yet indignantly descended to my tea, though no one alluded in the most distant manner to g—t—s of any kind, I seemed to see a suspicious twinkle in every masculine eye, which was very trying; and to this day I don't know the fate of that maltreated woolen friend in need.

Feeling that nothing was worth looking at after Mount

Washington and that we never could be surprised anymore, Laura and I retired to our rooms, there to fight our battles over again, anoint our burned noses, bandage our bruised ankles, and congratulate ourselves that though we hadn't seen the Alps and the Andes, no one could twit us with not having seen Mount Washington.

IV

"Come, Tot, put on your habit and ride up to see the Imp before tea."

Will addressed this remark to me as I sat on the piazza, in a group of beflounced and bejeweled ladies, pretending to embroider, with an absurd little workbasket on my knee and a puckered bit of cambric in my hand. His masculine eye saw at a glance that it was no place for me, and he rescued me from my genteel martyrdom, like a kindhearted creature as he is. Up I flew and, leaving four models of elegant ennui behind me, speedily equipped myself for one of the pleasures which I am destined never perfectly to enjoy.

When I came down, the horses not being ready, I sat on the doorstep endeavoring to recall all the equestrian rules and regulations I had ever heard, that I might not disgrace my cavalier. But I must confess that, never having been to riding school, my ideas of the matter were somewhat confused and hitherto I had confined myself to the simple laws of getting on and staying on. These had served me very well so far, though my Amazonian sister had confided to me her opinion that my appearance, when enjoying myself on my favorite steed, was that of a meal bag on a cantering cow. Now, with the eyes of Gorham upon me, I wished to present a correct deportment and, while waiting with apparent serenity, was secretly murmuring, "Elbows down, shoulders back, head up, reins in left hand, whip at the side, don't touch the pommel, one, two, spring!" etc.

When the beasts appeared, I ran down the steps without waiting for Will, who was tightening his hatband. The truth was, I saw a party of gentlemen approaching and I wanted to be off before the arrival of these connoisseurs. So, mounting the horse block, I sat down in the saddle as if it had been a rocking chair, a proceeding which would have disgusted my more accomplished sister, who regards anything but a scientific toss-up disgraceful in the extreme. Somebody on the piazza laughed—I don't wish to know who—and the small hostler grinned as he handed my whip—I should like to ask why. Then Will gave me a hoist and a smooth and swung himself up with a "Now, then!" that caused me to cluck to my horse, bow to my friends, and prepare to ride gallantly away. Nothing of the sort, however, occurred. Squab, my interesting steed, merely put back his ears, whisked his tail, and began to describe a circle with his hind legs, while his forelegs remained stationary, or nearly so.

"Give him a cut behind, miss. He always acts ugly at first, but I guess he won't throw you," remarked the hostler with his hands in his pockets.

There was a cheering speech for you! But with the inviting prospect of presently alighting on my head, I gingerly tickled the saddlecloth in the rear with a few flaps of my whip. The only visible effect was an acceleration of the circular prance, a general smile, and a disagreeable certainty that I resembled a bad circus rider; which last idea incited me to give Squab a vengeful slash over head and ears that effectually conquered his objections to progression. With a plunge that sent my heart into my mouth, he bolted off, throwing me into such mental and bodily confusion that I suspect my elbows went up, my head went down, and all my good intentions came to naught. I know I did "touch the pommel," not to say clung to the same, while the "one, two, spring!" movement was performed every half second, with a velocity that induced Will to observe ironically:

"Fine exercise, isn't it?"

"Ve-ry fi-ne in-deed," chattered I, bound not to give in while I could hold on.

In this graceful and dignified style, we trotted out of sight, and I was just collecting my scattered wits when the landscape abruptly reversed itself and I found myself seated in the dirt, with the saddle on Squab's belly instead of on his back. Finding repose of any kind extremely grateful, I remained where I was, and Squab so entirely coincided with me that he strolled to the roadside, feeding leisurely as he went. Will's face was a study as he dismounted, exclaiming with mingled mirth and anxiety:

"My dear girl, are you hurt?"

"I'm very comfortable, thank you," responded the dear girl, still reposing in the dirt.

"Well, shall we go on?" he asked presently.

"Yes, why not?" and rising from the dust, I shook myself, wiped my hot forehead, and stood ready to remount, though my cowardly heart beat like a trip-hammer; and my face would have been a little palish with alarm if it had not been decidedly reddish with heat. This time it was literally a "toss-up," for whether I should come down "heads" or not was an open question in my mind. Fortunately I hit aright, and as we moved on, Will said:

"Try jockeying. That is a hard horse, but the best I could get for you."

"Haven't I been jockeyed enough?" thought I, but replied with all possible alacrity, "Yes, I will," and immediately asked myself what it meant "to jockey." Something about rising in the stirrup and taking the motion of the horse floated mistily through my mind. However, I proceeded to bounce vigorously, wondering why it was considered easier than to be passively bounced, till it struck me that I had made a mistake somewhere and that in riding, as in dancing, it was necessary to keep time; for as I came down, the horse was always going up, and instead of my "taking the motion," the motion was taking me, and very unpleasantly, too.

"Christopher Columbus! How will it end?" groaned I, vainly endeavoring to hit the proper moment for an easy bounce. Will seemed to think we were getting on excellently, and began to dilate upon the beauties of nature, while I responded to the best of my ability.

"It is a perfect day for seeing the Imp's profile to advantage, clear, and cool, and dry."

"Yes"—bump—"we couldn't"—chatter—"have had"—bump—"a better"—chatter, bump—

"There's a chatty old woman in one of the houses that stand in the meadow where we go for the view, and you must make her talk."

"Does she"—chatter—"live there"—bump—"all alone?"—chatter, bump—chatter, bump—

"No, she has neighbors. You find Squab easier now, don't you?"

"Oh, very"—bump, bump—"much easier"—chatter, chatter—bump—chatter—bump.

At this point the brute's patience gave out as the woman's had long ago, and I don't blame him, for a more miserable pair than rider and ridden it would be hard to find. Coming to a millpond, he suddenly whirled about, backed down the bank, and began to shake himself as if I was a horsefly—so I was in one sense of the word, for, goodness knows, I would gladly have put a greater distance between us than the length of a hyphen. At this new and somewhat perilous demonstration, I called upon gods and men, Will seized the bridle, and we all floundered back into the road together.

"Confound the beast! He acts so because he knows you are afraid of him," fumed Will.

"I'm not afraid now, I'm mad. Lash him well while I hold on," scolded I, feeling ready to break my horse's neck and my own, also, just then.

A great ramping and scuffling ensued, and after the dust had subsided, the spirit of the hills might have beheld a hot, begrimed, and bedraggled female pelting along the road, with hat awry, staring eyes, and desperation in every feature of her face. How we reached the meadow is more than I can tell. That we did reach it at all I regard as one of the most felicitous events of my life; for when we paused, my arms were stiff, my eyes literally danced in my head, and "the dews of exhaustion bathed my brow," as they did Consuelo's some half dozen times during her subterranean search for her lunatic lover.

Turning at a certain spot, Will bade me look up; I did so, and there, clear against the deep blue behind it, stood out the profile of the Great Stone Face. Starr King, in his *White Hills,* has said all that can be said, in the way of rapture, quotation, and description, of this as of all the other wonders of this region; therefore, his picture of the profile shall stand instead of mine.

It seemed as if an enormous giant had sculptured his own likeness on the precipice. There was the broad arch of the forehead; the nose, with its long bridge; and the vast lips, which, if they could have spoken, would have rolled their thunder accents from one end of the valley to the other. The whole profile is about eighty feet in length. The expression is really noble, with a suggestion partly of fatigue and melancholy. The upper portion of the mouth looks a little weak, as though the front teeth had decayed and the granite lip had fallen in. Those who can see it with a thunder cloud behind and the slaty scud driving thin across it will carry away the grandest impression it ever makes on the beholder. But when, after an August shower late in the afternoon, the mists that rise from the forest below congregate around it and, smitten with sunshine, break as they drift against its nervous outline and, hiding the mass of mountain which it overhangs, isolate it with a thin halo, the countenance, awful but benignant, is "as if a mighty angel were sitting among the hills and enveloping himself in a cloud vesture of purple and gold."

So we saw it from the low-lying meadow, green and still, the very contrast enhancing the beauty of each; for almost weary of the immensity of all about me, it was often a relief to rest my eyes and mind in some sunny spot where ferns were the only forest, a brook the tranquil river, mossy stones the hills, with dragonfly and gnat to play the parts of hawk and eagle.

My meditations were brought to a close by Squab, who, after fidgeting and fussing like an evil-disposed beast as he was, turned around and stared me in the face with an intelligent look—I hate him, but I'm bound to say he had an intelligent eye, fiendishly intelligent, if I may use so forcible an expression—a look that said as plainly as words, "If you don't want to be pitched into the brook, ma'am, you'd better get off and let me drink."

Will appeared to understand him and proposed that I should pay a visit to the old lady while he watered the horses and talked politics with somebody at the barn. As every bone in my body ached and I regarded even a temporary divorce from Squab a foretaste of heaven, I agreed, and in ten minutes found myself seated by a breezy window, a fan in one hand, a saucer of raspberries and cream in the other, and my hostess knitting away in front of me. I suspect the worthy woman was kept rather short of the food so essential to her feminine constitution, namely gossip, for hardly was I seated before she began.

"Be you stayin' to the Glen?"

"No, ma'am, at the Alpine."

"He's a harnsome, likely-lookin' man," with a nod in the direction of the invisible Will.

"Very much so."

"I mistrusted who you was the minute I see you," and a significant smile accompanied the words.

"Dear me, can she know anything about my little 'works of Shakespeare,'" thought I, feeling quite Fanny Burneyish on a small scale. Not knowing what else to do, I also "put up my fan and simpered"; to "rouge high," as she describes her modest blushes, was out of the question, my complexion being quite as rubicund as that of the hollyhocks outside the window. Still nodding and smiling like an amiable Chinese mandarin, the old lady continued:

"Yes, I've heard of you. There was another couple here this mornin', and they said they guessed you'd be along, it's such pretty ridin' in these parts for such as you and him."

"What a peculiar old person," thought I, adding aloud, "Yes, ma'am, I enjoy it very much, for I've spent here some of the happiest days of my life."

"That's jest what they all say, and ef young folks would only start right, they might keep on sayin' of it a consid'able spell longer than they gen'rally do. Now, I've had experience, and I can see as plain as anything that you're one of the up-and-down sort, and I shouldn't wonder a mite ef there come a hitch by'm'by, for all you are so fond a one another now."

"Bless the woman! What is she driving at?" muttered I, with a mouthful suspended halfway to my lips. Her next words enlightened me, and my literary vanities received a blow.

"I don't wish for to take no liberties, but havin' seen a slight more o' life than young folks, I always say my say when new married couples come philanderin' out here; and whether they like it or not, I feel as ef I'd done my duty by 'em, for a word in season is wuth a whole sermon too late."

As she paused to pick up a stitch, I came to the conclusion that owing to Will's injunctions to "rest and cool yourself, my dear," the old lady had taken it into her head that we belonged to the bridal swarm that infested the neighborhood. The idea amused me mightily, and for the joke's sake, I did not inform her that my valuable affections were still unwon, except by the ghost of a youthful sweetheart, who wooed me on a haycock with a Jew's-harp serenade full fifteen years ago. So I quenched a dawning smile and answered soberly:

"Very true, ma'am. Pray speak freely. I shall be glad to receive any advice you may like to offer, for I suspect I shall be very likely to err in the manner you suggest, being as fond of having my own way as most women."

"I ain't a doubt of it, so let me tell you to begin with, don't never try to drive your husband into nothin', for the best of 'em turns contr'y and pigheaded ef drove. It's our place for to bear all things in meekness of sperrit, as we was ordered when that Saint Paul said, 'Wives submit yourselves to your husbands.'"

"I don't agree to that, ma'am, though a dozen Saint Pauls said it, and never intend to submit to anyone but the Lord. It is my opinion that the bearing and forbearing should be mutual, and as men are eternally calling women angels, they should be more willing to be guided by them. They certainly could not be managed worse than they usually manage themselves."

"Lord a massy, child, ef that's your belief. There never was anybody more off the track than you be, and it's my 'pinion, before the year's out, you'll be in a wuss scrape than I was oncet."

She appeared so shocked at my doctrine, and so eager for a convert of her own, that I did not hesitate to say, with an appearance of deep interest:

"Suppose you tell me your scrape, and perhaps it will help me to avoid a similar one."

"I ain't no objection in the world, for though it ain't much of a story, it's a warnin' which you'd do wall to take in case o' need. I've told it a sight o' times, and folks laugh as ef it was ruther humorsome. It warn't to live through, you'd better believe." And leaning back in her creaky chair, her tongue rattled as briskly as her needles while she reeled off the following "warnin' to young married folks."

"I was raised in York State, and when I married, we settled in Vermont. I declare I ain't seen a prettier place sense I left; and the old sayin's come true: 'A cow don't know the wuth of her tail till she's lost it.' Silas was a master hand to his trade, a careful and a savin' man, so for three, four year we was as comfortable as a pair o' old shoes. My nighest neighbor was a widder. She'd berried a couple o' husbands and was lookin' round for another as chipper as you please. You see, havin' few pies of her own to make, Mis' Millet was amazin' fond o' puttin' her fingers in her neighborses. But she done it so neat, folks ruther liked it till they found she was takin' all the sass and leavin' 'em all the crust, as you may say. I never mistrusted her for a long spell, not knowin' widder's ways.

"I thought luck was in my dish, surely. But it warn't, and I had to eat my mess o' trouble, which was needful and nour- ishin', ef I'd only had the grace to see it so.

"Silas got into a lawsuit about his wages, and it seemed as if everything was at sixes and sevens all to onct. He was a high-sperrited man and had the right of it, but them lawyers made a snarl out o' nothin' and sent the bill to him. It was a long job and made him terrible fractious while it lasted. I thought he'd better give up than muddle along that way, and it fretted me past bearin' to have him dingin' away about that three hundred dollars continual, so I got as fractious as him. The children seemed to ketch the fit, for they acted like time in the primmer, with croup and pins and hoopin' cough and temper. I declare I used to think the very pots biled over jest to spite one another, to say nothin' o' me. Of course I told Mis' Millet my werryments, and she seemed to sympathize real hearty, telling me to keep a taut rein or I should never get the upper hand all my days. 'Train Silas well,' ses she. 'Don't give up nothin', but show him you've a will o' your own, though he don't take your advice. A woman has a sight o' power if she only knows how to use it, and can fetch a man to 'most any- thing from blacking her shoes to marryin' of her. Jest keep vit- tles low, buttons oncertain, and kisses scurse, and he'll soon give up beat, for peace and quietness sake. That's how I keep my blessed Jabez and Nathan under.'

"In them days I thought consid'able as you do, and so, when Mis' Millet put it into my head that I was picked upon, I thought it was about time for me to set up my Ebenezer and make things stan' round my way. I went and done jest what she told me, for I didn't see through her a mite then or guess that settin' folks by the ears was as relishin' to her as bitters is to some. Merciful sus, what a piece o' work we did make on't. I scolded, Silas swore, the children carried on like all pos- sessed, and the house was gettin' too hot to hold us when we was brought up with a round turn and set straight in time to see the sense of our redicklous doin's."

"When I spoke of not submitting, I didn't mean to have any

fighting or scolding about it, ma'am. But each yields a little, and though two strong wills may not work quite smoothly at first, a constant and gentle friction will probably polish off the angles and make a match at last."

The old lady was somewhat in the dark as to my meaning, but after a moment's meditation, illuminated herself with an explanation to suit her own views:

"You're about right there, though I didn't see it at fust. It *is* like rubbin' a friction match, and many a house has been sot afire from such small beginnins, both reelly and what you call figger o' speech way. I 'most done the job for myself, as I was tellin' of you, and though we was common sort o' folks, I reckon it's pretty much the same with the grand folks, for I've seen fine ladies snap at their husbands and get a right good settin' down for their pains, only it was all done what you call elegant. Wal, one day Silas come home madder'n a hornet's nest; for the suit seemed goin' aginst him, he'd had a lecter from his boss, and one o' the neighbor's cows had spiled every one o' the mellions he sot so much by. I was dishin' up dinner, feelin' anything but comfortable; for a whole batch o' bread was burnt to a cinder, my Nathaniel had sca't me 'most to death swallerin' a cent, and the steak had been on the floor more'n oncet, owin' to my havin' three babies, a dog, two cats, and no end o' hens under my feet. Silas looked as black as thunder, hove his hat away, and come along to the sink where I was skinnin' pertaters, and as he wasked his hands, I asked him what the matter was. Bad news is hard enough to tell at the best o' times, but when a man's cross, it's wuss'n rubbin' their nose the wrong way, a gret sight. He muttered and slopped, and I couldt' git a word o' sense out on him nohow. Being riled myself didn't better it, and so we fell to hectorin' one another right smart till we both felt ekle to 'most anything. Presently he said something that dreened the last drop o' patience in my biler. I gave an aggravatin' answer, and fust I knew, he up with his hand and struck me. It warn't a hard blow, only a kind of a wet spat side o' the head. But I thought I should a flew, for I see a million sparks in a minnit. All the blood in my body went tearin' up to my head, and I felt as ef I'd been knocked down. You never see a man look so shamed as Silas did, but he didn't say a word. I just pitched fork, dish, pertaters, and all into the pot, put on my bunnet, and said as ferse and high as you please: 'When you're ready to treat me as a man oughter treat his wife, you can come and fetch me back, but you won't see me before, and so I tell you.' Then I made a beeline for Mis' Millet's, told her all, asked her to let me stay till he come round, had a good cry, a mouthful o' dinner, and was ready to go home in half an hour, though nothing would have fetched me to ownin' of it.

"Wal, that night passed—sakes! What a long one it was, and me without a wink o' sleep, thinking o' Nat and the cent, my emptins, and the baby. Next day come, but no Silas, no message, no nothin', and I'd begun to think I'd got my match, though I had a sight o' grit in them days. I sewed, and Mis' Millet, she clacked, but I never heard what she said, only worked like sixty to pay for my keep, 'cause I warn't goin' to be beholden to her for nothin'. At last I begged her to go and git me a clean gown; for I'd come off jest as I was, and folks kep' droppin' in as soon as they heard of the job, as Mis' Millet took care they should. She went, but ef you'll believe it, Silas wouldn't let her in! He jest handed the things out o' winder and told her to tell me they was gettin' on fust rate with Florindy Walsh to do the work, and hoped I wouldn't expect him for a spell, as he liked a quiet house and had got one now. When I heard that, I knew he must be terrible pervoked, and could a streaked straight home and crawled into the winder ef he hadn't opened the door; but Mis' Millet wouldn't let me go and kep' stirrin' on me up till I was ashamed to eat 'umble pie fust and waited to see what would come on't. But you see, he had the best on't, for he'd got the children and lost a cross wife, while I'd lost all and got nothin' but Mis' Millet, who grew hatefuller and hatefuller, for I begun to mistrust that she was a mischief maker, seein' how she pampered up my temper and seemed to like the querrel.

"I thought I should o' died more'n once; for as true as I'm settin' here, it went on pretty nigh a week, and of all the miserable creeters, I was the miserablest. When Saturday come, a tremendous storm set in, and it rained guns all day. I was hankerin' after the baby and dreadful werried about the others, all bein' croupy, and Florindy, with no more idee of sickness than a baa-lamb. The rain come down like a regler Deluge, and I didn't seem to have the leastest mite of an ark to run to. Everything got into a fluster as night come on; for the wind blew off the roof o' Mis' Millet's barn and smashed the buttery winder, the brook riz and went streamin' every which way, and such a mess you never did see. I was as nervous as a witch, but kep' on sewin' and listenin' to the tinkle-tankle of the drops in the pans we'd sot round, for the house leaked like a sieve. Mis' Millet was down suller putterin' about, for every kag and sass jar was afloat; her brother was lookin' after his stock and tryin' to stop the damage. All of a sudden he bust in. Lookin' kinder wild and settin' down his larntern, he ses, ses he:

"'You're ruther an unfortunate woman tonight, ma'am. The spilins have give way up in the rayvine; the brook's come down like a river and stove in your back kitchen, washed your gardin slap into the road; and while your husband was tryin' to get the pig out o' the pen, the water jest swep' him clean away, as ef he warn't no more'n a cabbage leaf.'

"'Oh, my Lord! Is he drownded?' ses I, with only breath enough for that.

"'Guess he is,' ses he. 'A chuck over them falls gen'lly makes things ruther cur'ous sights next time you see 'em, ef you ever do see 'em.'

"It come over me like a streak o' lightenin', everything kinder slewed round, and I dropped in the fust faint I ever had in my life. I'd no idee what was to pay for a long spell, but the next thing I knew was Silas huggin' of me and cryin', fit to kill himself. I thought I warn't woke yet, and only had wits enough to give a sort of promiscuous grab at him and say:

"'Oh, Silas, ain't you drownded?'

"He fetched a great start when I spoke, swallowed down his sobbin', and said as lovin' as ever a man did in this world:

"'Bless your dear heart, Sophy. It warn't me, it was the pig!'

and then fell to huggin' on me agin till, betwixt laughin' and cryin', I was 'most choked."

The old lady had told her tale so often that she had learned to embellish it with dramatic effects, which gave it a peculiar charm to me. At the slapping episode, she flung an invisible "fork, pertaters, and dish" into an imaginary pot and glared. When the catastrophe arrived, she "sallied back into her chair" to express fainting; gave my arm the "permiscuous sort of a grab" at the proper moment; and hiccuped out the repentant Silas's benediction, with an incoherent pathos that forbade a laugh at the sudden introduction of the porcine martyr.

"Well, ma'am, did you exult over him and make him promise to let you have your own way forever after? It was a fine opportunity. I hope you improved it."

"Oh, law, no. Of course I went right home and kissed them children for a couple o' hours stiddy," answered this weak-minded "Sophy," as if but one conclusion was possible.

"A great mistake, ma'am. But did all your pride and spirit go down with the pig?" I asked, much disappointed.

"Wal, no, it didn't, but I learned a sight by that week's work, and so did Silas. For though we sometimes edged back to the raspin' state, we never come to blows agin, and was so mortified we kep' our werryments to ourselves and give Mis' Millet a wide berth, for there wern't no end to the lies she made out o' that scrape of ourn. For a long spell we was as sweet as honey pots. I never tried to be boss agin, but cooked the best o' vittles, let them children walk over my naked nose, and petted the hull on 'em 'most to death. Silas was so lovin', I declare for't, I used to say the old courtin' days was come back, for he was as meek as a whole flock o' lambs and only got as red as fire when twitted about that job of ourn, which was doing well for a hot-sperrited man by nater. When I felt fractious or like drivin' on him anyhow, I jest thought o' that time and shet up; and often after a cross fit, Silas would bust out larfin' and say, 'Lord bless you, Sophy! It warn't me, it was the pig.'"

As the old lady paused to chuckle in character, I obeyed Will's summons, saying as I rose:

"Thank you, ma'am, I will remember your experience and tell my husband (when I find him) how to manage me if I should happen to forget, though I'm afraid a box on the ear would settle the matter so effectually that I should prefer the salvation of the bacon to that of the boxer."

Laying her brown hand on my arm, my hostess administered a parting bit of advice, with a warning wag that made her cap frill tremble.

"Don't expect too much of human critters, child, and bein' as you're one o' the outspoken sort, you'd better hang onto them two sayin's—'Every path has its puddle,' and 'It's better the feet slip than the tongue.'"

"Good-bye, ma'am, and allow me to offer one in return: 'Women must have their will while they live, because they make none when they die.'"

I ought not to close this letter from but not about the mountains without mentioning that, owing to a late repentance or some striking suggestions of Will's, Squab took me home like a bird and I had the satisfaction of trotting up to the hotel door in a style which I fervently trust effaced all recollection of my inglorious departure.

SKETCHES OF EUROPE

UP THE RHINE

At nine o'clock that lovely August morning, we gladly left the evil-smelling city which so belies its name—Cologne—and steamed away into fairyland. At least it seemed so to one member of the party, who, as soon as she landed at Ostend, felt as if she had walked into a romance and found every new chapter more delightful than the last.

The boat was full of travelers, all enjoying themselves in their different ways. The English sat bolt upright with a somewhat grim and defiant air, as if they had made up their minds to be surprised at nothing and warned everyone to let them alone. The French chattered and pranced, "bon jour"-ed every mortal who approached, and made themselves at home in the most cheerful manner. The Germans began to smoke and eat the moment the boat started, and kept up those amusements vigorously all day. The men tended their meerschaums, the women their babies; and all ate with an air of placid satisfaction which made them resemble a row of cattle meditatively chewing their cud. The Americans stared and asked questions; the gentlemen, hands in pockets, examined the steamboat and would have harrowed the soul of the captain by praises of American boats, could they have spoken French or German well enough. The ladies sketched, took notes, and laughed privately at the droll groups all about. A party of English lads from Rugby pervaded the boat—rosy, well-bred, gay, and altogether refreshing in their boyish enthusiasm and hearty relish for everything under the sun. One capital little fellow I called Tom Brown, and I felt strongly tempted to ask how cricket flourished at Rugby and why East was not of the party. As Tom had not reached the famous "heliotrope" period, I could not allude to Mary, though from the glances of admiration the lad bestowed on a little French girl, it was evident that time was fast approaching.

There is no use in trying to describe the Rhine beyond saying that it is not wonderful nor magnificent like Niagara, the Mississippi, or Mount Washington. It is exquisitely beautiful, and it is like sailing through a gallery of ever-new, ever-lovely landscapes, painted with a skill no human artist can attain. Vineyards, summer palaces, gray ruins, charming villages, mountains, green valleys, and ancient churches follow one another in such picturesque succession that one can hardly believe they are real. Here is an outline of one of these scenes. Steaming around a bend in the river, a great gorge opened before us, high cliffs on each side crowned with the ruins of two famous castles called "The Brothers." Just beyond, at the water's edge, a quiet village lay basking in the sun, with gay gardens, flocks of goats among the rocks, and funny babies in black silk nightcaps and wooden shoes playing about the doors. Church bells were ringing from a quaint old chapel halfway up the cliff, and several boatfuls of people were floating down the river, singing as they went. The men in blue caps and blouses; the women in bright skirts, black bodices, and white sleeves, with gilt suns on the flat plaits of hair behind or, prettier still, lace and muslin handkerchiefs thrown loosely over their heads. Sturdy brown folk with little beauty, but honest, peaceful faces, full of pious feeling as they warbled Dutch, with their tired hands at rest for one day in seven.

Everyone knows the famous sights to be seen on the Rhine: the Lorelei Rock; the Mouse Tower; Stolzenfels; the fine castle owned by William of Prussia, who entertained Victoria there once upon a time; the Sieben Jungfrauen, or Seven Sisters, as the seven rocks are called; Boppard, the gloomy town with

Roman ruins; the Mouse and Cat; St. Goar; Altar of Bacchus, where the fine wines are made; Assmannshausen, where grapes are grown in such steep spots that earth is carried up to them in baskets, and in some places the vineyards are one thousand feet above the river, in crannies of the rock; the copper and silver mines; the Devil's Ladder at Lorch; the fortress of Monksburg; and Bonn, with flocks of jolly students rioting about the walls and kissing their hands from the windows as the steamboats pass.

But even on the Rhine one must eat. And at noon long tables were spread on the deck, and we luxuriously took scenery with our salad, castles and cheese, vineyards and cabbage, ruins and boiled cucumbers, picturesque donkeys and famous wine. It was jovial beyond description, and the Major and I enjoyed it immensely, especially one party of Germans, who emptied nine bottles and devoured everything they could lay their hands on, to the great wrath of an old Englishman, who tried to take his dinner in solemn state. One stout young charmer in bright yellow, with a golden dagger through her black braids, seemed to be the belle and was overwhelmed with tender mottoes from the bonbons which were brought on at dessert. Three youths from some military school and a long-haired student were devoted, while her elderly lover blandly filled her glass, heaped her plate, and toasted his "Liebchen," without a frown for the young Werthers who surrounded his Charlotte. Hard-boiled eggs are henceforth associated with the grand passion in my mind, for these German lovers consumed a dozen at lunch, dividing each one between them, as they sat with their arms about one another in the most artless manner, quite undaunted by the scandalized glare of several British spinsters opposite. The old gentleman cherished a firm conviction that the elderly German would drop in a fit after the dinner, and watched him eagerly all the afternoon—feeling, doubtless, that apoplexy was but a just retribution for the sin of eating coriander seeds in bread, rose water on mashed potato, and plums in the gravy. The placid unconsciousness of the German and the fussy interest of the Englishman were intensely ludicrous, and when Meinherr ordered refreshment at four o'clock and fell to with renewed relish, John Bull's indignant amazement made me fear that he would fall a victim to his own dark prophecy.

We passed the night at Koblenz, and I spent a greater part of it in the little balcony outside my window; for the midsummer moon was at the full, and the scene it showed me was too beautiful to lose in sleep. Opposite towered the famous fortress of Ehrenbreitstein; at its feet lay villas, bathing houses, and hotels; on the heights stood watchtowers; and between fortress and town flowed the great river, where steamers, boats, and rafts came and went all night long. Just before the hotel was a bridge built on boats, and over this passed a constant succession of picturesque figures. Peasant girls with gold and silver arrows shining in their hair; old women spinning with the distaff or knitting as they went; donkeys laden with fruit, fish, vegetables; priests, soldiers, artists, and strangers. At midnight a regiment crossed from the fortress, with the band playing, bayonets glittering, and the steady tramp that made my heart beat fast, as it recalled the days when so many of our own dear boys marched away, never to return.

All my dreams were waking ones that night, yet they were very happy; and though I travel the world over, I think I never shall enjoy anything more truly than I did that midsummer night's dream at Koblenz.

Another pleasant day looking at the great picture book, "as we sailed, as we sailed," ended rather dismally. Before we reached Biberach, our proper stopping place, poor little Mademoiselle gave out and implored to be put ashore anywhere and left to rest. A hasty conference with the captain decided us to stop and trust to fortune for food and shelter. Armed with the address of a certain amiable old wine dealer, who the captain was sure would take us in, we three with our five trunks were set ashore at sunset in the little town of Oestrich. A group of peasants waited in blank amazement to receive us, for what two strange women and a young man with all that luggage could possibly want in that primitive place puzzled their slow wits to discover. Boldly pronouncing the magical name, we formed ourselves into a sort of procession and marched upon the town. First, five large trunks on the shoulders of five small men; several geese by way of band came next; then the Major, anxious but calm, with Mademoiselle on his arm; a tall lady in brown, with a face to match, and a somewhat bewildered expression, stalked after, bearing bottles, bags, shawls, notebooks, and herself with as much dignity as circumstances would permit; more geese, with a donkey or two; and a sprinkling of young Teutons in the black nightcaps closed the train.

In this order we went to our doom, and when the trunks vanished into a courtyard, we ladies camped on the doorsteps while the Major went in to make arrangements. He presently reappeared with an air of dismay, which he tried to conceal under a smile, for the Major never allowed himself to be agitated by any mishap.

"Is it the wrong place?" I asked, for Mademoiselle was past talking.

"Oh, dear, yes. Nothing could be more so. It seems the captain made a great mistake, and the old gentleman here, though very polite, is much amazed at our taking his house for an inn. He speaks very little French and won't hear of our stopping."

"What shall we do?" I demanded.

"Haven't the slightest idea" was the answer, given with exasperating cheerfulness. Here Mademoiselle moaned pathetically, and in sheer desperation I fell upon one of the men and demanded a hotel, in a lucid mixture of good English, bad French, and worse German.

"Nein, nein" was all the comfort I got; and despair was rapidly descending upon us when a pretty young girl came running out, full of sympathy and goodwill. She understood French, and soon our woes were made known. It was impossible to receive us there, but Adam Petri kept a *Gasthaus* and perhaps could take us in for a night. Meanwhile, we should rest and let Monsieur go to inquire. Up into her pretty room she took us, and while Mademoiselle reposed, I tried to talk with the young girl and kept watch over our baggage, which had now become a sort of magnet to attract all the idlers of the town. A group of men stood about it, trying to decipher the various labeis which adorned it and by means of which they were able to trace our route. Coming to the dingiest one, the man who acted as reader let fall the end of the trunk, lifted his hands, and exclaimed in a tone of wondering awe: "Livartpool! Ach, Gott, Livartpool!" All the others echoed him and fell to staring at the trunks, as if they came from the North Pole or some equally remote locality. I could not resist popping my head out of the window and adding "Amérique," with a gesture toward the luggage and myself.

They all looked up, pulled off their caps, and stood with their mouths wide open, staring as if the dusty, weary individual at the window was as much of a curiosity as one of Peter Wilkins's flying ladies.

The rumble of a carriage roused them from this trance of astonishment, and the Major came bustling in to say that Petri would take us and the town chariot was at the door. With many thanks we set forth again—trunks and men in front; band playing as it waddled before the horse; carriage proceeding slowly, the streets being too narrow and rough to permit of speed; boys laughing, donkeys braying, and geese hissing as they brought up the rear. And so in time we came to the much needed *Gasthaus*.

Adam was not visible to the naked eye; but a large damsel with no teeth and a bandage around her head welcomed us in Dutch and showed us to a room which might have been used by Noah and not opened since he quitted it for his little voyage—so musty, dusty, hot, and old-fashioned was it. Poor Mademoiselle was got to bed after a series of superhuman exertions on the part of Gretchen and myself, for neither understood a word the other said; and when I mildly demanded a blanket, I got an egg; when I asked for fruit, she brought a paper of rusty pins; and when I implored a foot warmer, I got

a cool salad. At last, in despair, I ordered supper in pantomime, and was overwhelmed at the sight of clean towels and
a flatiron, neither of which articles could assuage the pangs of
hunger which now consumed me.

By seven o'clock I managed to find a room and something
to eat; and after refreshing myself with cold coffee, sour black
bread, bad butter, and three plums, I soothed my ruffled spirit
by sitting at my window and examining the town. It seemed as
if the world stood still here and as if nothing had changed
since the place was first built. Hardly a sound broke the silence and few people passed, though Petri's was in the main
street. Now and then a woman with a tub of water on her
head went by, a child with a long loaf like a log on his shoulder, a man driving a cow harnessed to a queer cart, or a
stately goose promenading like one of the oldest and most respected inhabitants. The houses opposite had high stone walls
directly on the street, with little grated windows, through
which I caught glimpses of clean chambers and tidy kitchens,
full of bright pots and pans, where fat fraus cooked onions
and cabbage, while the blond, moon-faced daughters peeped
through the bars at the American gentleman who sat outside
Petri's door with his feet up in the national attitude. On a distant chimney top was a stork's nest, and the great bird, medi-
tating on one leg, was clearly defined against the red evening
sky, carrying me back to Hans Christian's fairy tales so vividly
that I almost expected to see Ole Luck Oie coming down the
street. I should have welcomed any old friend heartily, for it
was a very forlorn place; and being tired, worried, and homesick, I should have been in a very forlorn mood but for the
row of white-breasted swallows that sat on the ridgepole of
the house opposite, twittering so cheerily in the sunshine that
the familiar little song comforted me like sounds from home.

All night a watchman blew his horn to tell us the hour, and
ushered in the dawn with a "tootle-too-too," which made it
impossible for any but the deaf to slumber. I went out for an
early walk and had a charming one through a vineyard near
the river. The road was bordered with wildflowers; little pink

and white morning glories starred the grass and climbed up about the stone image of a saint with a broken nose that stood in a wayside niche; scarlet poppies, blue succory, yellow Saint-John's-wort, purple heath, and a misty-white flower that was very lovely, with feathery grasses, ferns, and grape tendrils, made a pretty bouquet wherewith to greet Mademoiselle when she woke.

The Major came in to breakfast with glad tidings, for he had found a man who had been years in America. And this worthy Mr. Crist had smoothed away all difficulties; had explained our plight to the old wine merchant, who was rather lofty because he had been at Waterloo; had opened the heart of the invisible Petri and placed the town at our service. At noon he escorted us to the station, which we reached just in time to precipitate ourselves into the train and tear away, leaving all our luggage behind us. How we laughed as the queer little town vanished, with the sentinel stork at his post, the blue-bloused men staring, the nightcapped babies waddling, and the geese bidding us a musical adieu, leaving us consumed with curiosity to discover whether the children took care of the geese or the geese of the children—with a strong suspicion that the latter supposition was the true one.

LIFE IN A PENSION

Five tall poplars stood before the house, their yellow leaves quivering in the October winds that blew across the lake whose waters washed the terrace wall. Behind, a vineyard and rose garden sloped up to the old chateau and chapel on the hillside. To the right lay Vevey, with its quay, its great hotel flying the flags of three nations, its narrow streets full of gay visitors and picturesque peasantry. To the left, the gray towers of Chillon, sunny Montreux, and gloomy St. Gingolph in the perpetual shadow of the Dent du Midi range. Opposite, far across the lake, beyond Lausanne and Geneva, rose the white Alps of Savoy, shining in the sun like some celestial country seen in dreams.

Pension Victoria was pleasant, well kept, and as full as a beehive with a motley collection of lodgers from all quarters of the world: a Russian baron, page to the Czar; an English colonel and family; an Irish lady, daughter, and governess; a consumptive young Pole; two Scotch sisters; one fat Frenchman; a cosmopolitan lady and daughter; a retired English physician, wife, and friend; a family of rebels from South Carolina; and two young ladies from Boston.

As I glanced down the long tables on the first day, I could not help wondering how this heterogeneous assemblage of people would get on together in such close quarters, and amused myself from that time forth by taking notes.

Baron Eugene Wopoloffski, on a furlough for his health, was a stout, comely, turbulent young barbarian, who beguiled his time by smoking, playing billiards, and falling madly in love with the handsome Southern girl. She did not smile upon his passion, and this caused him to moon about in the most despairing manner. He did not reply when addressed, tramped up and down the corridors half the night, and sat brooding with his hair in his eyes during mealtimes. His only solace seemed to be walnuts; these he ate desperately, cracking and crunching them, as if revenging himself on the obdurate Antoinette. I mention this mode of relief in the friendly hope that some other suffering youth may benefit by it; for Baron Eugene never failed to brighten a little and sigh less tempestuously when his plate was heaped with shells—as if he found a soothing oil for his wounds in the fresh walnuts.

Colonel W. was abroad with his family for the winter. The gigantic powers of this man will be better understood when I add that he was traveling with seven children, an invalid wife, and two maids, who spoke nothing but English; also that he carried on the education of the children himself. Six pale little girls filed in to meals three times a day, all dressed alike, all apparently of an age, all painfully well-bred and accomplished. They read, wrote, and spoke three languages beside their own; sang, played, drew, painted, and had mathematical, geological, and astronomical foreheads, which made one shy of addressing them lest they should playfully respond with an algebraic problem or bewilder one with the date of every event since the Flood. Six little pairs of shoes stood outside their door at night; six little damsels, with six little camp-stools and sketchbooks, went out walking each morning like a seminary. Six little curtsies were made and six kisses were bestowed all around when the young ladies retired; and doubtless six little prayers were duly said before the six weary little heads found rest on six welcome little pillows. The seventh child was a boy, and *not* a phenomenon, but rosy, plump, and gay, which was a great relief to eyes saddened by the sight of his pale, overtasked, unchildlike sisters. The handsome, courtly papa was devoted to his offspring, and they clustered about him like bees about a honey pot while he airily discussed with them the Spanish Inquisition, the population of Switzerland, the politics of Russia, and other lively topics equally well suited to infant minds. Mama was a pale, placid little woman, who partook copiously of chops and porter, talked religion, and looked ready to be translated at any moment, as well she might with such a family.

The Irish lady was a big, bony matron, nearly extinguished in crepe and never seen without black gloves. She ate in them, read in them, made tatting in them, and, it was my private belief, slept in them. The daughter was a colorless, prim girl, so bent on improving herself that she had no time to help anyone else. The governess was a fiery-faced little woman, who spoke with a lisp and an odd mixture of Irish brogue and French accent. The three grimly marched in and out—Mrs. H. apparently buried in memories of her sainted spouse, Edith absorbed in Greek and Hebrew, Miss W. struggling with her rebellious color and traitorous tongue.

Mr. Joseph—the fat Frenchman—labored under a delusion that he resembled the Emperor, and was continually striking Napoleonic attitudes. The airs and graces of the corpulent dandy were very amusing. He had a closely cropped head, strongly suggestive of a scrubbing brush; round black eyes; a purple nose; and plump hands, of which he was intensely vain, wearing a big ring and wide wristbands turned back, that he might gracefully move his hands when paying a compliment, twirl his dyed mustache with a martial air, or quirk the little finger wearing the diamond when he flirted his napkin and imbibed his wine. As he languished across the table with a high-shouldered bow, or fell back in his chair in fits of apoplectic merriment at his own wit, he was so like old "Joe Bagstock" I almost expected to see the natives pat him on the back.

Mrs. Chatterly was a brisk widow, who had been all over the world and passed for a lady while she spoke French and German. Her cockney English betrayed her—especially as, in her native tongue, she rattled away in the most comical manner, addressing the company in general with a shrill voice and much gesture.

"Ann, me daughter" was a lively, brown-eyed "girl" of five-and-thirty, who thought she knew everything, and offered her opinion upon every subject under the sun. A Teutonic admirer smoked cigarettes at the shrine of Ann and proved the depth of his passion by teaching her Italian in German.

The wiggy doctor and his faded wife were the toadies of a rich old lady who traveled with them. A stately, solemn, handsome woman, so like Marie Antoinette that everyone observed it. She was a mystery, for the little that was known about her was peculiar. Somebody was dead for whom she was inconsolable; certain subjects of conversation caused her to leave the room with somewhat startling abruptness; she never ate in public, as all her food had to be ground up in a mysterious machine; and no one but her maid was allowed to enter her room. Dr. B. escorted her down every evening for a game at long whist, but through the day she was invisible, except an occasional glimpse of a massive purple bonnet on the back terrace.

Marget and Ellen Glennie were two maiden ladies, on their way to Rome, as confiding and simple as the babes in the wood, telling their plans, asking advice, and enjoying everything as enthusiastically as if they were sixteen instead of sixty. They were connections of Walter Scott, and intensely national in every respect—speaking with a pleasant Edinburgh accent and carrying a fresh, feathery atmosphere about with them.

The young Pole Stanislas W.—two hiccups and a sneeze will give the last name better than letters—was an interesting youth of twenty, who fought with his fellow students in the last Polish outbreak and ruined his health by exposure and suffering during the campaign. Altogether captivating and romantic was the boy, in his blue and white university suit, with his charming manners, many accomplishments, and the fatal malady, of which he seldom spoke. Poor, alone, and ill, it was impossible for anyone to long resist his pleading eyes, and he became the pet of the ladies, especially of one who had a weakness for brave boys in blue. With a great interest in free America and an intense longing to hear about our war, the barrier of an unknown language did not long stand between us. Beginning with my bad French and his three words of English, we soon got on capitally, giving each other lessons; and in his he made astonishing progress, though he often slapped his forehead with the despairing exclamation, "I am imbecile. I never can will shall to have learn this beast of English!" His music was the delight of the house; and being an enthusiast in this, as in everything, he gave us delightful little concerts with the help of Madame Teihlin, who played like a Russian Saint Cecelia, with a cropped head and a gentlemanly sack, cravat, and collar. The longer they played, the more inspired they got, and the more impossible it seemed to stop them. The piano vibrated, the stools creaked, the candles danced in their sockets, and everyone sat mute while the four white hands chased one another up and down the keys till we almost expected to see instrument and performers disappear in a musical whirlwind.

Of the American ladies, nothing need be said, except that one was an invalid, the other an observing spinster, who sat in the corner and studied human nature.

The first day at dinner, when our neighbor, the Baron, asked what part of America had the happiness of being our home and I replied, "Boston, Massachusetts," I saw that a look of intelligence went from our end of the table to the other, where sat a tall, sallow, dissipated-looking man with long gray hair and mustache; also a handsome, haughty black-eyed lady and a girl with the head of a Clytie. They all glowered at us so darkly that I was not surprised to find they were Colonel Polk and his family from South Carolina. As they had lost five hundred slaves, all their property, and been thoroughly beaten, I could not wonder that we were unwelcome neighbors, and tried not to show any ungenerous exultation, though I must confess the blood of a born abolitionist simmered—not to say boiled—when I heard the tales they told, found myself insulted daily, and learned that nearly everyone in the house sided with them.

The English gave us to understand that they were "strictly neutral." The Scotch ladies, being as timid as a pair of tabbies with a strange dog in the house, implored us to be careful what we said, for the Colonel was a desperate man; and whenever at table any allusion was made to America, Miss Marget broke in with anecdotes of Sir Walter, or Miss Ellen gave recipes for sheepshead broth and bannocks. The French shrugged, sighed, and politely declined to say anything about "this so unhappy affair." But the Russian and the patriotic Pole were on our side, and with these allies we carried on the war with spirit.

Polk solaced his exile with cards and brandy, often being unfit to appear, at which times his wife would pathetically bewail the sufferings which had destroyed his health. This well-bred lady used her tongue with a freedom which in time disgusted even the "neutral" English. Her favorite evening amusement was to entertain the company with accounts of Northern barbarity, cowardice, treachery, and meanness, varied by tales of the happiness, fidelity, and devotion of their slaves, who had been *forced* away by the Yankees and who were longing for their master to return. As the drawing room was small, we could not avoid hearing her conversation, and feeling strongly tempted to return her fire by a few remarks upon Andersonville, Belle Island, and Wilkes Booth. Colonel Polk amused himself by standing in the doorway and scarcely deigning to move when we wished to pass; boasted how many Yankees he had shot; and audibly forbade his daughter to speak or look at "the cursed Northerners." It was decidedly disagreeable; but—taking a lesson from Stanislas, who said, when I wondered at the polite greetings exchanged between himself and the Baron: "It is true we are enemies, but we are also gentlemen"—we let the rebels politely alone and in time found a change in public opinion which surprised us as much as it did them.

They had a black nurse for the youngest child, and having

spoken a few times to poor, lonely Betty, she was moved to come into our room one day and tell her story. Mrs. Chatterly and Ann happened to be there, and as the slave described her wrongs with the simple eloquence of truth, the English-women listened with indignant tears and went away no longer "strictly neutral." Having convicted Mrs. Polk of one falsehood, they lost faith in her; for when asked if it was true that the Colonel's slaves were *forced* away and longed to have him back, Betty replied with a sniff of intense scorn:

"De young ones runned de fus ting, widout waitin' for de blessed Yankees. De old ones jes stayed where dey was, sayin', 'Massa had all de good ob us, an' we's worn out slaven for him. Now he may jes take kere ob us.' But he runned away hissef an' lef 'em to starve. Dat's de troof, missis, an' it's easy nuf to see de sense ob it—kase my boy never had no wages for sixteen years, and now he gets fifty dollars a munt an' his livin' on a steamboat. We likes money an' freedom, as well as Massa, an' we's got 'em now, bress de Lord and de Yankees."

When asked if she was free, as Mrs. Polk affirmed, Betty nodded with a significant gesture over her shoulder and an irrepressible laugh:

"She says I is *here,* kase she knows I couldn't git on alone and don't kere fer no one dis side de water. She's gwine home to see what she can git, and I'm gwine too. She specks I'm comin' back wid little Missy, but once safe over dar, I specks I spints missis a heap."

I hope she did, for unconsciously Betty served us a good turn. Gossipy Mrs. Chatterly whispered her story about behind the scenes, and before we came away, this and the conduct of the Polks had such an effect upon the little community that the tables were completely turned and the North won the day again.

A little incident is perhaps worth recording, as it shows a Southerner's opinion of Johnson a year ago. The room next to mine was occupied for a day or two by a young English couple, who gave themselves great airs and talked as if lords and ladies were their bosom friends, but as we afterwards discovered, Mr. W. was only an agent for a hardware concern in Birmingham. Dr. B. and the Colonel often visited them, and one evening I heard Polk talking excitedly. Wishing to let them know I was there, I poked my fire with a clatter and knocked my books about, whereupon the cautious doctor cried:

"Hush!—they are there."

"The d—d Northerners? Then I'll swing open the door and see what they'll do," said Polk. Which threat caused one Northerner to prepare for war.

"Sit down and speak low, I beg of you, or they'll hear," said the doctor.

"Let 'em hear!" roared the Colonel.

"Thank you, I will," thought I, and was presently edified by the following conversation:

"I'm going back in a fortnight to take the oath. I'd rather go to h—ll, but I can't get a cent if I don't," began the Colonel when Mr. W. had produced brandy and water.

"You are wise," said the doctor, who toadied the Colonel for the sake of his wine. "It's hard, but I'd look at it in this way. It's a compromise of honor, but why be a martyr and let the blackguards enjoy their plunder? I'd go back, take the oath, get me property, and quit the country."

"I'll do as my friend Porter Brooks did: Get all I can and then turn Englishman," said Polk.

"We'll give you an 'arty welcome," returned the doctor. "Now, tell us about the Northern army. Was it composed of gentlemen, as they say?"

"Oh, Lord, no—of thieves, scum, rapscallions! And our army of the first and finest gentlemen in the country. Why, sir, the Yankees are the meanest race on the earth. They are mean enough to steal the sweetening out of a baby's ginger cake."

At which piece of wit they all laughed, and Mrs. W. said with withering scorn, "Worms! Let them crawl!"

"We have, ma'am, and to some purpose, I take the liberty of thinking," responded the wrathful worm on the other side of the door.

"Is it true that you starved your prisoners?" asked the innocent hardware agent.

"Not a word of it. All newspaper lies. We wanted to exchange honorably, and they wouldn't. Sherman, in the march they make such a noise about, destroyed our stores and surgical instruments, so we *couldn't* dress the wounds of either our men or theirs. We gave them as good food and shelter as we had ourselves, but you couldn't expect us to care much for such trash. I've killed a good many Yankees in my day, and I'll kill a few more if I can get the chance," said Polk with relish, which caused one Yankee to shake her fist at him.

"How about Davis?" asked the doctor.

"Davis is a fine man, sir. A mild, sensible, gentlemanly man, sir," replied Polk with an oath, which did not seem to offend the highly connected lady with whom he sat. Being so much with lords and dukes, she had doubtless become accustomed to it.

"What will they do with poor Davis?" she asked.

"Well, they've loaded him with chains and treated him so, he's entirely broken down and nearly blind. If old Lincoln was alive, they'd hang him. But *Johnson is all right, and he'll let him off.* There's a strong outside pressure upon Johnson, but he is coming around as fast as he dares."

"News from home," thought I, "and not agreeable ones, if true."

They talked of Sumner, and Polk told the Brooks assault as a Southerner would, while the listeners applauded and said it served Sumner right. Then followed charming tales of the Colonel's slaves, beautifully illustrating the refining and elevating influence of the "patriarchal institution" upon masters.

"I built 'em a church, sir—a church to Almighty God, sir—and it was rare sport to see 'em preaching and praying. I used to take my friends down to enjoy the fun. I let 'em marry, too, and gave away the bride myself. You'd roar to see 'em jump the broomstick."

"Did they understand what it all meant?" asked Mrs. Wood when the laugh subsided.

"No more than this cigar, but it pleased 'em and told well, you know. They got religion sometimes, and I let old Pete baptize a lot of 'em. But a couple got drowned, so I couldn't afford 'em any more religion."

Another story which struck the company as very funny was of a Yankee boy taken prisoner; and being put under ether to have a shattered arm amputated, the rebel surgeon took his leg off instead, that he might never fight again. With this sample of Southern chivalry the party broke up, after exchanging photographs and drinking "Luck to the South."

A week later Mrs. Chatterly, who studied the peerage devoutly, discovered that one of the American ladies had relatives living in a castle and that the other was descended from a famous archbishop; which intelligence, being industriously imparted to others, caused a mysterious change in the social atmosphere. To our great amazement, Mrs. Chatterly suddenly took us to her maternal bosom, Dr. B. begged to prescribe, the Colonel touched his hat, Antoinette was allowed to become conscious of our existence, and Mrs. Polk passed the salt, which act of Christian magnanimity was all that could be expected from that much-injured woman. This general conversion, though ludicrously sudden, was agreeable, and having been undeservedly sent to Coventry, we very willingly returned, though for a long while ignorant of the absurd means that shortened our exile.

Life in a pension was much pleasanter after this gracious change, and the November days were spent in drives to Chillon, Montreux, Vevey, Blonoy Castle, and the weird old chateau of La Tour, or rambles along the lake, tête-à-têtes in the sunny chateau garden, and lively shopping excursions in the town. The evenings were often very merry, for the little drawing room was a perfect Babel when all were assembled. Ann and her lover spoke Italian; Mrs. Chatterly practiced German with Miss H.; the Baron rumbled Russian; Mr. Joseph chattered French; Stanislas taught Polish; the doctor spoke English; the Polk drawled Southern slang; and the Northern ladies talked Bostonee like steam engines in full operation.

Music, lessons, flirting, politics, fancywork, High Church harangues, and card playing all found a place in Monsieur Vodoz's salon.

The whist table in the height of the season was a droll spectacle. They played for money, always quarreled, and broke up in a tumult. As they sat evening after evening at the green table, with the francs spread out before them, I often longed to sketch the party. Mrs. Reede, stately and handsome, with her rich black silks, her high cap, and gray hair, à la Marie Antoinette, would have suited the immortal "Martha Battles"—for with her, whist was a solemn ceremony. Her partner, the fussy doctor, was utterly absorbed in the game—his nose in his cards, his eye on the money, his very wig on the alert to catch a trick or play one. Mrs. Chatterly—thin, brisk, loquacious, and quivering with excitement—sat bolt upright, her eyes darting from one to the other and her tongue going ceaselessly. If she won, she exulted; if she lost, she lamented; if anyone played amiss, she scolded in three languages; if anyone blamed her, she flung down her cards and demanded an apology. Mr. Joseph, her vis-à-vis—a fat, yellow, pompous man—swayed in his creaking chair with an elephantine motion; sat with folded arms, trying to remind the observers of Napoleon at St. Helena; paid compliments to Mrs. Reede; snubbed the doctor, or contradicted his partner, who always responded with an explosive "Good gracious me! I 'aven't done anythink, upon my word!"

While the elders squabbled for money, the young folk applied themselves diligently to languages and love—for romances, like the roses, blossomed far into December. Sometimes grammars and dictionaries were thrown by, and games, gymnastics, or dancing went on in the big *salle à manger*. Cigarettes were allowed there, and as much laughing and as many pranks as we chose. Two Russian princes were the lions of our little world. Prince Gortschakoff, son or nephew of the Crimean general, was a Tartaresque individual with the face of an ogre and the manners of a savage. He dressed in velvet, with no visible linen; put one foot up in his chair; hung over his plate and fed himself as if he was pitching hay into a barn door. At dessert he passed around fireworks disguised as bonbons and enjoyed the confusion when they exploded, to the consternation of the ladies and children.

The other prince—with an unpronounceable name, without a vowel in it—was more agreeable and very amusing. "Prince Nosey," as we named him, possessed a Bulwerian feature, protuberant eyes, a great flow of language, and a lamb's-wool coat. He was proud of his English and bestowed much of his gracious society upon the lively Ann and myself, convulsing us with his Wallachian gallantry and droll speeches. Having told a story of the Empress visiting a hospital and being called "sister" by the patients, he suddenly pressed my hand— crochet needle and all—to the breast of his lamb's-wool coat, exclaiming with a melodramatic air and a concluding blunder that produced a general laugh:

"You, too, mees, are having been a nairse of the brave! I am a soldier, an invalid, and in the name of charity I say to you 'sister'! Is it not that we are sisters?"

Later in the evening he asked leave to stay longer, and when it was granted, he clasped his hands and cried with a burst of flowery gratitude:

"It is true, this that I say. When the Baron led me dark over many streets, I cry, 'Where have we going?' He says not, but takes me through plenty muds to this hall of brilliance, bliss, and beauty. Now you grant that I stay, for this I thank you and remain yet in Paradise."

The part of Vevey where we were was called Paradise, and doubtless, many Adams and Eves have found it so till the inevitable turning-out time comes. Our serpent entered in the guise of a telegram, and just then a general flitting took place. The season was over. All the little dramas were played out, and with a farewell festival of the dramatis personae, the curtain fell on that episode of foreign life.

A ROYAL GOVERNESS

As considerable interest is felt just now in Victoria and her books, it occurred to me that a little sketch of one of the royal ex-governesses might be amusing, if nothing more.

We hired an apartment for the winter of Madame Rolande, at Nice; and the moment we were settled, a tall, orange-colored lady, arrayed in black moiré and an imposing head-dress of somber crepe, rattling with bugles, came sailing in to pay her compliments. She had hardly folded her black-gloved hands in her lap before she informed us that for fourteen years she had been French governess to Victoria's daughters. As we received the startling news with becoming respect, she enlarged upon a subject which was evidently the pride of her heart.

The dear Queen, so truly amiable, bade her farewell with a pension, the sweet Princesses with a kiss; and all still wrote to their *"chère* Rollet" as affectionately as ever. They were perfect beings in her eyes, and never were allowed to forget their manners, but ordered by mama to beg pardon of any-one whom they had neglected or disobeyed, no matter how humble.

"All these so charming and precious souvenirs are from my beloved Princesses and Her Majesty," said Madame, moving her hand toward the étagères, filled with silver, china, books, and objects of virtu. Nearly everything in the rooms was the gift of the Saxe-Coburg family, and such a collection of ugly worsted work, chubby teapots, gay shepherds and shepherdesses, inlaid portfolios, and bronze Dianas with prancing deer and breezy drapery one seldom sees. The mirrors alone were enough to bewilder a modest person, there being three or four in each room, and the clocks drove us wild with their incessant ticking, not to mention the little dwarf who came every few days to wind them up and went gliding about or popping up in unexpected places like a goblin.

There was a perfect irruption of royalty all over the walls. The salon displayed Victoria, Albert, and three or four infants in one picture; also the Princess Royal as she went to her first drawing room, then in her wedding dress, with artificial orange flowers around the frame; Alice out walking, Helena playing with a fat dog, Prince Albert as a little tar, and the Prince of Wales in uniform.

In my room the Duchess of Kent simpered at me from under a turban like the Leaning Tower of Pisa. Victoria, in a massive hat and much-beflounced dress, guarded my bed. A photograph of the departed consort adorned my toilet table, and the chimneypiece was rich in a procession of one of the dozen christening parties. My friend's bower had Arthur Earnest Patrick Albert as a dropsical infant, chewing a doll; Alice in modern mourning at the tomb of her sire; and a grand conglomeration of Helena, Alice, Louise, Leopold, and Beatrice on a balcony—which looked hardly strong enough to support such an august load of stout young specimens of English royalty.

A gilded crown held up our bed curtains, British lions rampant glared at us from our fenders, and on the sideboard shone silver which had served tea and toast in Windsor Castle. It was all very regal and imposing, but being barbarians, we harrowed up the old lady's soul by bundling the stuffy bed curtains out of the way, trampled the British lion underfoot as we warmed our plebeian soles, and coolly put flapjacks in the sacred silver dishes. Vainly did Madame try to quench us by affecting to forget herself at times and call us *chère princesse,* or back out of the room with magnificent obeisances, or talk in half a dozen languages at once, with a rapidity that made my head spin and caused my friend to flee from her polyglot presence. We were not impressed, however; we didn't fall down and worship the ex-governess, but asked questions freely, laughed at and criticized the precious souvenirs, and behaved in all respects like savages from the wilds of America, as we were.

We certainly should have shown the poor lady more respect if her little domestic habits had not disturbed our freeborn minds. What may be the customs at court I can't say, but if listening at keyholes, reading private letters, rummaging boxes and drawers, and cross-questioning servants are the fashion, I'm glad I don't reside in a palace. It soon became the chief amusement of our quiet lives to head Madame off and keep her aristocratic fingers out of our domestic pies. If it had not been for Julie, our maid, we should have fared badly; for the old lady was as sly as a fox, and we never knew where to have her. She was a regular "Madame Beck," and seemed to feel it a duty to look well after the ways of the two lone strangers under her roof. After one lively skirmish concerning a dining room so strongly flavored with stable that we couldn't use it and didn't care to pay for it, though the queen's seventh portrait sanctified the spot, she ceased to rebel openly, but kept up a sort of guerrilla warfare, which was both annoying and amusing.

Having engaged her rooms because of their southern aspect, we expected to enjoy the sunshine freely, but Madame insisted on shutting blinds, windows, and curtains lest her velvet carpet should fade and her red damask furniture get dusty. So we locked the doors and reveled in the light, much to the old lady's wrath. Thinking to settle us, she got in one day in our absence and shrouded every shroudable article in brown linen. Whereat we rejoiced and ordered dinner to be served on the cherished round table, now bereft of its ornaments and covered with an old red cloth. This was a blow, but Madame revenged herself by using our charcoal and scolding our maid. But Julie, who could talk as much like a Tower of Babel as herself, defended her young ladies valiantly and instigated

Thérèse, Madame's servant, to open rebellion when the old lady became tyrannical.

Poor Thérèse regarded us in the light of angels, because we gave her a few trifles and treated her like a human being. She was a fat, brown, toothless damsel, who spoke nothing but Italian and spent her life in a dirty kitchen, hovering over the little pits of fire whereon Madame's messes were cooked. Wild fits of wrath seemed to be her only amusement, and in these she indulged with Southern zest. Being startled one day by howls of appalling shrillness, I rushed to the kitchen, to find the maid dancing frantically about, with a knife in one hand and a carrot in the other, as she poured forth maledictions in an unknown tongue. The mistress, in an unassuming *junon* of flannel, a fur-trimmed pelisse, slipshod shoes, and her most superb cap, was scrubbing the sink and scolding with a vigor which left nothing to be desired. The funniest part of the funny scene was Madame's utter unconsciousness of the ludicrous contrast between her cap and her shoes, her allusions to former grandeur and her present occupation. Being unable to assuage the storm, I enjoyed the prospect and retired much edified.

Half an hour afterward, Madame came rustling in, *en grande costume,* to show me a letter just received from Princess Helena. It was prettily written in French, and I was graciously permitted to copy it. As some young lady may like to know how a princess expresses herself, here it is:

Osborne,
Le 5er janvier, 1866

Ma chère et bonne Rollet:
     Je suis restée très longtemps sans t'écrire, mais tu sais bien que ce n'est pas faute de penser à toi et de t'aimer toujours autant qu'autrefois, mais les journées ne sont réellement pas aussi longues pour tout ce que j'ai à faire. Tu sais que j'ai assez à écrire pour ma chère maman, et en outre j'ai été bien occupée par ce que j'ai

à te dire, et que te fera plaisir j'espère, à cause de l'affection que tu me portes. Oui, ma chère Rolande, j'annonce avec plaisir que je suis fiancée depuis `le 1er décembre. J'aurais voulu te le dire plus tôt, mais cela m'a été impossible. C'est le Prince Chrétien de Schleswig Holstein Augustenberg que je vais épouser, et je n'ai pas besoin de te dire que je l'aime tendrement, et que je suis aussi heureuse que l'on peut être. Mon mariage aura lieu aussi bien vers le fin de juin.

Et toi, ma bonne amie, comment supportes-tu le commencement de cet hiver? J'espère que tu te soignes bien et que tu prends toutes les précautions nécessaires. Je fais des vœux bien ardents pour ton bonheur dans cette nouvelle année, et je serais bien heureuse de te revoir encore. Nous avons de bonnes nouvelles de nos deux sœurs Vicky et Alice. Je t'embrasse tendrement comme je t'aime, ma bonne Rolande, et je suis toujours,

Ta bien affectionée,
Hélène*

One cannot help wondering if the young princess is as happy now and if she continues to "love tenderly" her middle-

* My dear and good Rollet: I have not written you for such a long time, but you know that it is not for lack of thinking of you and loving you as much as before; but the days are really not long enough for all that I have to do. You know that I have a great deal to write for my dear mummy, and besides, I have been very busy with what I have to tell you, which I hope will please you because of the affection you have for me. Yes, my dear Rolande, I announce with pleasure that I have been engaged since the first of December. I wish I could have told you earlier, but this has been impossible for me. I am going to marry Prince Christian of Schleswig-Holstein-Augustenberg, and I do not need to tell you that I love him dearly and that I am as happy as one can be. My wedding is to take place toward the end of June.

And you, my dear friend, how are you tolerating the beginning of this winter? I hope that you are taking good care of yourself and taking all the necessary precautions. I send all my best wishes for your happiness in the new year, and I would be very happy to see you again. We have good news from our two sisters Vicky and Alice. I kiss you as dearly as I love you, my good Rolande, and I am always,

Your very affectionate, Helena

aged spouse, in spite of the German wife and seven children. Madame presented me with a sketch of Lady Jane Grey, by Helena, when sixteen; and another, of some fanciful individual, drawn and painted by Alice. She also showed me a portfolio of works of art by the Prince of Wales, which were excellent. I was at a loss to understand the cause of this unusual suavity till, with her most insinuating smile, Madame begged as a favor the loan of our salon for an hour that evening, to receive some friends who were to dine with her in honor of her fete day. We granted the favor and, feeling at liberty to amuse ourselves in Madame's own fashion, took sundry peeps at the festivities.

Madame's three grandchildren came at noon with a fine cake, a bottle of wine, and a nosegay, which they presented with a complimentary address such as French children alone could prepare and deliver. All the afternoon Thérèse, having been propitiated by the gift of a gay handkerchief, led the life of a salamander in that fiery furnace of a kitchen, where the pits blazed fiercely and the air was full of savory odors. At dusk two carriageloads of guests arrived, and Madame received them in true court style. *Grand Dieu!* What bows and curtsies, what embraces and compliments, what gossip, airs, and graces! Truly, it was *magnifique*. To behold Madame at the head of her table "was a thing to dream of, not to tell." Her cap was stupendous as the bugle ornaments clashed musically above her sallow brow; her moiré antique gleamed and rustled richly; her lace was dirty but priceless; and her aristocratic countenance glowed with an amiable complaisance in spite of her purple nose.

The fragrant little dining room was dressed with flowers in the royal vases; ablaze with candles in the royal sticks; gorgeous with china, glass, and silver from the royal hand; and odorous with the courtly perfume of garlic.

The guests were a handsome notary, who assumed the air of a prince, and did it very well, too; a pretty woman in melon-colored silk, with blue roses in her hair; a dried-up old lady, with such a big handkerchief she was occasionally lost in its voluminous folds and squeaked shrilly from behind that cambric barricade; two gentlemen, who apparently sat in the fireplace and were not visible from our point of view; and Madame's daughter, with her hair dressed so elaborately that it was a labyrinthine maze. Everyone ate copiously, talked incessantly, gesticulated violently, and all appeared to enjoy themselves immensely. Coffee and snuff were passed around in the salon, and at ten "the party went out," as children say; and Madame took to her bed for three days.

There was an agreeable lull in our civil warfare after this, and Madame behaved herself, offering to read French with us, opening her precious stores for our benefit, and regaling us with anecdotes of her brilliant life at court. According to her account, she had "enjoyed a varied career." Her spouse had been an ambassador, or something of that sort, to Spain; had come to grief in some way and laid his bones to rest in Genoa. She had known splendor, but in her time of adversity had found support from the hand of Her Majesty and "now reposed upon her pension." It was very interesting and romantic, and I daresay true; for among the wastepaper she gave us for kindling our fires, I found notes from countesses, English and French; lists of jewels, plate, and books sold by Madame's order; and several envelopes with big seals directed to "Madame Rolande de la Sage, Gouvernante de S.A.R. les Princesses à Windsor." One of the notes was as follows:

Osborne, March 22nd

Dear Madame:

I should be glad to know if *you* find it more difficult to teach the Prince of Wales *here* than elsewhere? *I* cannot make him attend nor remember anything, and he is very unruly. I fancy the sea air must have something to do with this change, but if you do not find the same difficulty, perhaps I am wrong. Excuse me for troubling you with this question. The Prince of Wales was going on so well that I am quite vexed to see him as I see him now; and I am anxious to know what you and Miss Ill-hart think of him and whether he is only so idle and inattentive with me.

Yours truly,
H. M. Birch

It is fortunate for the conscientious tutor that he no longer has the care of the Prince, for if idleness, inattention, and sea air disturbed him then, what would the poor gentleman say to his royal pupil now?

When we left, Madame, after trying to cheat us out of a few hundred francs and being disappointed in her amiable endeavor, kissed and blessed us and gave me letters to Miss Hildyard, another ex-governess, living in London, and to Mrs. Thurston, the housekeeper at Windsor Castle. Very French and funny were the letters, being a jumble of flattering commendations of "the American Miss"; regrets on the death of Sir Charles Phipps; congratulations to Sir Thomas Biddulph, master of the household; accounts of Madame's cutting off her hair; prayers for the royal family; and compliments to the "chère amie."

Miss Hildyard was out when I called. But the housekeeper received me at Windsor, some weeks later, in black satin, lavender kids, and blond cap, at eleven in the morning, and did her best to get leave for me to see the castle from Lady Caroline Somebody. But as one of the family was at the castle, etiquette would not permit strangers to see more than the chapel, terrace, and tower. I spoke of Madame, and Mrs. Thurston, the "bien aimie amie," disposed of the old lady with British brevity.

"Rollet meant well, but she was—French."

And the royal housekeeper bowed me out with the air of one resigned to the mournful fact that Madame Rolande de la Sage never would become English enough to keep inquisitive Americans from calling on Her Majesty at unseasonable hours.

RECENT EXCITING SCENES IN ROME

Rome,
December 29, 1870

My dear Mr. ——:

As we are having very exciting times just now, I will send you a little account of the two last "sensations," though I daresay the news will be rather old by the time you receive it.

Yesterday morning at breakfast our maid, Lavinia, came flying in from market with the news that the Tiber had overflowed its banks and inundated the lower part of the city; that people just outside the walls were drowned, others in the ghetto were washed out of their houses, the Corso was underwater, and the world generally coming to an end. We instantly went out to see how things stood, or rather floated, and found that Lavinia's story was true. The heavy rains and warm winds had swelled the river and melted the snow on the mountains till the Tiber rose higher than at any time since 1805 and had done much damage in a few hours.

When we reached the Piazza di Spagna, it seemed as if we were in Venice; for all the long streets leading up to it from the lower part of the city were underwater, and rats and boats were already floating about. The Piazza del Popolo was a lake, with the four stone lions just above the surface, still faithfully spouting water, though it was a drug in the market. Garrett's great stables were flooded, and his horses and carriages were standing disconsolately on the banks about the piazza. In at the open gates rolled a muddy stream bearing haystacks and brushwood from the country along the Corso. People stood on their balconies, wondering what they should do, many breakfastless; for meals are sent in, and how were the trattoria boys to reach them with the coffeepots across such canals of water? Carriages splashed about in the shallower parts with agitated loads of people hurrying to safer quarters; many were coming down ladders into boats; and flocks stood waiting their turn with little bundles of valuables in their hands.

THE SOLDIERS AND PRIESTS

The soldiers were out in full force, working gallantly to save life and property—making rafts, carrying people on their backs, and later going through the inundated streets with boatloads of food for the hungry, shut up in their ill-provided houses. It has since been said that usually at such times the priests have done this work, but now they stand looking on and smile maliciously, saying it is a judgment on the people for their treatment of the Pope. The people are troubled because the priests refuse to pray for them; but otherwise they snap their fingers at the sullen old gentleman in the Vatican, and the brisk, brave troops work for the city quite as well (we heretics think better) than the snuffy priests. Some of the saintly young Jesuits amused themselves by throwing stones at the soldiers while they were working during the flood; for which cowardly trick the aforesaid heretics feel a strong desire to box the long-coated boys' ears and cast their shovel hats in the mud. By the way, I heard that one whole college of lads left in a body and went to the free school the King has opened, demanding to be taken in and taught something, being disgusted with their Jesuitical masters—a sure sign that young Italy is waking up. Three cheers for the boys!

THE FLOOD

To return to the flood. In the ghetto the disaster was really terrible, for the flood came so suddenly that the whole quarter was underwater in an hour. At five no one dreamed of such a danger; at seven all the lower part of the city was covered, up to the first story in many places. A friend who promptly went to the rescue of the Jews told us that the scene was pitiful; for the poor souls live in cellars, packed like sardines in a box, and, being washed out all of a sudden, were utterly destitute. In one street he saw a man and woman pushing a mattress before them as they waded nearly to their waists in water, and on the mattress were their little children—all they could save. Later in the day, as the boats of provisions came along, women and children swarmed at the windows, crying, "Bread! Bread!" and their wants could not be supplied in spite of the generosity and care of the city authorities. One old woman who had lost everything but her life besought the rescuers to bring her a little snuff, for the love of heaven; which was very characteristic of the Italian race. One poor man, in trying to save his wife and children in a cart, upset them, and the little ones were drowned at their own door. Tragedy and comedy, side by side.

Outside the city, houses were carried away and people saved with difficulty, so sudden and rapid was the overflow. A bridge near the ghetto was destroyed, and a boatful of soldiers upset in the current and several men drowned. In the Corso the finest shops were spoiled, and many people are ruined by the mishap. Friends of ours from Boston were cut off from supplies for two days, and lived on bread and water till help came. A pleasant little experience for the Christmas holidays.

We fared better, for our piazza is on the hill and our Lavinia, foreseeing a famine, laid in stores; among them live fowls, who roost in the kitchen with the cats and L.'s relatives, who infest that region in swarms. If the heavy rains continue, we may come to want; for the wood yards are underwater, the railroads down in all directions, and the peasants from outside cannot get in to bring supplies, unless the donkeys swim. So far we enjoy the excitement, for the sleepy old city is all astir; and we drive about, seeing unexpected sights in every direction. Being a Goth and a Vandal, *I* enjoy it more than chilly galleries or moldy pictures. It thrills *me* more to see one live man work like a Trojan to save suffering women and babies than to sit hours before a Dying Gladiator who has been gasping for centuries in immortal marble. It's sad, but I can't help it.

DARKNESS

Last night the gas went out in many parts of the city, and people were ordered to put lamps at their windows—for thieves abound. We prepared our arms, consisting of one pistol, two daggers, and a heavy umbrella, and slept peacefully, although it was possible that we might wake to find ourselves floating gently out at the Porta Pia. My last idea was a naughty hope that the Pope might get his pontifical petticoats very wet, be a little drowned and terribly scared by the flood, for he deserves it.

NOVEL SCENES

Today the water is abating, and we are becoming accustomed to the sight of boats in the marketplace, gentlemen paying visits on the backs of stout soldiers, and family dinners being hoisted in at two-story windows. All the world is up on the Pincio looking at the flood, and a sad sight it is. Outside the Popolo Gate a wide sea stretches down the valley, with roofs and trees sticking up dismally from the muddy water. A raging river foams between us and the Vatican, and the Corso is a grand canal where unhappy shopkeepers float lamenting. The Pantheon is underwater over the railing, the post office has ceased to work, the people have become amphibious, and Rome is what Grandmother Rigglesty would call "a wash."

THE POOR

The city officers are working splendidly, having fed and housed the poor. But there will be much misery, and beggars already begin to come to us with long tales of their woes. Lavinia's five grandmothers, six aunts, and two dozen small nephews and nieces will settle for the winter in our tiny kitchen probably, although none of them have suffered by the flood; and we shall not have the heart to object, they will look so comfortable and be so easy about it. Lavinia herself is as good as a whole opera troupe, she is so dramatic and demonstrative. Ristori is feeble beside L. when she shakes her fist at the Pope and cheers for the King, with a ladle in one hand and her Italian eyes flashing as she prances with excitement, regardless of our polenta burning in the frying pan.

January 1, 1871

THE CLIMATE AND THE KING

A happy New Year to you and a pleasanter day than we have here in balmy Italy, which, by the way, is the greatest humbug in the way of climate that I ever saw. Rain, wind, hail, snow, and general disorder among the elements. Boston is a paradise compared to Rome just now. Never mind; we had a new sensation yesterday, for the King came in the first train from Florence to see what he could do for his poor Romans. He arrived at four A.M., and though unexpected, except by a few officials, the news flew through the city, and a crowd turned out with torches to escort him to the Quirinal. Lavinia burst in like a tornado to tell us the joyful news; for the people have begun to think that he never would come, and they are especially touched by this prompt visit in the midst of their trouble. He is to come on the tenth of January and make a grand entry; but the kind soul could not wait, so came as soon as the road was passable, and brought 300,000 francs for the sufferers with his own royal hands.

VICTOR EMMANUEL

Of course we rushed up to the Quirinal at once, though it rained hard. Before the palace stood a crowd waiting eagerly for the first sight of the King and cheering heartily everyone who went in or out.

There was a great flurry among the officials, and splendid creatures in new uniforms flew about in all directions. Grand carriages arrived, bringing the high-and-mighty to welcome the King. General Marmora, looking like a seedy French rowdy, went in and out, full of business. Dorias and Collonas gladdened our plebeian eyes, and we cheered everything, from the Commander-in-Chief to somebody's breakfast, borne through the crowd by a stately "Jeames" in a splendid livery. We stood one mortal hour in a pelting rain and then retired, feeling that the sacrifice of our best bonnet was all that could reasonably be expected of a freeborn American. We consoled ourselves by putting out Lavinia's fine Italian banner, supported by our two little ones proudly bearing the Stars and Stripes, and much perplexing the boys and donkeys who disport themselves in the Piazza Barberini.

Feeling that neuralgia would claim me for its own if I went out, I sat over the fire and read *Roma di Roma,* while M. and A. took a carriage and chased the King all over the city till they caught him at the Capitol. They had a fine view of him as he came down the steps of the Capitol, through a mass of people cheering frantically and whitening the streets with waving handkerchiefs.

ENTHUSIASTIC RECEPTION

My enthusiastic damsels mounted up with the driver and cheered with all their hearts, as well they might, for it certainly was a sight to see. They had another view of the King on the balcony of the Quirinal; for the people clamored so for another sight of "Il Rè" that the Pope's best velvet hangings were hastily spread on the balcony and Victor Emmanuel came out and bowed to his people, "who stood on their heads with rapture," as one young lady expressed it. He was in citizen's dress and looked like a stout, brown, soldierly man, M. said. He hates ceremony and splendor and would not have the fine apartments offered him, but chose a plain room and said, "Keep the finery for my sons, if you like; I prefer this." He asked the city fathers to give the money they intended to spend on welcoming him to the poor. But they insist on giving him a Roman welcome when he comes on the tenth. He only passed one day here and went back to Florence last night at five. All Rome was at the station to see him off. Ladies with carriages full of flowers were tearing by at dusk, and there was a great demonstration, for this kingly sympathy has won all hearts.

We are preparing to decorate our balcony for the tenth and have our six windows full of cheering Yankees; for our rooms are directly on the street he will pass by, and our balcony on the piazza, where two great arches are now being set up. The prudent A. suggests that we let these windows and make our fortunes, but we decline and intend to hurrah our best for the "honest man," as they call Victor Emmanuel—and that is high praise for a king.

LITERARY WORK

I hope the New Year opens well and prosperously with you. I was just getting well into my work on *L. M.*, when sad news of dear "John Brooke's" death came to darken our Christmas and unsettle my mind. But I now have a motive for work stronger than before; and if the book can be written, it shall be, for the good of the two dear little men now left to my care, for long ago I promised to try and fill John's place if they were left fatherless.

We all send best wishes, and I am as ever

Yours truly,
L. M. A.

CONCORD, MASSACHUSETTS

WOMAN'S PART
IN THE CONCORD CELEBRATION

Being frequently asked, "What part the women took in the Concord Centennial celebration?" I give herewith a brief account of our share on that occasion.

Having set our houses in order, stored our larders, and filled our rooms with guests, we girded up our weary souls and bodies for the great day, feeling that we must do or die for the honor of old Concord.

We had no place in the procession, but such women as wished to hear the oration were directed to meet in the town hall at half past nine and there wait till certain persons, detailed for the service, should come to lead them to the tent, where a limited number of seats had been provided for the weaker vessels.

This seemed a sensible plan, and as a large proportion of ladies chose the intellectual part of the feast, the hall was filled with a goodly crowd at the appointed hour. No one seemed to know what to do except wait, and that we did with the patience born of long practice. But it was very trying to the women of Concord to see invited guests wandering forlornly about or sitting in chilly corners, meekly wondering why the hospitalities of the town were not extended to them as well as to their "menfolks," who were absorbed into the pageant in one way or another.

For an hour we women waited. But no one came, and the

sound of martial music so excited the patient party that with one accord we moved down to the steps below, where a glimpse of the approaching procession might cheer our eyes. Here we stood, with the north wind chilling us to the marrow of our bones, a flock of feminine Casabiancas with the slight difference of freezing instead of burning at our posts.

Some wise virgins, who put not their trust in men, departed to shift for themselves, but fifty or more obeyed orders and stood fast till, just as the procession appeared, an agitated gentleman with a rosette at his buttonhole gave the brief command:

"Ladies, cross the Common and wait for your escort."

Then he vanished and was seen no more.

Over we went, like a flock of sheep, leaving the show behind us, but comforting ourselves with the thought of the seats "saving up" for us and of the treat to come. A cheerful crowd, in spite of the bitter wind, the rude comments of the men swarming by, and the sad certainty which slowly dawned upon us that we were entirely forgotten. The gay and gallant presence of a granddaughter of the Doctor Ripley who watched the fight from the Old Manse kept up our spirits; for this indomitable lady circulated among us like sunshine, inspiring us with such confidence that we rallied around the little flag she bore, and followed where it led.

Patience has its limits, and there came a moment when the revolutionary spirit of '76 blazed up in the bosoms of these long-suffering women. For when some impetuous soul cried out, "Come on, and let us take care of ourselves!" there was a general movement; the flag fluttered to the front, veils were close reefed, skirts kilted up, arms locked, and with one accord the Light Brigade charged over the red bridge, up the hill, into the tented field, rosy and red-nosed, disheveled but dauntless.

The tent was closely packed, and no place appeared but a corner of the platform. Anxious to seat certain gray-haired ladies weary with long waiting, and emboldened by a smile from Senator Wilson, a nod from Representative May, and a pensive stare from orator Curtis, I asked the president of the day if a few ladies could occupy that corner till seats could be found for them.

"They can sit or stand anywhere in the town except on this platform; and the quicker they get down the better, for gentlemen are coming in to take these places."

This gracious reply made me very glad to descend into the crowd again, for there at least good nature reigned; and there we stood, placidly surveyed by the men (who occupied the seats set apart for us), not one of whom stirred, though the grandmother of Boston waited in the ranks.

My idea of hospitality may be old-fashioned, but I must say I felt ashamed of Concord that day, when all I could offer my guests, admiring pilgrims to this "Mecca of the mind," was the extreme edge of an unplaned board; for when the gods were settled, leave was given us to sit on the rim of the platform.

Perched there like a flock of tempest-tossed pigeons, we had the privilege of reposing among the sacred boots of the Gamaliels at whose feet we sat, and of listening to the remarks of the reporters, who evidently felt that the elbowroom of the almighty press should not be encroached upon even by a hair's breadth.

"No place for women," growled one.

"Never was a fitter," answered a strong-minded lady standing on one foot.

"Ought to have come earlier, if they come at all."

"So they would, if they had not obeyed orders. Never will again."

"Don't see why they couldn't be contented with seeing the procession."

"Because they preferred poetry and patriotism to fuss and feathers."

"Better have it all their own way next time."

"No doubt they will, and I hope we shall all be there to see."

So the dialogue ended in a laugh, and the women resigned themselves to cold shoulders all around. But as I looked about me, it was impossible to help thinking that there should have been a place for the great-granddaughters of Prescott, William Emerson, John Hancock, and Dr. Ripley, as well as for Isaac Davis's old sword, the scissors that cut the immortal cartridges, and the ancient flag some woman's fingers made. It seemed to me that their presence on that platform would have had a deeper significance than the gold lace which adorned one side, or the senatorial ponderosity under which it broke down on the other, and that the men of Concord had missed a grand opportunity of imitating those whose memory they had met to honor.

The papers have told the tale of that day's exploits and experiences. But the papers did not get all the little items, and some of them were rather funny. Just before the services began, a distracted usher struggled in to inform Judge Hoar that the wives of several potentates had been left out in the cold and must be accommodated. Great was the commotion then, for these ladies, being bobs to political kites, could not be neglected; so a part of the seats reserved for women were with much difficulty cleared, and the "elect precious" sat thereon. Dear ladies, how very cold and wretched they were when they got there, and how willingly the "free and independent citizenesses" of Concord forgave them for reducing their limited quarters to the point of suffocation, as they spread their cloaks over the velvet of their guests, still trying to be hospitable under difficulties.

When order was restored, what might be called "the Centennial Breakdown" began. The president went first—was it an omen?—and took refuge among the women, who I am happy to say received him kindly and tried to temper the wind to His Imperturbability as he sat among them, looking so bored that I longed to offer him a cigar.

The other gentlemen stood by the ship, which greatly diversified the performances by slowly sinking with all on board but the captain. Even the orator tottered on the brink of ruin more than once, and his table would have gone over if a woman had not held up one leg of it for an hour or so. No light task, she told me afterwards, for when the inspired gentleman gave an impressive thump, it took both hands to sustain the weight of his eloquence. Another lady was pinned down by the beams falling on her skirts, but cheerfully sacrificed them and sat still till the departure of the presidential party allowed us to set her free.

Finding us bound to hear it out, several weary gentlemen offered us their seats after a time, but we had the laugh on our side now and sweetly declined, telling them their platform was not strong enough to hold us.

It was over at last, and such of us as had strength enough left went to the dinner and enjoyed another dish of patriotism "cold without"; others went home to dispense hot comforts and thaw the congealed visitors who wandered to our doors.

Then came the ball, and there all went well. For Woman was in her sphere, her "only duty was to please," and the more there were, the merrier; so the deserted damsels of the morning found themselves the queens of the evening and, forgetting and forgiving, bore their part as gaily as if they had put on the vigor of their grandmothers with the old brocades that became them so well.

Plenty of escorts, ushers, and marshals at last, and six chairs apiece if we wanted them. Gentlemen who had been grim as griffins a few hours before were all devotion now, and spectacles that had flashed awful lightning on the women who dared prefer poetry to polkas now beamed upon us benignly and hoped we were enjoying ourselves as we sat nodding along the walls while our guests danced.

That was the end of it, and by four A.M. peace fell upon the exhausted town, and from many a welcome pillow went up the grateful sigh:

"Thank heaven we shall not have to go through this again!"

No, not quite the end; for by and by there will come a day of reckoning, and then the taxpaying women of Concord will not be forgotten, I think—will not be left to wait uncalled upon, or be considered in the way—and *then,* I devoutly wish that those who so bravely bore their share of that day's burden without its honor will rally around their own flag again and, following in the footsteps of their forefathers, will utter another protest that shall be "heard round the world."

REMINISCENCES OF
RALPH WALDO EMERSON

As I count it the greatest honor and happiness of my life to have known Mr. Emerson, I gladly accede to a request for such recollections as may be of interest to the young readers for whom I write.

My first remembrance is of the morning when I was sent to inquire for little Waldo, then lying very ill.

His father came to me so worn with watching and changed by sorrow that I was startled and could only stammer out my message.

"Child, he is dead" was his answer.

Then the door closed and I ran home to tell the sad tidings. I was only eight years old, and that was my first glimpse of a great grief, but I never have forgotten the anguish that made a familiar face so tragical and gave those few words more pathos than the sweet lamentation of the threnody.

Later, when we went to school with the little Emersons in their father's barn, I remember many happy times when the illustrious papa was our good playfellow.

Often piling us into a bedecked hay cart, he took us to berry, bathe, or picnic at Walden, making our day charming and memorable by showing us the places he loved; the wood people Thoreau had introduced to him; or the wildflowers whose hidden homes he had discovered; so that when years afterward we read of "the sweet rhodora in the wood" and "the burly, dozy humble-bee," or laughed over "The Mountain and the Squirrel," we recognized old friends and thanked him for the delicate truth and beauty which made them immortal for us and others.

When the book mania fell upon me at fifteen, I used to venture into Mr. Emerson's library and ask what I should read, never conscious of the audacity of my demand, so genial was my welcome.

His kind hand opened to me the riches of Shakespeare, Dante, Goethe, and Carlyle, and I gratefully recall the sweet patience with which he led me around the book-lined room till "the new and very interesting book" was found; or the indulgent smile he wore when I proposed something far above my comprehension.

"Wait a little for that," he said. "Meantime, try this, and if you like it, come again."

For many of these wise books I am waiting still, very patiently, because in his own I have found the truest delight, the best inspiration of my life.

When these same precious volumes were tumbled out of the window while his house was burning some years ago, as I stood guarding the scorched, wet pile, Mr. Emerson passed by and, surveying the devastation with philosophic calmness, only said in answer to my lamentations:

"I see my library under a new aspect. Could you tell me where my good neighbors have flung my boots?"

In the tribulations of later life this faithful house friend was an earthly Providence, conferring favors so beautifully that they were no burden, and giving such sympathy in joy and sorrow that very tender ties were knit between this beneficent nature and the grateful hearts he made his own.

Acquaintance with such a man is an education in itself; for "the essence of greatness is the perception that virtue is enough," and living what he wrote, his influence purified and brightened like sunshine.

Many a thoughtful young man and woman owe to Emerson the spark that kindled their highest aspirations and showed them how to make the conduct of life a helpful lesson, not a blind struggle.

> "For simple maids and noble youth
> Are welcome to the man of truth;
> Most welcome they who need him most,
> They feed the spring which they exhaust,
>   For greater need
>   Draws better deed."

He was, in truth, like his own Saadi, "a cheerer of men's hearts."

"Friendship," "Love," "Self-Reliance," "Heroism," and "Compensation," among the essays, have become to many readers as precious as Christian's scroll, and certain poems live in the memory as sacred as hymns, so helpful and inspiring are they.

No better books for earnest young people can be found. The truest words are often the simplest, and when wisdom and virtue go hand in hand, none need fear to listen, learn, and love.

The marble walk that leads to his hospitable door has been trodden by the feet of many pilgrims from all parts of the world, drawn thither by their love and reverence for him. In that famous study his town's people have had the privilege of seeing many of the great and good men and women of our time and learning of their gracious host the finest lessons of true courtesy.

I have often seen him turn from distinguished guests to say a wise or kindly word to some humble worshiper, sitting modestly in a corner, content merely to look and listen, and who went away to cherish that memorable moment long and gratefully.

Here, too, in the pleasant room, with the green hills opposite and the pines murmuring musically before the windows, Emerson wrote essays more helpful than most sermons, lectures which created the lyceum, poems full of power and sweetness and better than song or sermon; has lived a life so noble, true, and beautiful that its wide-spreading influence is felt on both sides of the sea.

In all reforms he was among the foremost on the side of justice and progress. When Faneuil Hall used to be a scene of riot and danger in antislavery days, I remember sitting up aloft, an excited girl, among the loyal women who never failed to be there, and how they always looked for that serene face on the platform and found fresh courage in the mere sight of the wisest man in America, standing shoulder to shoulder with the bravest.

When woman's suffrage was most unpopular, his voice and pen spoke for the just cause, undaunted by the fear of ridicule which silences so many.

His own simple, abstemious habits were his best testimony in favor of temperance in all things, while in religion he believed that each soul must choose its own aids and prove the vitality of its faith by high thinking and holy living.

When traveling in various countries, I found his fame had gone before and people were eager to hear something of the Concord poet, seer, and philosopher.

In a little town upon the Rhine, where our party paused for a night, unexpectedly delayed, two young Germans, reading the word Boston on the labels of our trunks as they stood in the yard of the inn, begged to come in and see the Americans, and their first question was—

"Tell us about Emerson."

We gladly told them what they asked, and they listened as eagerly as we did to anything we could hear concerning their great countryman Goethe.

A letter once came to me from the far West, in which a girl asked what she should read to build up a noble character. It was a remarkable letter, and when I inquired what books she most desired, she answered, "All of Emerson's; he helps me most."

A prisoner just from Concord jail came to see me on his release and proved to be an intelligent, book-loving young man, who had been led into crime by his first fit of intoxication. In talking with him, he said Emerson's books were a comfort to him and he had spent some of the money earned in prison to buy certain volumes to take with him as guides and safeguards for the future.

In England his honored name opened many doors to us, and we felt as proud of our acquaintance with him as Englishmen feel of the medals with which their queen decorates them—so widely was he known, so helpful was his influence, so ennobling the mere reflection of his virtue and his genius.

Longfellow was beloved by children, and of Emerson it might be said, as of Plato, "He walks with his head among the stars, yet carries a blessing in his heart for every little child."

When he returned from his second visit to Europe after his house was burned, he was welcomed by the schoolchildren, who lined his passage from the cars to the carriage, where a nosegay of blooming grandchildren awaited him; and escorted by a smiling troop of neighbors, old and young, he was conducted under green arches to his house.

Here they sang "Sweet Home," gave welcoming cheers, and marched away, to come again soon after to a grand housewarming in the old mansion, which had been so well restored that nothing seemed changed.

Many a gay revel has been held under the pines, whole schools taking possession of the poet's premises, and many a child will gladly recall hereafter the paternal face that smiled on them, full of interest in their gambols and of welcome for the poorest.

Mrs. Emerson, from her overflowing garden, planted flowers along the roadside and in the plot of ground before the nearest schoolhouse to beautify the children's daily life. Sweeter and more imperishable than these will be the recollections of many kindnesses bestowed by one who, in the truest sense of the word, was a friend to all.

As he lay dying, children stopped to ask if he were better, and all the sunshine faded out of the little faces when the sad answer came. Very willing feet roamed the woods for green garlands to decorate the old church where he would come for the last time; busy hands worked till midnight, that every house should bear some token of mourning; spring gave him her few early flowers and budding boughs from the haunts that will know him no more; and old and young forgot for a little while their pride in the illustrious man to sorrow for the beloved friend and neighbor.

Life did not sadden his cheerful philosophy; success could not spoil his exquisite simplicity; age could not dismay him; and he met death with sweet serenity.

He wrote, "Nothing can bring you peace but yourself. Nothing can bring you peace but the triumph of principles"; and this well-earned peace transfigured the beautiful dead face so many eyes beheld with tender reverence, seeming to assure us that our august friend and master had passed into the larger life for which he was ready, still to continue—

> "Without hasting, without rest,
> Lifting Better up to Best;
> Planting seeds of knowledge pure,
> Thro' earth to ripen, thro' heaven endure."

RECOLLECTIONS OF MY CHILDHOOD

One of my earliest memories is of playing with books in my father's study—building towers and bridges of the big dictionaries, looking at pictures, pretending to read, and scribbling on blank pages whenever pen or pencil could be found. Many of these first attempts at authorship still exist, and I often wonder if these childish plays did not influence my afterlife, since books have been my greatest comfort, castle building a never-failing delight, and scribbling a very profitable amusement.

Another very vivid recollection is of the day when, running after my hoop, I fell into the Frog Pond and was rescued by a black boy, becoming a friend to the colored race then and there, though my mother always declared that I was an abolitionist at the age of three.

During the Garrison riot in Boston, the portrait of George Thompson was hidden under a bed in our house for safekeeping, and I am told that I used to go and comfort "the good man who helped poor slaves" in his captivity. However that may be, the conversion was genuine, and my greatest pride is in the fact that I have lived to know the brave men and women who did so much for the cause and that I had a very small share in the war which put an end to a great wrong.

Being born on the birthday of Columbus, I seem to have something of my patron saint's spirit of adventure, and running away was one of the delights of my childhood. Many a social lunch have I shared with hospitable Irish beggar children, as we ate our crusts, cold potatoes, and salt fish on voyages of discovery among the ash heaps of the wasteland that then lay where the Albany Station now stands.

Many an impromptu picnic have I had on the dear old Common, with strange boys, pretty babies, and friendly dogs, who always seemed to feel that this reckless young person needed looking after.

On one occasion the town crier found me fast asleep at nine o'clock at night, on a doorstep in Bedford Street, with my head pillowed on the curly breast of a big Newfoundland, who was with difficulty persuaded to release the weary little wanderer who had sobbed herself to sleep there.

I often smile as I pass that door, and never forget to give a grateful pat to every big dog I meet, for never have I slept more soundly than on that dusty step, nor found a better friend than the noble animal who watched over the lost baby so faithfully.

My father's school was the only one I ever went to, and when this was broken up because he introduced methods now all the fashion, our lessons went on at home, for he was always sure of four little pupils who firmly believed in their teacher, though they have not done him all the credit he deserved.

I never liked arithmetic or grammar and dodged these branches on all occasions, but reading, composition, history, and geography I enjoyed, as well as the stories read to us with a skill which made the dullest charming and useful.

Pilgrim's Progress, Krummacher's *Parables,* Miss Edgeworth, and the best of the dear old fairy tales made that hour the pleasantest of our day. On Sundays we had a simple service of Bible stories, hymns, and conversation about the state of our little consciences and the conduct of our childish lives, which never will be forgotten.

Walks each morning around the Common while in the city, and the long tramps over hill and dale when our home was in the country, were a part of our education, as well as every sort of housework, for which I have always been very grateful, since such knowledge makes one independent in these days of domestic tribulation with the help who are too often only hindrances.

Needlework began early, and at ten my skillful sister made a linen shirt beautifully, while at twelve I set up as a doll's dressmaker, with my sign out and wonderful models in my window. All the children employed me, and my turbans were the rage at one time, to the great dismay of the neighbors' hens, who were hotly hunted down, that I might tweak out their downiest feathers to adorn the dolls' headgear.

Active exercise was my delight from the time when, a child of six, I drove my hoop around the Common without stopping, to the days when I did my twenty miles in five hours and went to a party in the evening.

I always thought I must have been a deer or a horse in some former state, because it was such a joy to run. No boy could be my friend till I had beaten him in a race, and no girl if she refused to climb trees, leap fences, and be a tomboy.

My wise mother, anxious to give me a strong body to support a lively brain, turned me loose in the country and let me run wild, learning of nature what no books can teach and being led, as those who truly love her seldom fail to be—

"Through nature up to nature's God."

I remember running over the hills just at dawn one summer morning and, pausing to rest in the silent woods, saw through an arch of trees the sun rise over river, hill, and wide green meadows as I never saw it before.

Something born of the lovely hour, a happy mood, and the unfolding aspirations of a child's soul seemed to bring me very near to God, and in the hush of that morning hour I always felt that I "got religion," as the phrase goes. A new and vital sense of His presence, tender and sustaining as a father's arms, came to me then, never to change through forty years of life's vicissitudes, but to grow stronger for the sharp discipline of poverty and pain, sorrow and success.

Those Concord days were the happiest of my life, for we

had charming playmates in the little Emersons, Channings, Hawthornes, and Goodwins, with the illustrious parents and their friends to enjoy our pranks and share our excursions.

Plays in the barn were a favorite amusement, and we dramatized the fairy tales in great style. Our giant came tumbling off a loft when Jack cut down the squash vine running up a ladder to represent the immortal bean. Cinderella rolled away in a vast pumpkin, and a long black pudding was lowered by invisible hands to fasten itself on the nose of the woman who wasted her three wishes.

Little pilgrims journeyed over the hills with scrip and staff and cockleshells in their hats; elves held their pretty revels among the pines; and "Peter Wilkins's" flying ladies came swinging down on the birch treetops. Lords and ladies haunted the garden, and mermaids splashed in the bathhouse of woven willows over the brook.

People wondered at our frolics, but enjoyed them, and droll stories are still told of the adventures of those days. Mr. Emerson and Margaret Fuller were visiting my parents one afternoon, and the conversation having turned to the ever-interesting subject of education, Miss Fuller said:

"Well, Mr. Alcott, you have been able to carry out your methods in your own family, and I should like to see your model children."

She did in a few moments, for as the guests stood on the doorsteps, a wild uproar approached and around the corner of the house came a wheelbarrow holding baby May arrayed as a queen. I was the horse, bitted and bridled and driven by my elder sister Anna, while Lizzie played dog and barked as loud as her gentle voice permitted.

All were shouting and wild with fun, which, however, came to a sudden end as we espied the stately group before us, for my foot tripped and down we all went in a laughing heap, while my mother put a climax to the joke by saying with a dramatic wave of the hand:

"Here are the model children, Miss Fuller."

My sentimental period began at fifteen, when I fell to writing romances, poems, a "heart journal," and dreaming dreams of a splendid future.

Browsing over Mr. Emerson's library, I found Goethe's *Correspondence with a Child* and was at once fired with the desire to be a second Bettine, making my father's friend my Goethe. So I wrote letters to him, but was wise enough never to send them; left wildflowers on the doorsteps of my "Master"; sang Mignon's song in very bad German under his window; and was fond of wandering by moonlight, or sitting in a cherry tree at midnight till the owls scared me to bed.

The girlish folly did not last long, and the letters were burned years ago. But Goethe is still my favorite author, and Emerson remained my beloved "Master" while he lived, doing more for me, as for many another young soul, than he ever knew, by the simple beauty of his life, the truth and wisdom of his books, the example of a good, great man untempted and unspoiled by the world, which he made nobler while in it and left richer when he went.

The trials of life began about this time, and my happy childhood ended. Money is never plentiful in a philosopher's house, and even the maternal pelican could not supply all our wants on the small income which was freely shared with every needy soul who asked for help.

Fugitive slaves were sheltered under our roof, and my first pupil was a very black George Washington, whom I taught to write on the hearth with charcoal, his big fingers finding pen and pencil unmanageable.

Motherless girls seeking protection were guarded among us, hungry travelers sent on to our door to be fed and warmed; and if the philosopher happened to own two coats, the best went to a needy brother, for these were practical Christians who had the most perfect faith in Providence and never found it betrayed.

In those days the prophets were not honored in their own land, and Concord had not yet discovered her great men. It was a sort of refuge for reformers of all sorts, whom the good natives regarded as lunatics, harmless but amusing.

My father went away to hold his classes and conversations, and we womenfolk began to feel that we also might do something. So one gloomy November day we decided to move to Boston and try our fate again after some years in the wilderness.

My father's prospect was as promising as a philosopher's ever is in a money-making world, my mother's friends offered her a good salary as their missionary to the poor, and my sister and I hoped to teach. It was an anxious council, and always preferring action to discussion, I took a brisk run over the hill and then settled down for "a good think" in my favorite retreat.

It was an old cart wheel, half hidden in grass under the locusts, where I used to sit to wrestle with my sums and usually forgot them scribbling verses or fairy tales on my slate instead. Perched on the hub, I surveyed the prospect and found it rather gloomy, with leafless trees, sere grass, leaden sky, and frosty air. But the hopeful heart of fifteen beat warmly under the old red shawl, visions of success gave the gray clouds a silver lining, and I said defiantly, as I shook my fist at fate embodied in a crow cawing dismally on the fence nearby:

"I *will* do something by and by. Don't care what—teach, sew, act, write, anything to help the family. And I'll be rich and famous and happy before I die, see if I won't!"

Startled by this audacious outburst, the crow flew away, but the old wheel creaked as if it began to turn at that moment, stirred by the intense desire of an ambitious girl to work for those she loved and find some reward when the duty was done.

I did not mind the omen then, and returned to the house cold but resolute. I think I began to shoulder my burden then and there, for when the free country life ended, the wild colt soon learned to tug in harness, only breaking loose now and then for a taste of beloved liberty.

My sisters and I had cherished fine dreams of a home in the city, but when we found ourselves in a small house at the South End, with not a tree in sight, only a backyard to play in, and no money to buy any of the splendors before us, we all rebelled and longed for the country again.

Anna soon found little pupils, and trudged away each morning to her daily task, pausing at the corner to wave her hand to me in answer to my salute with the duster. My father went to his classes at his room downtown, Mother to her all-absorbing poor, the little girls to school, and I was left to keep house, feeling like a caged sea gull as I washed dishes and cooked in the basement kitchen, where my prospect was limited to a procession of muddy boots.

Good drill, but very hard, and my only consolation was the evening reunion, when all met with such varied reports of the day's adventures, we could not fail to find both amusement and instruction.

Father brought news from the upper world and the wise, good people who adorned it; Mother, usually much dilapidated because she *would* give away her clothes, sad tales of suffering and sin from the darker side of life; gentle Anna, a modest account of her success as teacher, for even at seventeen her sweet nature won all who knew her, and her patience quelled the most rebellious pupil.

My reports were usually a mixture of the tragic and the comic, and the children poured their small joys and woes into the family bosom, where comfort and sympathy were always to be found.

Then we youngsters adjourned to the kitchen for our fun, which usually consisted of writing, dressing, and acting a series of remarkable plays. In one, I remember, I took five parts and Anna four, with lightning changes of costume and characters varying from a Greek prince in silver armor to a murderer in chains.

It was good training for memory and fingers, for we recited pages without a fault and made every sort of property, from a harp to a fairy's spangled wings. Later we acted Shakespeare, and Hamlet was my favorite hero, played with a gloomy glare and a tragic stalk which I have never seen surpassed.

But we were now beginning to play our parts on a real stage and to know something of the pathetic side of life, with its hard facts, irksome duties, many temptations, and the daily sacrifice of self. Fortunately we had the truest, tenderest of guides and guards, and so learned the sweet uses of adversity, the value of honest work, the beautiful law of compensation which gives more than it takes, and the real significance of life.

At sixteen I began to teach twenty pupils, and for ten years learned to know and love children. The story writing went on all the while, with the usual trials of beginners. Fairy tales told to the Emersons made the first printed book and *Hospital Sketches* the first successful one.

Every experience went into the caldron, to come out as froth or evaporate in smoke, till time and suffering strengthened and clarified the mixture of truth and fancy, and a wholesome draft for children began to flow pleasantly and profitably.

So the omen proved a true one, and the wheel of fortune turned slowly, till the girl of fifteen found herself a woman of fifty with her prophetic dream beautifully realized, her duty done, her reward far greater than she deserved.

FROM *THE YOUTH'S COMPANION*
AND *MERRY'S MUSEUM*

A VISIT TO THE SCHOOL SHIP

One bright Sunday morning a pleasant party of us steamed out to the school ship, through the ice, with a fresh wind blowing and winter sunshine turning the snowy islands into pleasant pictures for our eyes. Some of us sat in the engineer's room for warmth and watched the mysterious cranks and wheels at their work; others flapped about the deck, trying to be romantic, with blue noses and tingling toes, while General Banks and the Judge settled the affairs of the nation in a place which we called the "cuddy."

A boat, manned by the boys, with a flag flying, came off to meet and escort us; and the rosy-faced lads in their blue uniforms looked very well as they rowed ahead, scrambled up the ship's side like so many monkeys, and stood ready to nod and grin when we came climbing up the stairs with a good deal of laughter and much handing-about by officers. There were a hundred and fifty boys aboard, I believe; and I was sorry to find that most all of them were there for some offense or other—setting houses afire, stealing, unruly conduct, and all sorts of naughtiness. As they stood about the decks, the ship did not look a bit like a prison, but like what it really is—a school, where these boys are kindly taught and helped to turn over a new leaf and begin again. A very wholesome place, I should think, for young rogues, with plenty of fresh air and exercise, good food and teaching, friendly faces around them;

and, best of all, they are safely guarded from the evil examples, temptations, and want which in many cases led them astray.

Presently they formed in two lines down the deck and marched below to the schoolroom, whither we followed, for the Sunday service. A pleasant place, looking like any schoolroom, except the little windows, queer beams, and odd corners. The good Judge conducted the services, and did it in a way that proved he was the right man in the right place. I couldn't help thinking that the memory of his own lovely little daughters made him so fatherly kind to these naughty, neglected boys, who seemed so fond of him. While he read, I watched the faces before me and found many interesting ones. Only here and there was there a really bad face, and I daresay, behind even the most sullen and brutal was a real boy's heart, with a soft spot in it, ready to be touched by the right influence when it came. I like to think so, for I feel sure that there always lurks a spark of good, even in the worst of us. Some of the faces were so young and bright and innocent that I wondered how they came there, especially two little lads who read out of the same book and seemed very fond of one another. Good little faces they had, and made a pretty picture as they leaned close together, like the chubby-cheeked cupids in old paintings, only cupids don't wear blue woolen shirts and trousers and crop their heads. I liked that little David-and-Jonathan pair, but did not dare ask what offense brought them there, lest I should be told that my cherubs were the naughtiest boys aboard. Some of the bigger ones looked sober and sad, and I've no doubt they had cause to look so, especially the tall one, who glowered at his neighbor and wouldn't sing. Some seemed sleepy, and one or two looked sick; but on the whole, I thought them a pretty jolly set of boys and longed to know what was going on in those cropped heads of theirs, for most of the eyes had a wide-awake look, as if very little escaped them.

One thing pleased me immensely, and that was the sight of several black boys among the white. That was as it should be;

and that little church set a good example to many a splendid one, for in it there was no Negro pew, but all were alike there, as they are in the eyes of the Father of all. The black sheep and the white were taken into the same fold, and the good work will prosper the better for the truly Christian spirit which makes room for all.

After reading and prayers the boys sang, and sang as only boys can, with all their might and main. Didn't they shout with a will when the tune permitted! Didn't they fold their arms and rock to and fro, as if entirely absorbed in the effort to get as much "sing" out of themselves as possible! And didn't the room ring with hearty music as these little varlets warbled away, with the sunshine on their faces and good words on their lips! My two chubby ones grew chubbier still and vibrated to and fro, chirping like two plump cock robins on a swinging bough. The black boys roared manfully, and their eyes danced in their heads during the "shout." The sleepy ones woke up; the sad ones brightened visibly; I think the sick ones felt better; and I know the naughtiest ones wished they "hadn't done it" then, if they never did before.

General Banks spoke to them, and I hope they were grateful to him for originating this beautiful and helpful charity. I was, and admired him more for that than for all the battles he has fought; for I don't like war, which fills hospitals and graves, and I do dearly love the philanthropy that turns prisons into schools and tries to make good men out of bad boys. So when anyone proposes "Three cheers for General Banks!" I'll throw up my hat and shout my best.

If I had not been told that his own kind heart took him there, I really should have thought the Judge had brought Mr. McC., as a sample of the manhood he wanted the boys to try to attain, for a better specimen of health, strength, comeliness, and courage I have not seen this many a day. Somebody whispered to me that he had been in the army with his father and six or seven brothers, and it was quite unnecessary to tell me that he fought gallantly. I knew it perfectly well; and so did the boys, I fancy, for their eyes turned oftenest to the fresh-faced young man, who nodded and smiled at them; sang when they sang; joined in their services; and when unexpectedly called upon to speak, up and did it like a man, though it wasn't fair of the Judge to take him unawares. He knew how to talk to boys; one saw that in a minute by the brightening of the faces; the twinkling of the eyes; the sly punches exchanged; the ready "Yes, sir!" "No, sir!" "Come again!" and so on, that accompanied his remarks. He didn't preach, but just talked to them like a big boy talking to his younger brothers. They felt that, loved him for it, I know, and heartily regretted his approaching absence, as they proved by asking me, when I went to speak to them after they had filed up on deck again, "I say, when is Mr. McC. going, ma'am?" "Will he stay long?" "Jest wish he'd take me!" "Hope we'll see him again 'fore he goes!"

As I had never met their hero before, I could not give them any consolation, but asked them all sorts of questions, while they stood around the cannon on which I sat, looking ready to talk and glad of a little attention. In summer they go on short cruises and work the ship themselves, which they consider "jolly fun." Several affably explained the different parts of the rigging to me, and one young man of ten, with a nose as red as his tippet, informed me that they fired the cannon sometimes themselves, which seemed to be his idea of earthly bliss. We were just beginning to get quite friendly when I was called away to examine the ship, and forty blue caps bobbed as I said good-bye.

Down below I saw the long tables set for dinner, with regiments of mugs, and the spoons stacked like muskets. I likewise tasted of their soup in the kitchen and found it very good. Everything was very nice, and if cleanliness is akin to godliness, these boys ought to be young saints. In the sleeping room, which was a big place with hammocks rolled and slung up by day, we found two lads ready to show us how they got into their high beds, which had comfortable little mattresses and coverings. As I thought of the wilderness of fun-loving boys collected in that big room every night, I couldn't help asking one of the young sailors if they didn't have splendid pillow fights there. He tried to say soberly, "'Tain't allowed ma'am"; but the other boy snickered, and the virtuous sobriety of Number One's face was not proof against the infectious sound. So we all laughed together, and I went on, sincerely pitying anyone who tried to bottle up the effervescent spirits of a hundred and fifty rollicking lads. I saw the clothes room, the workshop, the library, and the hospital; for every want seemed supplied, even to a brisk matron in a cheerful red jacket, and several teachers, who looked as if they did not have a very hard time. From Captain Mathews, the excellent superintendent, and Mr. Brooks, the teacher, we learned several interesting things. How one of the boys, who was friendless and sick, was taken to the house of a kind lady in New Bedford, who made his last hours happy and taught every boy in the ship a beautiful lesson, making them feel that they were neither forgotten nor despised because of their wrongdoing; but their self-respect was encouraged, and gratitude won, by such true charity. We also heard how one kind gentleman gave the boys an island of more than two acres in extent for a playground; how other friends made pleasant picnics for them, sent them a cabinet organ, good books, kind letters, and brought interesting people to see them; how Dickens paid them a visit and said in his speech, "Boys, just do all the good you can, and don't make any fuss about it"—advice which boys out of the school ship had better follow, as well as those in it. Many of the lads are sent off on whaling voyages and made good sailors. Others get places, but they don't forget their friends, and the officers often receive letters from them; and sometimes, on their return from voyages, the boys visit the old ship, even before they go home, which tells well for the kindness and faithfulness of these patient teachers. Winter on the briny deep is not exactly what one would choose, perhaps; neither is loss of liberty, homesickness, and the minor trials that afflict boyhood under such circumstances. But judging by what I saw, I should say that the school ship was an excellent place for the boys who can't keep out of mischief, and advise those who like to see good works underway to go and pay a visit to this floating hospital for wayward wills, feeble consciences, tempted souls, and erring hands.

I think this ship will have a prosperous voyage; that wintry winds will not visit it too roughly as it lies at anchor in the harbor; and that heaven's sunshine will be on it as it makes its summer cruises, manned by the waifs and strays whom its good commander has rescued from the great sea of poverty and sin, where so many little boats go down for want of a pilot to bring them safely into port.

LITTLE BOSTON

Just opposite my window is a kindergarten, and I derive much amusement and satisfaction from watching the children at their play.

This little world is very like the great one outside, and these small citizens enact many of the scenes that are taking place in the city that lies beyond their garden walls. So capitally do they play their parts that one can easily guess what is going on, and needs no playbill to give the dramatis personae.

The yard is divided by a wide flight of steps and a low wall. The boys play in the upper part, the girls in the lower, the steps being the boundary—a sort of society platform, beyond which neither may pass, but where both sides may meet when so minded.

Up in the paved yard the little lads mimic their fathers in many ways and unconsciously set their elders a good example in some things. I observe that any attempt at cheating in the traffic of marbles, string, knives, or apples, which goes on so briskly at times, is at once exposed and punished. Honesty is so plainly the best policy that these young businessmen promptly excommunicate swindlers, no matter if they wear velvet knickerbockers and live in swell-front houses.

I also observed that during the election these small politicians, though much interested, neither bribed, threatened, nor fought their opponents, but amicably discussed the merits of

231

the rival candidates, with a good deal of "My father says" and "My father thinks" to add weight to their arguments.

They marched and countermarched with paper lanterns minus all light except the sunshine of their own bright faces. They unfurled remarkable banners to the breeze, and when one side cheered heartily for "Horace Dreeley," the other side blithely responded with "Free 'rahs for Drant!" And often, in the enthusiasm of the moment, both parties cheered everybody promiscuously.

It gave me satisfaction to observe that none of these little gentlemen descended to unjust or ungenerous criticism, unmanly abuse, or coarse caricature of the future President, whichever man might win that uncomfortable honor.

The very worst they did in the heat of that exciting time was to have an old hat on a pole and put little sticks in their mouths for cigars. It was so funny to see how quickly these small men caught up the watchwords of their elders and imitated their jokes that I wished both candidates would set young America better examples in costume and habits. To me one very pleasing feature in this late election was the fact that many small women voted. They did not demand the ballot with loud protests, denunciations, or appeals; they did not even ask for it; but several bright-eyed little ladies sat on the upper step, watching the fun with such interest as they tore up an old copybook to make votes of, and offering such wise and witty suggestions, that it seemed to occur to the gentlemen that it would be but just, to say nothing of civility and gratitude, to ask these helpful friends to take part in the duties of the day.

"Ho, girls don't vote!" cried one little fogy in a plaid suit, which made him look like an animated checkerboard.

"Well, I don't see why they can't. Mamie gave us her copybook, and Nelly lent us all her pencils to write the names. 'Tisn't fair not to let 'em vote if they want to. Do you?" asked a rosy-faced gentleman with bright buttons sowed broadcast over his blue jacket.

"I like to play what you play, Willy," answered Mamie,

looking up at him with such a confiding air that Bright Buttons decided the matter at once by handing her a bit of paper, with the friendly explanation:

"If you vote for Greeley, put 'H. G.' on that, and if you go for Grant, put 'U. G.'"

"What shall you put on yours?" asked grateful Mamie with the amiable weakness of her sex.

"Shan't tell. You've got to do it all yourself"; and away went Buttons to put more votes into several chubby hands mutely outstretched to receive them.

"I say, Nelly, how do you spell 'Lysses Grant? 'L. G.,' isn't it?" asked the plaid gentleman, forgetting his prejudices as soon as the point was carried, and condescending to ask help of the weaker vessel, who gladly gave it without a word about past wrongs.

"You can't come into our yard, and we can't go into yours, so we'll pass a hat round, and you can put your votes in all nice, don't you see?"

And Buttons gallantly spared the ladies the unforgivable sin of quitting their sphere to go to the polls, by handing around his sailor hat, into which they carefully laid the crumpled papers with tipsy-looking letters scrawled on them.

'Lysses Grant was elected with such cheering, firing of popguns, and throwing up of hats that the cats flew off the sheds in all directions. Then the entire population took hands and danced around, singing a song not included in the campaign melodies, being a lively mixture of "Ring Around a Rosy," "Captain Jenks," and "Yankee Doodle."

A general game of tag followed, in which all party feeling was forgotten; and when a bell rang, the citizens returned to their duties none the poorer or the worse for the election.

Shutting my window, I went back to my own affairs much impressed by this quiet settlement of the vexed suffrage question, wondering how long the older women would sit at the top of the steps helping their friends while waiting to be asked to share the pleasures as well as the penalties of equal liberty; and I accepted the child's play as a good omen that the hat would soon be passed to them by some just and generous brother who believes that they have heads as well as hearts.

The late fire was all reenacted for my benefit on the little stage opposite. Alarm bells rang; firemen, with caps hind part before and jackets wrong side out, "ran with the machine" as briskly as the brave neighbors who dragged the larger engine twelve miles to help extinguish the real fire.

Ropes were thrown over the fence, and a great swarming up and down the walls followed, with shouts and cheers and an occasional smash of the old box, which represented the valuable stock of all the great firms that suffered.

There was no drunkenness, no thieving, and but very few arrests during this terrible conflagration, which spoke well for the order of the city.

When the first excitement was over, these curly-headed city fathers met on the wall and after much discussion set up a post office in the big box, which seems to work smoothly, if one may judge from the rapid delivery of letters and papers in all parts of the yard.

The ladies did their part nobly: first, in saving dolls of all sorts from a fiery death, then in nursing the sufferers, who lay in shawl beds on the steps, and running around with bundles of relief, like distracted ants on an anthill.

The boys make the most noise, I observe, but stick to the old games and do things according to rule. The girls play more quietly, but their inventive faculties are marvelous, and I am often puzzled by the new plays they get up.

Of course they imitate their mamas, gossip, "dress up," pay calls, have tea parties, and attend to their children. But even in their mimicry they improve upon the examples set them, in a way the mamas would do well to follow.

They take a great deal of exercise, which appears to have an excellent effect upon their nerves. They do not leave their children to the care of servants, and their housekeeping is of the simplest description.

If all the young ladies in Boston would dance the German in the morning, as these damsels do, take a good run around the Common, and dress as sensibly as my small neighbors dress, they would keep their youth and beauty longer and, what is better than either, their health.

These little mothers walk with their children, feed, teach, and wait upon them with a devotion beautiful to see; and I am sure that this generation of dolls will be the better for it.

It is delightful to find that in this circle clothes do not make the woman, for the little girl in a faded sack, with copper-toed boots and a shabby hat, is the queen of society, because she is the brightest, most honest, and sweetest-tempered.

They call her Hatty, and she leads them all, even the dainty Lilys and Mauds, in their embroidered cambrics, gay sashes, and fashionable hats with half a milliner's stock on the top.

Sometimes she keeps school for them, and then the dullest goes to the bottom of the class, no matter how splendid she may be. If anyone is rude or cross, Hatty leads her to a dim retreat under the steps and leaves her to reflect upon her sins for a time. But very soon she goes and peeps in, smiling sweetly as she beckons the small sinner out, kisses and restores her to society again without reproach or scorn.

If anyone is hurt in either yard, Hatty runs to comfort the sufferer. Even the noble beings up aloft call her to bind up their hurts with her microscopic handkerchief, to wipe away their tears, and send the wounded heroes back to the fray with a consoling pat and a cheering nod.

I am fond of this stouthearted, tender-handed Hatty, and fancy she will make her own way in the world by the magic of courage, cheerfulness, and goodwill. Her strong-mindedness seems to be of the right sort, womanly and winning, with good sense and tact at the bottom. I wish her all success and trust that the little feet in the copper-toed boots will not find the road before them very hard to travel.

One of the favorite games among these ladies is "honey pots," and I never see them playing it without wishing that we elders did the same, metaphorically speaking. I discover that whenever other games lose their charms, when squabbles seem imminent, or spirits begin to flag, some wise little soul calls out, "Let's play honey pots!" and at it they go, swinging and lugging one lively pot after the other till all are bubbling over with fun.

Why don't we find something that can do for us what this childish game does for these small women, and for a time at least, endeavor to forget our nerves, our cares, and our vanities in trying to see which can be the strongest and the sweetest?

Of course there is lovemaking in Little Boston, and very pretty lovemaking it is, too, without falsehood or maneuvering, very little coquetry, and, I trust, no worldly-mindedness. Simple and sincere are the loves of my young Romeos and Juliets, and very tender are the trysts they keep on the red steps or at the creaking gate.

Bright Buttons fondly adores a small charmer in a red hood, and often leans pensively on the wall watching her play below. At times his passion moves him to break all bounds; he slides down the baluster, give his darling a bite of his apple, a suck of his orange, or the large half of his candy, and then tears back again to play leapfrog with redoubled relish.

Little Red Hood returns these favors with smiles, throws him kisses, tosses back his ball when it comes over the wall, and lets him play with her bright hair when they trot home from school together.

Another pair, like Pyramus and Thisbe, talk not through a chink, but around a post, and no lion molests them. On one occasion, though, a small "rough" hustled Thisbe, so that she fell down a step or two and was picked up with great lamentation by her mates. He never did the base deed again, for Pyramus fell upon him as he retired, and so pummeled him that he roared for mercy, when the wrathful lover cast the ruffian's cap into the street with direful threats for the future, while all the other gentlemen applauded wildly.

On the whole, their little loves seem to run smoothly, and no one cares who is the richest, who has the most grandmothers, or whose father is in the genteelest business.

An arcadian state of things that even the most sanguine be-

liever in the millennium can hardly hope to see established—
but it is very pretty to watch, and it keeps one's faith fresh in
the old-fashioned idea that love makes all equal if it only be
strong and pure enough.

A bell rung by some invisible hand daily calls the little people from play to study, and trooping in, they leave the garden
empty. But presently the sound of many childish voices ringing
sweetly makes music for the street, and passersby pause a
minute to listen, then go on with a smile and a tender thought
for the small singers.

As I shut my window, I end the little sermon I have been
preaching to myself by wondering if Big Boston, the city of my
love and pride, will ever be like the kindergarten over the
way. A little world full of busy, happy souls, helping and loving one another, obeying promptly the call of an unseen
teacher when summoned from their pleasures to their duties,
and making cheerful music of their lives till it shall be heard
above the turmoil of the world, singing such brave, sweet
songs that strangers passing by shall stop to listen, and go on
with a grateful smile, the better for the lesson unconsciously
bestowed.

HOW WE SAW THE SHAH

Certainly the compensation of a sight at this distinguished personage should be great, for he seems to have turned everybody's head and disturbed the general peace to such an extent that even our little household has felt some inconvenience from his visit.

Our chief annoyance has been the refusal of the neighboring stable keepers to let us a vehicle of any sort large enough to carry a party of fourteen, with the hampers and wraps necessary for a day's picnic at Hampton Court or Kew. Each thrifty Briton was so sure that as soon as the program of the royal movements was made public, he could get high bids for every sort of carriage, he was naturally slow to accommodate us at the usual rates.

Much disgusted, we were about to give up our trip when a right-minded man was discovered, who agreed for a moderate sum to let us have a barouche which would hold five, "if we were not proud," he said, "for one gentleman could sit with the driver, who should wear his best livery, free of extra charge."

So on a lovely June day it was announced that our "carriage stopped the way." Five happy souls soon filled it. With many wishes for a pleasant trip, in four different languages, from gentlemen of four nationalities on our balcony, we drove away for a visit to Kew Gardens.

Much impressed with the elegance of our turnout, for the coachman was a stately being in gold lace, white tie, top boots, etc., we drove through the marble arch into the park and found ourselves surrounded on all sides by an expectant crowd.

Our yellow plush condescended to inform us that the "Shay," as he pronounced it, was going to Richmond in a royal barge and the people were waiting for him, as he must pass this way on his road from Buckingham Palace.

Having expressed an utter contempt for His August Highness, especially his morals and manners, we decided that it was not consistent to wait for him, but as he would probably overtake us, we could then honor him with a casual glance of our freeborn eyes.

In this lofty, imposing frame of mind we rolled on, passing fine drags with gentlemen driving four-in-hand, coaches with outriders, ladies in phaetons, and whole families looking very domestic and happy in small omnibuses.

By the Albert Memorial, with its Byzantine shaft and finely sculptured marble base, by Kensington Gardens, haunted to my fancy by Trollope's, Thackeray's, and Dickens's heroes and heroines, through the great gates we went, and came into the more countrylike region of Hammersmith.

Still flocks of people lined the road. Every balcony was full, and all high steps and walls swarmed with men and boys. So eager were they to see *something* that every head was turned as we drove by, and judging from their remarks, many were firmly persuaded that my companion, who occupied the seat of honor, shrouded in a blue veil, was the only wife of the "Shay" not sent back to Persia in disgrace for wanting to see and join in the festivities at Moscow.

At last our cry of "Sister Ann, sister Ann, do you see anything coming?" was answered by my opposite neighbor, who commanded a fine view of the wide road behind us.

"I see the glitter of the Queen's horse guards, many carriages, and much dust."

At this our indifference changed suddenly to interest, for

there *is* something rather exciting in the approach of royalty, even if it be only a half-savage Persian with more diamonds than decency.

Soon the gilded helmets adorned with long horse tails, the glittering lances and gay uniforms of the guard, appeared and flashed by, followed by eight state carriages, so shut up that little could be seen of the golden idols within. At last came the vehicle on which all eyes were fixed; but great was the disappointment, for all that could be seen were glimpses of a dark face, with fine eyes, surmounted by a hat like a muff set on end, with some very brilliant ornament in front. Then came more state carriages with gold-laced beings inside, more gay guards, clouds of dust, and—we had seen the Shah.

It was all over in such a minute that I hardly know what he was like; still, there is an infinite satisfaction in the thought that I can truly say in answer to the one question now asked by everybody all over England:

"*Have* you seen the Shah?"

"Yes, I have, and I did not pay anything for the spectacle, either."

Congratulating ourselves upon this piece of luck, we left the great road and, taking to the pretty lanes, came at length to the bridge crossing the Thames at Kew.

A livelier sight can hardly be imagined, for all the world was abroad. The riverbanks were lined with gaily dressed people, and the water covered with boats of every sort—great pleasure barges, small steamers, canal boats tugged along by used-up horses, club boats with their eight oars keeping perfect time, and such inviting shells that I could not resist the temptation which then and there beset me.

As the carriage stopped near the bank, I turned to my English friends and invited them to take a row with me. Ignoring a slight hesitancy on their part in accepting my proposal, I headed the procession and, marching up to an old boatman, asked, pointing to a captivating little craft floating below, if I could have it for an hour.

"It won't hold but three and is very cranky, so if the ladies are nervous, I'd rather row you in a bigger boat," replied the bare-legged patriarch.

Then it was that the full audacity of my project dawned upon the party, for, having explained that I proposed being skipper, coxswain, oarsman, all in one, horror fell upon all my friends. With the utmost politeness they explained that though ladies rowed in England, it was always in the chaste seclusion of "Papa's grounds" or some more retired portion of the river than that now before us.

But the boating fever was on me, and I could no more keep from the water than a Newfoundland dog. With a naughty satisfaction in asserting my Yankee independence, I boldly replied to their gentle hints and kindly advice:

"Very well; if you don't like to go, I'll go alone, for a row in the *Rose* I *must* have, in remembrance of my own boat and quiet river at home."

Resolutely stepping in and feathering my oars in my most scientific manner, I pulled vigorously up the stream, with the true Harvard stroke, as nearly as one of the uninitiated can hope to come to it.

Wasn't it lovely? And didn't I enjoy the exercise? For after weeks of painting my arms positively reveled in a sturdy pull, and got it, too, as the current was strong and all England looking on. Yes; utterly regardless of the chaff of the boys, the dismay of my lady friends, and the amusement of my gentlemen ditto, I heartily enjoyed the brief trip. I longed to stop and book some of the lovely pictures up and down the river: the gray stone arches of the bridge, the gay crowds on the one bank, the great trees and pagoda of the garden on the other, and all the water dappled with soft shadows and green glimmers as I floated near the shore.

With a delightful sense of having had my own way, I presently rejoined my party, and strolling away under the oaks, we lay on the grass watching the fine toilettes in the principal avenue. I was tired and, turning from nature to art, became absorbed in watching two splendid beings in mauve silk and muslin, with bonnets, gloves, and parasols of the same color, golden hair hung curling to the waist; and the tall, graceful creatures leaned and languished on the arms of lemon-kidded beaux in the most aristocratic style. I was wondering whether they were lords and ladies, or actors and actresses, when someone said, "Let's have tea," and we all instantly clamored for refreshment.

A mysterious basket made one of the party and was now borne in state as we followed our matron to a retreat where we could enjoy our lunch in the open air. Through winding ways we went, catching glimpses of pretty vistas on either hand, usually adorned with a tender couple in a high state of bill and coo.

We came at last to a series of what I, in my ignorance, called "little backyards"; but each had a sign, bearing in gilt letters the words "Tea Gardens," "Flora's Bower," "Cupid's Retreat," and other pleasing legends. On entering we found many little tables, each in a nest of vines, as if especially intended for lovers to feed at.

All, however, were full, so we wandered vainly to and fro till at last we subsided about an empty table in a dismal nook overhung with earwiggy shrubbery and decorated with the tails of many departed shrimps.

Hailing an exhausted waiter, we asked for hot water, and were told we could not have it unless we took a whole lunch, when hot water was included; for it is the fashion to carry one's own tea and make it on the spot, with more solid refreshments added.

We left indignantly, bearing our obnoxious basket, and after much search, found a little house with the sign "Tea and coffee, eight pence each; hot water, two pence extra."

An old woman welcomed and led us through several small rooms, all full, to an upper perch in this pigeon box, where one vacant table was discovered and engaged, none too soon, for we were literally "dropping for our tea" by this time.

The basket proved to be a mine of comfort, and we partook copiously of its treasures. It was a new style of picnic to me, for we were wedged in so closely that one could not leave his seat without disturbing the whole party. Our hats and bonnets were laid out of a window, on the roof of the little porch; for each nook in the little room was filled with china dogs of every size and color. Mirrors hung on every nail. Limp muslin curtains would sweep over the table and flap in our faces with every breeze, while much pink tissue paper fluttered and rustled mildly from the ceiling.

I felt so much like one of Miss Burney's heroines that I involuntarily looked in the nearest mirror to see if I had not a "full-dressed head," and kept recalling the tragic scene in the tea garden, where Evelina's lover implores the timid maid—

> "To stay and sip one dish of tea;
> She sipped one dish, and flew."

We not only sipped, but flew also, for someone, popping out his head to recover the hats, reported that clouds were gathering and a shower coming up.

Away we went in hot haste toward home, but not fast enough to escape the great drops that soon came pattering down. Passing what had been the gay crowd of an hour before, it now presented a most forlorn appearance, for the women had their smart gowns bundled up, their best bonnets under their shawls, and their faces full of vexation at the impending damage. Unhappy lovers or surly husbands, with handkerchiefs tied over their hats, sat on fences beside the ladies, like fowls at roost, or hung about tavern doors, seeking comfort in beer.

The half top of our carriage and a good rug kept us quite dry, so we could enjoy the woes of our fellowmen at our ease.

Down came the rain, thick and fast, laying the dust delightfully, but tarnishing our Jeames's gold lace and baptizing liberally his amiable comrade on the box.

No pleasure party in England can end properly without a shower, so we were quite in order. Yet we arrived in style, nevertheless; for the clouds parted before we reached home, the rain ceased, and we drove up triumphantly in a burst of sunshine, all feeling heartier and happier for a merry English outing.

LONDON BRIDGES

I have often said to friends on their return from England, "Well, did you try the penny boats going up and down the Thames all day, and so get fine views of St. Paul's, the Houses of Parliament, Westminster Abbey, and the Bell Tower?"

"No, we didn't know that strangers did that."

"Did you ever take a drive on one of the coaches, and so have gone dashing off to Sunbridge, Wells, or Dorking for the pleasure of viewing the country from the top of one of these once famous mail coaches?"

"No, we never tried it."

"Did you see the immense wine vaults, where the visitor wanders for miles, apparently, candle in hand, as if among the Catacombs?"

"Never thought of such a thing."

"Nor bought hot roasted potatoes from the ovens kept by sleepy women at street corners in the night?"

"Bless me, no!"

"Nor gone to the Zoo to hunt up the wombat and see if he really were 'hairy and obtuse,' as Christina Rossetti says in one of her poems; and, being there, ride on camels and disport yourself like children among the animals?"

"We went, of course, but a man showed us around."

"I won't harrow up your feelings any further, but end my questioning by the triumphant assertion, I *know* you didn't see London bridges by moonlight."

"You are right, it did not occur to us."

"Then it seems to me you have missed some of the best sights of London and have only followed in the beaten track laid down by Murray and made very dull and dusty by the feet of many travelers like yourselves."

Some would have thought it quite impossible for a lone woman, even an enterprising American, to have done these things, and perhaps I *should* have found it so, had not a kindred spirit of the opposite sex, but an American, been raised up to me.

My grandson, as he respectfully calls himself, being my junior by some years, is a youth of an inquiring turn, an adventurous soul, a persuasive tongue, and makes a capital guide, guard, comrade, and friend.

A delightful unexpectedness attends our trips and gives them zest, so we always keep in light marching order and never are surprised at any suggestion from the other.

On the evening of the Fourth of July, as we sat on the balcony enjoying the lovely moonlight that glorified all London, I was suddenly seized with a desire to do something revolutionary and independent in honor of the day. So instead of sitting decorously in an easy chair and taking my moonlight like a well-conducted young woman, I rose up, and pointing vaguely to the horizon in general, I said, "Let us go somewhere."

"We will," promptly responded my ever-ready grandson, and in a moment we were walking forth into time and space with the delicious sense of freedom so dear to the Yankee soul.

"Where shall we go?" said I, as we came out of the quiet square.

Now, most men would have suggested a concert, call, or a romantic stroll in the park, but C. knew better and gave me something far finer than any of these.

"Come and see the bridges by the moonlight," he answered, like an inspiration.

Away we clattered in a cab to the Thames embankment, that wonderful piece of work which turned the riverbank, with its tumbledown houses, old wharves, and dangerous dens, into a magnificent drive, with the city on one hand and the busy river on the other.

We alighted at Blackfriars Bridge, and here, standing in one of the niches built in a half circle over each abutment, we took a long survey, for it was a view which no one should lose.

Behind us rose St. Paul's, its great white dome thrown out in strong relief against the soft haze of the sky beyond. Nearer the water were the enormous breweries which seem to line the Thames, almost always surrounded by a stone lion or some other device, which in that magical light made them look more like palaces than establishments for satisfying what seems to an American the unquenchable thirst of the British nation.

Still nearer to us were many Dutch vessels, with their uncouth hulks, queer rigging, and the bright-colored sails that so enliven the river by day, now lost in black shadows or closely reefed, for no large craft is allowed to ply up or down after dark.

While expressing my wish that John Bull would change some of his laws to suit my private taste and let the penny boats run by night, we strolled across the bridge, meeting crowds of the common people out for refreshment like ourselves.

Each niche had its pair of lovers, and I had just said how happy they seemed, when in a smaller nook I caught sight of the crouching figure of a woman so suggestive in attitude and figure of "one more unfortunate" that I involuntarily moved towards her, remembering the other lines:

> "Alas for the rarity
> Of Christian charity
> Under the sun."

But C. drew me away, saying sagely, "Don't waste your sympathy. These people are usually humbugs, and this is not the bridge where the real tragedies happen."

Feeling rather crushed, I went on; but when we returned,

the dark, despairing figure was still there, and it haunted me all that night.

On Waterloo Bridge such sights are common, for the poor souls who are in earnest pay a halfpenny toll and, thus escaping the idlers so thick on the free bridges, drown themselves as privately as possible.

My mind was so full of these sorrowful images that I followed my guide silently up the long flight of stone steps leading to the iron turnstile. Here, while C. paid our toll, the policeman who keeps guard there turned the light of the little lantern fastened to his belt full upon my face, for I daresay its solemn expression raised a doubt in his mind as to my intentions.

But there never was less reason for anxiety; for life was wonderfully attractive to me that lovely night, and there were few happier mortals than I, when a little later I sat in a light boat and we went swiftly with the tide along that line of moonshine which always seems like a silvery path to heaven.

Many small sailboats were out, and we found much amusement in hearing the comments of the strollers on both banks concerning our rowing. I took an oar and we went down in gallant style. But coming back was hard work; for around the piers of the bridges the current ran swift and strong, and we had a famous pull before we landed at Westminster pier and crossed to the Lambeth side.

Here the embankment (which, by the way, cost three million pounds) runs before the fine Lambeth Hospital, built on the new plan of having the contagious diseases in separate buildings connected by handsome arcades. These command such charming views up and down the river, with the turrets and spires of the Houses of Parliament opposite and Lambeth Palace not far off, that I almost wished myself a convalescent patient able to enjoy it every day.

On we went to the Suspension or Lambeth Bridge, and standing between this and the Vauxhall above, I was perplexed to decide which was most beautiful, each was so fine in its way.

In spite of Ruskin's sneers at Blackfriars, it is charming to me, with its different-colored stones. The long arches of old Westminster are the most perfect, and the airiness of Lambeth is very striking. Hungerford adds the charm of variety, and the one which spans the curve of the river at Greenwich is a delight to look upon.

Being warned by the deep tones of Big Ben from the clock tower that it was getting late, I proposed turning homeward, but C. would not hear of it till I had admired Lambeth Palace, which is most interesting, with its square gray towers, deep gateway, portcullis, and high walls, all looking particularly impressive just then, with the dark figure of a sentinel passing to and fro behind the barred entrance.

All the way back to Westminster the moon shone brightly on the venerable abbey. St. Paul's gloamed in the purple shadows of the distance; the dark bridge and massive stonework of the hospital rose upon the right, and on the left were the brightly lighted Houses of Parliament, dropping countless yellow reflections on the water below, where the superb eight-oared club boats rose and fell with the tide.

It was a very happy walk home, for I refused to drive, being bound to enjoy my midsummer night's dream to the uttermost. From the sublime to the ridiculous is but a step, and we took it when, leaving the more crowded and brilliant streets behind us, we turned into a quiet quarter and nearly fell over a queer black object, like an oddly shaped wheelbarrow in mourning, while a sleeping woman sat on the curbstone folded in a dark shawl.

The whole thing looked mysterious, and I could not pass without stopping to investigate. C. satisfied my curiosity by giving the shrouded sleeper a gentle poke and demanding two hot potatoes. Up rose the woman; open flew a little door, disclosing an oven; and out came two immense potatoes baked to a turn. Producing a pepper pot with salt in it, the now wide-awake lady obligingly offered to break the skins and add the necessary savor. But we preferred to bear our warm purchases home, there to feast royally on them, with bread, butter, and sardines added.

Not a romantic termination of our moonlight ramble, but very acceptable and more wholesome, as we morally decided, than ices and cake at a restaurant or a heavy tea at some social board. Our walk and our row made us delightfully tired, and in our dreams we saw again, more wonderful and bright than ever, the famous bridges we had visited "in the glimpses of the moon."

A NEW WAY TO SPEND CHRISTMAS

In spite of rain and fog, our party met at the appointed hour on board of the boat bound for Randall's Island.

This is one of the three islands that lie in East River and are used for charitable purposes. Blackwell's Island is full of hospitals, alms- and workhouses; Ward's has a hospital for immigrants, a lunatic asylum, and the Potter's Field; but Randall's is devoted to the children.

On it is a nursery in which children over two years old are placed and kept until parents or guardians are able to provide for them. If not claimed, they are bound out at a proper age to respectable citizens to learn some useful trade. There are now in the nursery six hundred and forty-two boys and three hundred and twenty-one girls. A school for idiots is also on this island, and a hospital for sick babies.

"SHE'S COME! SHE'S COME!"

For thirty years has the lady who led our party (a worthy daughter of good Isaac T. Hopper) visited the poor children in their various refuges, taking upon herself the duty of seeing that this holiday was not forgotten, but kept as it should be, with "goodies," gifts, kind words, and a motherly face to make sunshine in a shady place.

The Mayor and a commissioner went also; but the heartiest

welcome was given to Mrs. G., for hardly had we landed when several excited boys, after one look at the boxes piled up in the carriage, raced off in various directions to spread the glad tidings, "She's come, she's come!"

To the chapel first, and there, seated on the platform draped in flags, we looked down upon rows of children, who looked up, smiling and nodding at the good friend, who nodded and smiled back again, as if she had been the proud grandmother of every one of them.

The big boys in gray suits sat back; the little fellows in white pinafores, with cropped heads and clean faces, came next on one side; and a flock of girls in blue gowns and white aprons sat on the other side. They were nearest me, and I observed them carefully, thinking at first what a pretty group they made, with gay ribbons in their hair and the innocent look, which they seem to keep longer than the poor little men who so early begin to "see life."

But among forty girls, I counted fifteen with defective eyes, nine deformed, and seven lame ones, for the blight of poverty, neglect, and bad birth was on nearly all, if one examined closely. Here and there a smiling little face shone out like a daisy in the grass, and I longed to take these young creatures into some safe corner, to grow up in the sunshine and pure air they needed.

Singing followed a very brief speech from the commissioner, who vanished immediately afterward, leaving Mr. and Mrs. G., a young reporter, and myself to enjoy the simple exercises offered us.

SWEET MUSIC

It was touching to hear the small boys stand up and sing away with all their might a song about a "little white angel," whom they begged to leave the gates of heaven ajar, that they might get a peep in, if no more, when some of the poor dears looked as if they had never known a home, or expected to till they got back to the heaven so lately left.

I love to hear white-robed choirboys chanting as they pace demurely to and fro in handsome churches, but on this Christmas morning the song of these small orphans in white pinafores sounded through that charity chapel with a sweeter music to my ears than any Latin hymn I ever heard, even from the Pope's choir in St. Peter's.

The girls alternated with the boys in songs and recitations, the former showing most ease of manner and the best memories, the latter gesticulating with great energy and stumbling manfully through their tasks, as if bound to do or die.

I felt highly complimented and much pleased when a bullet-headed orator of twelve or thirteen gallantly gabbled a Christmas hymn of my own, coming to great grief, however, over some of the lines, for "chanting cherubs" were evidently unknown animals to him and "mistletoe and holly" a trial to his feelings. But the last line met his views exactly, and Richard was himself again as he stretched out two grimy hands with a hearty "Merry Christmas, everyone!"

As the public labored under the delusion that I was the Mayoress, I could clap with the rest and enjoy the joke in private.

Mrs. G. made a speech which ought to have cheered their little hearts, for she assured them that as long as she could, she should always come to see them on that day and, when she was gone, her own children would still continue the pleasant custom in memory of her for another thirty years, if need be.

It was not necessary for the teacher to give the signal for cheers and clapping of hands after *that* speech—"it did itself"—and as the girls passed us to go to dinner, the tap on the shoulder from the old lady's hand, with a kindly word and a motherly smile, was evidently considered an honor worth hustling for.

We had a look at them in the first rapture of dinner, and it was a sight to remember, especially the small boys, who fairly swam in soup and cheered the banquet by a chorus of happy voices with a lively accompaniment of drumsticks.

THE HOSPITAL

Then we went to the hospital, and I have rarely passed an hour fuller of the satisfaction which is made up of smiles and tears than the one spent in dealing out gifts to these afflicted children. It was good to see a whole roomful brighten as we went in, nurses and all, for *they* knew Mrs. G.; and the poor babies understood at a glance the mission of the dolly woman and the candy man, for the young reporter lent a hand like a brother and lugged around a great wooden box of sweeties with a goodwill which caused me to forgive all the wrongs suffered at the hands of his inquiring race.

"Dolly!" "Tandy!" "Me, me!" was the general cry, with every manifestation of delight the poor things could show. Some hobbled on their little crutches; half-blind ones groped their way, as if by instinct; sick babies sat up in their beds, beckoning with wasted hands; while others could only look beseechingly from the corner where infirmity imprisoned them.

Alas, how sad it was to see such suffering laid on such innocent victims and to feel how little one could do to lessen it! No Christmas sermon from the most eloquent lips could so touch the heart and teach the tender lesson of Him who took the children in His arms and healed their ills.

A LITTLE SUFFERER

One tiny creature, cursed with inherited afflictions too dreadful to describe, lay bandaged on its little bed and could only move its feet impatiently, with a pleading sort of moan, as its one dim eye recognized the gay dolls in the laps of its mates. I wanted to give one, but there was no hand to grasp it. Even the bonbons must be denied, for in that poor little mouth even sweets were bitter; and all we could do was to prop up a brilliant dolly at the bed foot, leaving baby to lie contentedly blinking at it, with the moan changed to a faint coo of pleasure.

She will never see another Christmas here, but as I hurried away, with eyes so full that I could not tell the pink candy from the white, it was a comfort to think that, thanks to a good woman's faithful pity, I had given poor baby one hour of happiness in the short life that was all pain.

As if this wasn't heartache enough, we ended off by visiting the idiot house, the memory of which will supply me with nightmares for some time to come. "All ready and waiting, ma'am," said the matron, whose bonny face cheered me at the first glance, and as we went up, outstretched heads and eager hands verified her words.

Rows of big boys and girls were ranged on either side of a long hall, with a table full of toys in the middle, all innocents, as I prefer to call them, yet all wise enough to turn with one accord and give a good shout of welcome as the little lady hurried in, waving her handkerchief and crying heartily, "Merry Christmas, children!" like a fairy godmother, in a Quakerish bonnet and brown waterproof instead of the pointed hat and red cloak, of blessed memory.

She had brought some gay pictures as an experiment, and dropping the doll and candy business for a time, the rosy-faced reporter helped me show these brilliant works of art.

PRESENTS GIVEN

On holding up two white kittens lapping milk, all the girls went into ecstasies, mewing, laughing, and crying, "Cat, Puss, O pretty, pretty!" in the most gratifying manner. A ship with a display of canvas that would have carried a man-of-war clean out of the water in the gale that was blowing had such an effect upon the boys that they fairly howled, and when I changed it to a big spotted horse with three legs in the air and a fierce-looking Turk holding on for dear life, every boy that could see it pranced as rampantly as the Arab steed.

A fresh relay of dolls was unpacked for the girls, and it was pathetic to see how tenderly young women of eighteen embraced the poor counterfeits of the only children they can ever know and love.

The boys waited patiently till the ladies were served, and appreciated the dolls so highly that several requested to be supplied with interesting families likewise. But they were invited to choose from the toys instead, and one didn't know whether to laugh or cry when these bearded babies picked out painted dogs, ninepins, or blocks, and went proudly back to show their treasures. One dwarf of thirty-five got a Noah's ark and a squeaking lion and sat brooding over the wooden family with a vacant smile, too feeble to comprehend how the squeak was made in the brown beast, which he hugged and patted fondly.

We saw their schoolroom, the neat copybooks and drawings, various methods for teaching form and color, and heard many interesting facts from the gentle teacher, whose devoted life seemed blessed to her, since, in spite of the sad imprisonment she freely endured, she was as fresh and cheerful as if heaven's sun and dew found her out even there.

HEAVEN-BORN CHARITY

The tidy dormitories were kept in order by the girls themselves, and the boys worked at other tasks well and willingly, we were told. Several seemed intelligent enough, but each had a mental weakness of some kind, which unfitted them for self-help and government; so one could not but be truly grateful that men and women were ready to give, as some had done, twenty-five years of life to this work of Christian charity.

We got some splendid cheers as we departed, and leaving boxes here and there on our way, drove at last to the boat, tired and hungry, but well content with the day's work.

To my eye there seemed to be a sort of halo around the little black bonnet that had led us to and fro all these hours, and it was not difficult to believe that the serene old couple who folded their empty hands with a sigh of satisfaction and sat cheerfully telling over new charities with the soft "thee and thou" that made the sad words "poverty" and "sin" almost sweet were really Christmas angels in disguise.

I shall always think so, and I fancy the young reporter

never will regret that he did not return *early* with the Mayor and the commissioner, since by staying he saw scenes far better worth recording than brutal executions or vain hunts after the great swindlers who escape with golden keys.

For my part, though I lost my dinner, I felt as if I had feasted sumptuously on the crumbs that fell from the children's table, and though the smiles, broken words, or dumb gratitude of orphans, idiots, and babies were the only gifts I received that day, they were precious enough to make forever memorable the Christmas spent at Randall's Island.

AN EVENING CALL

"Now, what would you like to see in New York? Stewart's big store, I suppose; ladies usually make their first pilgrimage there," said a friend soon after my arrival in that queer mixture of London and Paris.

"I don't care a pin for any big store! I want to see the Newsboys' Lodging House and School" was my answer, for I felt as if that building was more beautiful than the white marble square of the millionaire, splendid as it is.

So arrangements were made, and one cold evening we set out to see the boys in the Newsboys' Lodging House. We arrived just too late for the evening school, but I was quite resigned to that because I could see schools anywhere, but not a hundred and eighty independent business boys "taking their ease at their inn."

YOUNG AMERICA

All around the great hall were rows of little cupboards, and it was a fine sight to see a boy come in, pay six cents for his lodgings, put his surplus funds into the savings bank, register his name, receive his key, and leisurely deposit his cap, jacket, and shoes (if he possessed any of these articles) in his own private cupboard. One lad had nothing but an old cap, yet he laid it away and locked it up with such an air of satisfaction and importance that it did one good to see him.

Some were reading, and the master told us that they would read half the night if he would let them, so eager were they for amusement or information. Some were talking over the affairs of the day, lounging in easy attitudes on the benches, with newly washed bare feet and smooth heads, which seemed to be prepared for morning, to save time; for we were told that many were up and away by five o'clock to sell early papers on trains and boats.

Shirts and trousers, more or less tidy, were the prevailing costume, and the free and easy manners of the young gentlemen were amusing to watch. But on the whole, they behaved wonderfully well. And it was very comforting to see so many lads safe, and warm, and clean and happy in this home, instead of being left out in the streets to sin and suffer, uncared for just when most needing care.

PATSEY

One little chap of six was trotting about among the larger boys, as busy as a bee with his small affairs, and when we asked about him, we were told something that made him a very interesting Patsey, to me at least.

It seems that the parents were dead, and this child and a nine-year-old brother were left alone in the world. One would have thought two such babies had no refuge but an orphan asylum, but brother Pete preferred to support the family himself and did so with the help of this newsboys' friend. Actually, little nine-year-old took care of his brother, buying or begging his clothes, paying for his bed and food, and getting on bravely with business meantime. I longed to see this small hero, but he had not yet come in, being one of the boys who sell late papers.

The idea of this child knocking about at night in the busiest places and coming in, tired out, to pay for "self and family," like a little man, was so comic and so pathetic that it quite haunted me for days afterward and I longed to see and know both the boys and learn how they turn out in the years to come.

Patsey was called up to see us, and though he had seemed a lively mite when left to his own devices, he was as meek as a mouse when he stood before us, in a tidy blue shirt and trousers that had evidently been "built" for a larger man. His little face was scrubbed till it shone, and his yellow hair stood straight up in an independent sort of way, while a pair of quick blue eyes peeped at us with the sidelong glance of one used to looking out for squalls and dodging blows.

If I had not thought it would look sentimental, I should have liked to take him up and have a good chat with him to find out how things seemed to such a lonely creature. I fancy his views of life would not have been very extensive, but eminently practical and cheerful, for Patsey evidently appreciated his present well-being and had no fears for his future, no doubts of brother Pete's entire ability to steer their boat into some safe harbor.

Bon voyage, brave little brothers, and thank God that you have so soon found one of the blessed school ship, whence you can set sail by and by for the long voyage, with the memory of past kindness warm at your hearts and the white flag of the Children's Aid Society flying from the masthead.

Upstairs we saw the dormitories, with the long rows of neat beds, in tiers of two; and the vision of one hundred and eighty boys snugly tucked up there was so delightful and amazing that I could not realize it as a sober fact. The other vision of a hundred and eighty boys all enjoying a general scrimmage was even more delightful, and that I could realize fully.

When I asked our conductor by what magic he got this brigade of boys into their beds and kept them there, he laughed and said:

"You see, ma'am, the poor chaps are so tired after being out at work all day that they are glad to keep still when night comes. Now and then new boys try to get up a breeze, but we have a watchman and he keeps things quiet."

UNDER THE COVERLETS

How I should like to be that watchman, for a time at least, and see these "poor chaps" peacefully asleep under the blue coverlets—if any lay awake with a pain or a trouble, to ease it if I could, and say the word, or give the soothing pat that strengthens weak will and conquers temptation by the thought that "somebody cares." To tuck up the little ones and give a good-night kiss, if they wanted it, trying to keep soft the hearts that often grow so hard or hungry for the lack of love.

But I fancy there is a special angel sent to keep guard over these motherless boys, else how is it that they do so well, and often come back from Western homes to thank those who helped them, and to go and do likewise?

The gymnasium must be a lively place when the lads are there; for even hard work does not exhaust all their energies, it seems, and they give vent to their buoyant spirits before bedtime by swarming up and down ladders, turning somersaults, and swinging so high that the ceilings would suffer if boards full of nail points were not put up to restrain their soaring ambition.

Downstairs we saw the dining room, with tables all set out, ready for morning. Some of the well-to-do fellows decline the breakfast of tea and bread and syrup here provided and go away to feast sumptuously on coffee and cakes. These dissipated youths also clamor at times to have their bank opened before the month is out, even offer to pay for the favor, so that they may waste their substance in riotous living—go to the theater, have a supper, and then for a time sleep in the street and live as they can.

MONEY IN THE BANK

Once a month the bank is opened, and the boys can take their money to use as they like. Some spend it, some hand it over to the proper persons, who invest it for them, so that when they get homes, they have something of their own for an outfit.

A prize is sometimes offered to the lad who saves up the most in the month. As we were told this, standing by the wide, low table full of slits, each numbered and leading to a small safety vault below, a boy came in and dropped a handful of pennies down the hole belonging to him.

"How much have you got this month?" asked my friend.

"Fourteen dollars, sir."

And this boy walked off with the air of a millionaire.

This arrangement encourages industry and economy, yet leaves the lad quite independent, and that suits the masculine mind, however young or ignorant.

One feature of the establishment was peculiarly interesting to me, and that was the charming variety of cats and kittens that pervaded the lower regions. Boys and cats being the pets dearest to my heart, I felt that this house, so rich in both, would be a truly delightful retreat when other hopes and labors failed; and if a matron is allowed, I shall apply for the place in a few years.

THE MIMIC

I was struck with the decent appearance and good behavior of the boys, for I had expected to see a somewhat disorderly set. They were certainly not well dressed nor polished in manners, but looked intelligent, were generally tidy, and minded their own affairs in a capable sort of way that both amused and pleased me.

One big fellow with a very dirty face glowered at us, as if he decidedly objected to us and considered our call impertinent. I inferred from his manner that "shines" had not been plentiful that day, and nothing but the immediate offer of the boots of the company would brighten the cloud of gloom and blacking that obscured his countenance.

Another boy agreeably relieved the monotony of general virtue which prevailed by whisking a newspaper over his shoulders, like my cloak, and prancing behind our backs with such a comical imitation of the tall woman's walk that I was immensely tickled.

The rapidity with which he retired behind that paper when I caught him at it was so very funny we all laughed together, and grins kept breaking out on the faces of that group of boys every time I met their eyes afterward.

I trust they felt that a kindred soul lived under the big cloak, and if that droll fellow ever sees this article in any of his papers, he will own that the laugh is on my side now.

I enjoyed my call so much that I mean to go again some Sunday and see how my young men appear then. Or on Christmas, if possible, and make sure that little Patsey has one present, at least, whether he has a sock to hang up or not.

A VISIT TO THE TOMBS

"Hark, from the tombs a doleful sound,
Mine ears attend the cry."

These lines of the old hymn were ringing in my mind one bright morning as I walked briskly along the Bowery, on my way to visit the great New York prison.

I had seen its grim exterior more than once and always felt a strong desire to see what lay behind it. Now, thanks to a city missionary, I was about to do so, and went to prison very willingly, taking a look at Five Points as we passed.

Coming to the Tombs at last, we found that our promised guide had not arrived, and while waiting in the low, wide hall which led to the warden's office on one side and the grated entrance to the prison on the other, I saw

VARIOUS SIGHTS

which interested me very much. A constant stream of people ebbed and flowed, most of them friends and visitors of the prisoners within. Each had to present an order and receive a pass before they could enter, and delay was unavoidable when many came at once.

It was a curious study to watch the faces of these people, and I was struck by the differences between the men and women.

The former waited patiently, lounging about the hall, laughing and chatting, with few signs of agitation or anxiety. But the women came hurrying in, pale and eager, and if not admitted at once, got as close to the grating as possible and clung there with restless gestures, wistful faces, and frequent presentations of the precious pass which would let them in to carry what comfort they might to those whom they loved so loyally.

Officials of all sorts came and went—the doctor and his assistant, with a tray full of bottles; policemen with fresh offenders, clerks with books, and keepers with jingling keys—while the busy warden kept popping in and out of doors in a most tantalizing way to us, for still our guide did not come and we were getting impatient.

My friend went off to reconnoiter, and while I waited, I saw two little scenes which impressed me very much by the mere force of contrast.

A RELEASED PRISONER

An old Irishman had been wandering about for some time, evidently waiting for someone.

I had heard him talking in a loud, excited tone to the group of men about the grate, behind which an official seemed to be making out papers of some sort; and by the general interest taken in the old man's affairs, I felt sure that his mission was a happy one.

The name "Mike" occurred often in his talk, and every time the inner door slammed, he rushed to the outer one, with an expression of joyful expectancy, which beautified his withered old face.

It was impossible to help sympathizing with him, so frank and genuine was his emotion, and I found myself watching the heavy doors almost as eagerly as if some friend of my own was coming out.

Each time they opened, everyone leaned forward to look at the old man's face for news, and each time it showed disappointment, a glance of sympathy went around and someone said a cheering word to the poor old soul, who often wiped his hot face with a half-droll, half-pathetic—

"Be the powers, it's kilt intirely with this waitin', I am!"

At last his hope was fulfilled, for a good-looking young fellow came out, swinging on his coat, as if in haste to be off, and glancing about him with the eager look of one to whom sun, fresh air, and merry faces were very welcome.

The turnkey opened wide the gate to let him pass, but before they could close it, with a real Irish whoop of delight the old man fell upon the young one, crying brokenly:

"Long life to ye, Mike! It's safe out ov it ye are, me b'y, and the saints be praised, it's howld ov ye I've got at last!"

And "howld" of his "b'y" he kept, clutching him so close that no one could pass, till the son said in a rough tone that belied the honest feeling his face betrayed:

"Whist, Father! Whist till we're clear of this!" and drew the old man away with a grip of the hand that made me sure Mike was not quite spoiled yet.

In the street more friends awaited him, and with the old father on his arm, he went away to a better life, I sincerely hope.

Just then my friend returned, bringing our passes, and with a secret shiver I followed him through the iron gate, clutching my yellow ticket, marked "Visitor," as if it was my only chance of ever getting out again.

First we went into a stonyhearted yard, with gray buildings all around it, the walls of which were pierced with rows of narrow slits to light the cells within.

At the door of the largest of these buildings we showed our passes and, with much turning of keys, were let into the men's part of the prison. Alas, how large it was, how full! And how heavy the air with the dreadful prison smell, worse even than the evil odors that haunt a hospital.

THE CELLS

Long and narrow, with three or four tiers of cells, balconies all around, winding stairs, with a gate at the top of each flight and keepers to unlock them as we passed.

All was iron and stone, and peeping through the half-open inner door of each cell, we saw a little whitewashed room, just big enough for a narrow bed, a chair, and table. High up in the wall a grated slit, to admit all the light allowed the occupant of the living tomb.

The moods and occupations of the prisoners were as different as their faces, for some seemed asleep; others sat disconsolately on their beds; a few were reading, many smoking, and still more pacing to and fro as restless as tigers in a cage.

Some never looked up as we passed; some turned their backs; many stared boldly at us or pressed their faces so closely to the bars that we looked into their eyes before we knew it, and very strange expressions we read there.

PERHAPS A TRAGEDY

Our attention was attracted by a groaning and scuffling in one of the lower cells, and looking in, we saw two men struggling together. One was evidently a keeper, the other a prisoner—an old man who seemed making a last effort to get out of that dark hole, if only to die free.

Glancing up from the ghastly, panting creature under his knee, the keeper bade us "call one of those men, quick!"

My friend did so, and I followed him, not wishing to see more. But the man to whom we spoke only shrugged his shoulders and answered in a superior tone:

"Never you mind, sir. It's only one of their dodges."

Leaving him to his newspaper, we went upstairs and were passing along the gallery when a cry from below made us look down in spite of ourselves. We were just opposite the cell where the struggle was going on, but the keeper's call for help had been more successful than ours, and several men were half in, half out, evidently trying to do their best in some emergency.

Presently the prisoner was brought forth on a dirty mattress, quiet now, except a feeble moaning, and wearing on his face the gray shadow which assured me that for him captivity was nearly over.

As he vanished on his way to the hospital, we turned around to see another scene in prison life, sadder even than that which death was mercifully ending.

SENTENCED

A young woman came hastily up the iron stairs, asking breathlessly as the turnkey unlocked the little gate:

"How's Jim?"

"Just back from court," answered the man, with a look that made the woman cry out:

"O my God, he's sentenced!"

The man nodded and was about to speak when she said in a desperate sort of way:

"Don't tell me! I can't bear it yet!" and rushed down the gallery to a cell at the far end.

Involuntarily my eye followed her and saw a pair of hands thrust between the bars to seize hers, saw her lay her face down on them and break into passionate weeping while she listened to the voice which, inaudible to us, was telling the heavy news.

Then my own eyes got too dim for seeing, and with one impulse my friend and I went down the opposite gallery, that we might not interrupt that sad interview.

WOMAN'S SYMPATHY

But there was no escape from misery of some sort, for here were more women breaking their hearts over some beloved sinner and bravely bearing their share of the trouble, whatever it was. One pretty girl was kissing her lover between the bars and trying to smile through her tears.

A colored woman was talking earnestly to a bright boy, who smoked while he listened. Another young man hid his face as we passed, and the motherly-looking woman at his wicket laid her hand on the bent head, as if to assure him that no sin or shame could estrange *her* love and hope.

A soldierly fellow sat on the bench outside of his cell, reading a magazine, like one who, for some reason or other, was permitted unusual privileges, and enjoyed them.

The faded blue coat caught my eye, and the brown face, frankly lifted up as we approached, made me long to stop and talk, for it looked honest in spite of the stone walls about him.

But my companion was a man, and I knew by experience that the presence of one of his own sex would seal the lips of my soldier to the utterance of any but the most commonplace remarks.

So I only nodded as I went by, with a half-involuntary motion of my hand to my temple, for I could not resist the impulse to salute a comrade in misfortune. It was good to see how quickly he caught the idea and how heartily he returned the salute, not only with the hand, but a grateful look and the first smile I had seen on any face within those walls.

WOMEN PRISONERS

Leaving this part of the prison, we went to the quarters of the women. A chatty old lady in the matron's room told my companion that he must wait for me there, as men were not admitted.

So I followed a forlorn-looking woman through the lower hall, where only a few colored girls, shut up in large cages, were to be seen.

They made faces and called out impertinent remarks as we passed, and I felt no desire to stop and speak with them.

The matron had cautioned me "not to talk to them, for you'll get the worst of it, certain sure, mum, if you try." And I felt the wisdom of her advice, for these poor girls seemed far more repulsive and depraved than any man we saw, and so lost to self-respect that it filled me with a sort of fear merely to look at them.

Most of the women were at chapel, my guide told me, and when I asked why the men were not there also, she said:

"O there's too many of 'em, and they ain't to be trusted."

I was glad that the women were to be trusted, and being

shut into one of the empty cells "to see how it seemed," I made a chapel of it for a moment and prayed a very hearty prayer for every unhappy sister who might come after me.

It was a dreadful place, that narrow, white tomb—no sun, no books, no work, and, to those who usually inhabited it, nothing to do but think bitter thoughts of the sin or sorrow that brought them there. I did not wonder that they grow frantic or pray for companionship to keep them sane, and hoped that the benevolent young lady who visits the Tombs so often to comfort condemned murderers sometimes came to these women, who need help to bear the burden of life quite as much as the men about to lay it down forever.

THE JUVENILE PRISONERS

As there was little to see here, we went to find the boys and, entering the juvenile department, were instantly surrounded by a flock of sharp little lads, all asking for money and looking quite ready and able to help themselves if we gave them a chance. I should have liked to stop and chat a bit, but their attentions were so pressing that we could hardly breathe, and our attention was so unpleasantly divided between our pity and our pockets that we escaped from the clutches of these young Jack Sheppards after a very brief call.

Before leaving the buildings, as I stood looking about me, remembering all I had seen that morning, I could not help wishing that those who are tempted to do evil could first visit this dreary place and see it as it is, with no romance about it, only the hard, grim reality—the atmosphere of sin and shame, the chill of captivity and loneliness, the shadow of the gallows over all, and one long tragedy, in many acts, forever going on behind those gloomy walls.

Never had sun and air seemed so bright and welcome, or liberty so sweet, as when we came out into the world again, sadder yet wiser people for our brief sojourn in the Tombs.

THE MAYPOLE INN

A PLACE OF HOLIDAY STORIES

"Will you go sometime?"

"I will."

This was the question asked and answered at the conclusion of a glowing description of the charms of a walk to the ancient church at Chingford, England, and the possibility of taking a shortcut through the hedgerows and green lanes to the famous Maypole Inn, where we could "quaff a beaker" to the memory of old John Willett and pretty Dolly Varden.

This proposition, coming as it did on a bright May morning just as my friend and I were leaving our lodgings for a day's work, instantly fired me with a desire to tramp away into the country, now looking its loveliest after the late rains.

So without more ado I said, "Let us go at once and make sure of this perfect day. It is barely nine o'clock, so we have plenty of time. Do you cut your books, and I will give up my painting, and let us be off for a cheap and wholesome frolic."

"Done!" replied the ever-amiable C——, and away we went, ready for anything from a summer shower to the Gordon Riots all over again.

Making for the underground railroad, we came, after many windings through the busiest part of this endless city, to the Shoreditch Station. This is the quarter of many levels, the intricacies of which it takes great grasp of mind to fathom, for there are three grades of railroad, known as the upper, middle, and lower levels.

After long confabulations with many officials at many small windows, our disappointments and trials began. It appeared that though we were early birds, we were not early enough to get the worm we wanted, in the shape of a train to Angel Road, the nearest station to Chingford, but must wait nearly three hours for the next.

This was very trying; but with the pluck peculiar to Americans when impatient with the seemingly unnecessary red tape of this slow-going nation, the more trouble we found in getting to the Maypole the more resolved we were upon going, even if we walked the twelve or fourteen miles.

So with a cheering smile C—— proposed trying the lowest level of all as a last resource, and remembering that Hope lay at the very bottom of Pandora's box, we took a downward plunge. Many steps led us to what seemed a backyard, but on a careful inspection it proved to have an outlet through a low arch leading to a large, airy station in the bowels of the earth.

Here, to our great joy, we found a man of mind in the booking office, who took a kindly interest in our proposed excursion and had imagination enough (a rare thing in an Englishman) to plan out a route by which we could approach the old church from a different point, putting the last touch to his favors by adding that a train for Silver Street left in about twenty minutes.

Our relief was great; for our disappointment would have been bitter if we had been obliged to return to our work, when we were in just the mood for play and the day seemed made on purpose, being warm and bright, with a fresh wind blowing countryward.

As we waited, I read a packet of home letters put into my hands as I left the door, and so pleasantly beguiled the time that the train came rumbling in before we had thought of getting impatient.

Stepping into an empty carriage, we were soon among the

red-tiled roofs and well-kept gardens so thick in the outskirts of London.

Mind you, we traveled second-class, for this was to be a cheap frolic in good earnest, and my comrade, rather against his will, let me have my way in all things.

Leaving the train, we struck into a pretty country road winding along between hawthorn hedges, pink and white with bloom, the pathways making pleasant walking, with the dust well laid and the grassy banks all starred with flowers.

After a good stretch to rest our limbs and fill our lungs, admiring all creation most enthusiastically as we went, it occurred to us that we might as well find out if we were going right or wrong.

It being Whitsun week and Holy Day time, the common people were all abroad, so we hailed the first party we met. Several bluff fellows going a-fishing in the Lea told us we were all right and, by "going over the bridge by the mill and taking the path through the fields, we should save a mile or two."

But our fisher friends did *not* add that at intervals in these fields were many stiles, most trying to the female mind, not to say skirts. Certainly no woman less than five feet seven inches could have gone at them as I did, and with one wild plunge have surmounted what seemed an almost insurmountable barrier.

These gymnastics raised my spirits finely, and I accomplished the rest of the way like a scientific walkist. Coming to the graveyard of the church, a halt for repose was found both agreeable and necessary, for just then large drops began to fall. Seated on a gravestone, while my devoted C—— held a big umbrella over me, we enjoyed the little shower without anxiety, for a short stay in England teaches one how to dress sensibly and to be sublimely indifferent to the elements.

Through this moist medium we took our first view of this fine old ruined church. Its square Norman tower, quaint side porch, the pure line of its double stone doors, and the colonnade of arches supporting the ruined roof, through which hung luxuriant festoons of ivy, were enough to delight the most unartistic eye.

Added to this was the historical Epping Forest as background; the Alexandra Palace, with its great glass dome glittering in occasional gleams of sunshine on the one hand; on the other, a quiet English landscape of green meadows with the river Lea winding through them, thatched cottages with their hayricks and hedges of golden gorse and rosy hawthorn, making far more picturesque boundaries than the ugly walls and fences of America.

Cows and donkeys fed about us, and a small boy in a red cap (with an eye to effect, I fancy) leaned against a broken window, the graceful arch of which made a perfect frame for the little figure in the foreground.

Then it was that I groaned in spirit for my sketchbook and unwillingly owned that hasty starts had their drawbacks. As a solace for this loss, I picked sprays of ivy for relics and demanded food.

Rapidly descending the hill, we reached an inn called the Two Horseshoes, and here I declared, in spite of many carts before the door suggesting many rough drivers within, that I *must* have some bread and cheese and a pint of ale foaming in a pewter pot, according to the fashion of English wayfarers.

C—— obediently put his head in at the door, but withdrew it hastily, to report that this was no place for me. Much disappointed, we were about to move on when a woman appeared, said we could have a quiet parlor upstairs, and led the way to it at once.

A queer, old-fashioned room furnished with a spinet, on which my companion "discoursed fine music," while I amused myself with the pictures on the walls. One was of Dick Whittington with his pack on his back listening to the advice of the bells. The other works of art were, of course, a much flattered likeness of the Queen and a very ghastly view of the dear departed Nelson, who haunts one's steps here as persistently as do pictures of the Father of Our Country at home.

Presently our Hebe appeared with a lunch which would

have horrified a genteel young lady, for at first sight even I, who pride myself on a hearty appetite, was a little startled. Two great plates of cold beef, piles of bread, much butter and cheese, and the foaming mugs so generally set before travelers.

It was exceedingly jolly, and we soon proved that the English estimate of the powers of the human stomach was a perfectly correct one, for when we left the table, not a vestige of food remained but a morsel of cheese and a few crusts.

The bill was the best of the joke, for, use of spinet included, the cost of this most satisfying lunch was two shillings and sixpence.

And now, though the rain had stopped and all looked propitious, arose my first doubt as to our ever reaching the Maypole Inn, for, according to our landlady, it was so far off she could not even begin to direct us to it. Ten miles at least lay between us, and the morning was far spent.

Undaunted, however, we set forth, mightily refreshed by our beef, and tramped off in what we hoped was the right direction. While C—— enjoyed a brief rest, I picked gorse to be immortalized on a black panel and sang all the old English ballads I could remember.

Mile after mile we walked, often asking our way, but as all differed in their statements of distance, the result was not cheering. On the outskirts of a town, we met a policeman and threw ourselves upon him, feeling that it was his duty to know *everything*.

But a more discouraging official I have never met, for he began by saying it was utterly impossible to reach the Maypole Inn, still a good eight miles away by most intricate roads. This cheering statement he followed up by advising us to go on three miles farther and take the train to London at the next station.

We scorned his advice, however, and pegged along at a great pace, for now our blood was up and we were bent on succeeding, if we died in the attempt.

A postman was our next victim, and him we found even

more depressing than the policeman, for he said we must go back a mile and then strike into the great road leading to Romford.

At this juncture I showed signs of giving out, and a word from me would have sent us back in the most ignominious manner to London. But "No surrender!" is my motto, so I cried, "Forward!" and on we went, till another long stretch brought us at last to the desired spot and my eyes actually beheld on a creaking sign the well-known words "Maypole Inn."

It was not the fine, picturesque ruin which the artist's pencil had made familiar in the illustration of Dickens's work. But it was pleasing and poetic, and here indeed was rest for the weary travelers—footsore now, but in the best of spirits after a walk of fourteen miles.

A buxom hostess received us cordially, and was much pleased at our desire to visit the old place, and much amused at my ordering bread and milk. As I feasted thereon, she told me all about the place—how the original old building had been moved back and was now a private house, as we could see; how Mr. Dickens often came and sat in that very room, having his dinner by the long window where I was sitting, and how he often joined in the singing, dancing, or fun going on below. As if to make the story quite perfect, there was a sound of jollity at the moment she spoke, for a flock of country people were dancing jigs to the sound of a fiddle.

As I sat there in the delicious state of weariness that follows healthful exercise, the words "Maypole Inn" seemed to bring up before me all the characters in *Barnaby Rudge* and make them live again. I saw the old kitchen with fat John Willet staring at the "biler," while Parkes, Tom Cobb, and little Solomon Daisy sat in a row waiting for him to "bring his powerful mind to bear" on some vexed question. Rough Hugh seemed to be lounging in the stables; elegant Mr. Chester was taking snuff in the dreary best chamber and gloomy Haredale stalking up the wide stairs to defy him.

A rustle in the porch suggested pretty Dolly caught and kissed behind the door by her devoted Joe. A hearty laugh certainly came from dear old Gabriel Varden, the locksmith, and a woman's scolding voice assured me that his shrewish, sanctimonious wife still lived to torment him. A shrill giggle so forcibly recalled the inimitable Miggs that I turned my eyes to the door, sure that I should see that acid virgin enter, with a "Ho, indeed, mim!"

Down the road I seemed to see poor Barnaby come prancing, with his feathers fluttering and Grip on his shoulder, drawing corks with a burst of "Never say die! I'm a devil! Polly put the kettle on. We'll all have tea."

At this point someone did say "tea"—not the raven, but my long-suffering C——, who was mildly suggesting that I had better wait till I was in the homeward-bound train before I indulged in naps and that we should not get home until late if we did not start at once.

So my pleasant dream vanished, and I awoke to the sad fact that it was nearly six, and how were we to get home?

C—— had an idea there was a station not far off, and summoned the landlady to confirm his statement. To our dismay she answered blandly, "Oh dear, no, the nearest station is four miles off, and the omnibus that goes twice a day has just left."

So nothing remained but for us to foot it, and having done what we started to do, we found such support in the reflection that we trudged stoutly away, with a handful of pink hawthorn as a trophy.

The sunset was lovely and the green leaves fragrant all the way. C—— bore up like a man and a brother, and we came at last to the little Woodford Station just in time to skip into a second-class carriage and roll away toward London.

Here we laughed over our adventures and counted up the cost of our day's excursion. Six shillings apiece was not an expensive trip, we thought, for the sunshine, air, exercise, and pleasure we had enjoyed were worth far more. Lamps were lighted when we reached London, and hailing the first hansom we saw, we were soon dashing through the busy streets at the breakneck pace which so delights me.

Our fellow boarders received us with joy, for dire predictions concerning our fate had been made and much anxiety felt at our disappearance. But being Americans, any odd pranks were forgiven us, and we were soon asleep and dreaming of the Maypole Inn.

SELECTED BIBLIOGRAPHY

Flower Fables (1855) – stories
Hospital Sketches (1863) – nonfiction
The Rose Family (1864) – story
On Picket Duty, and Other Tales (1864) – stories
Moods (1865, 1882)[1] – novel
The Mysterious Key, and What It Opened (1867) – story
Morning-Glories, and Other Stories (1868) – stories
Three Proverb Stories (1868) – stories
Little Women (1868, 1869)[2] – novel
An Old-Fashioned Girl (1870) – novel
Will's Wonder Book (1870)[3] – stories
Little Men (1871) – novel
Aunt Jo's Scrap-Bag I (1872) – stories
Aunt Jo's Scrap-Bag II (1872) – stories
Work (1873) – novel
Aunt Jo's Scrap-Bag III (1874) – stories
Eight Cousins (1875) – novel
Silver Pitchers (1876) – stories

1. Originally published by Loring in 1865. The revised version was published by Roberts Brothers in 1882.
2. *Little Women* originally appeared as two separate volumes. Part First was published in 1868 and Part Second in 1869.
3. Originally published anonymously; edited by Madeleine Stern and republished in 1975 as *Louisa's Wonder Book*.

Rose in Bloom (1876) – novel
A Modern Mephistopheles (1877) – novel
Aunt Jo's Scrap-Bag IV (1878) – stories
Under the Lilacs (1878) – novel
Aunt Jo's Scrap-Bag V (1879) – stories
Jack and Jill (1880) – novel
Proverb Stories (1882) – stories
Aunt Jo's Scrap-Bag VI (1882) – stories
Spinning-Wheel Stories (1884) – stories
Lulu's Library Vol. I (1886) – stories
Jo's Boys (1886) – novel
Lulu's Library Vol. II (1887) – stories
A Garland for Girls (1888) – stories
Louisa May Alcott: Her Life, Letters, and Journals (1889) – letters and journals
Lulu's Library Vol. III (1889) – stories
Comic Tragedies (1893) – plays
Behind a Mask (1975) – stories
Plots and Counterplots (1976)[4] – stories
Diana and Persis (1978) – story
The Selected Letters of Louisa May Alcott (1987) – letters
A Double Life (1988) – stories
The Journals of Louisa May Alcott (1989) – journals
Freaks of Genius (1991) – stories
From Jo March's Attic (1993)[5] – stories
A Long Fatal Love Chase (1995) – novel
The Inheritance (1997) – novel
The Poems of Louisa May Alcott (2000) – poems (Ironweed, ISBN 0-9655309-5-7)
The Early Stories of Louisa May Alcott, 1852–1860 (2000) – stories (Ironweed, ISBN 0-9655309-6-5)

4. Republished in 1995 as *A Marble Woman*.
5. Republished in 1995 as *The Lost Stories of Louisa May Alcott*.

ORIGINAL PUBLICATION SOURCES

HOSPITAL SKETCHES

Hospital Sketches (Boston: James Redpath, 1863). Chapters III–VI originally appeared in *The Commonwealth,* May 22 and 29 and June 12 and 26, 1863.

"The Hospital Lamp": *The Daily Morning Drum-Beat,* February 24 and 25, 1864.

"Preface to *Hospital Sketches* (1869)": In *Hospital Sketches and Camp and Fireside Stories* (Boston: Roberts Brothers, 1869).

LETTERS FROM THE MOUNTAINS

"Letters from the Mountains": *The Commonwealth,* July 24 and 31 and August 7 and 21, 1863.

SKETCHES OF EUROPE

"Up the Rhine": *The Independent,* July 18, 1867.

"Life in a Pension": *The Independent,* November 7, 1867.

"A Royal Governess": *The Independent,* July 9, 1868.

"Recent Exciting Scenes in Rome": *Boston Daily Evening Transcript,* February 3, 1871.

CONCORD, MASSACHUSETTS

"Woman's Part in the Concord Celebration": *The Woman's Journal,* May 1, 1875.

"Reminiscences of Ralph Waldo Emerson": *The Youth's Companion,* May 25, 1882.

"Recollections of My Childhood": *The Youth's Companion,* May 24, 1888.

FROM *THE YOUTH'S COMPANION* AND *MERRY'S MUSEUM*

"A Visit to the School Ship": *Merry's Museum,* March 1869.

"Little Boston": *The Youth's Companion,* June 12, 1873.

"How We Saw the Shah": *The Youth's Companion,* August 14, 1873.

"London Bridges": *The Youth's Companion,* July 23, 1874.

"A New Way to Spend Christmas": *The Youth's Companion,* March 9, 1876.

"An Evening Call": *The Youth's Companion,* April 13, 1876.

"A Visit to the Tombs": *The Youth's Companion,* May 25, 1876.

"The Maypole Inn: A Place of Holiday Stories": *The Youth's Companion,* December 14, 1882.

A NOTE ON THE TEXT

The sketches are drawn directly from their original publication sources. Obvious errors have been emended; however, to preserve the original text, certain nineteenth-century practices, such as the use of dangling modifiers ("never having been to riding school, my ideas of the matter were somewhat confused"), have been allowed to stand. Where appropriate, modern standards in spelling and punctuation have been imposed to enhance readability.